WAITING FOR ALLAH

VIKING
Penguin India

WAITING FOR ALLAH

PAKISTAN'S STRUGGLE FOR DEMOCRACY

CHRISTINA LAMB

VIKING

VIKING

Penguin Books India (P) Ltd., B4/246 Safdarjung Enclave, New Delhi- 110 029, India
Penguin Books Ltd, 27 Wrights Lane, London, W8 5TZ, England
Viking Penguin, a division of Penguin Books USA Inc.
375 Hudson Street, New York, New York, 10014, USA
Penguin Books Australia Ltd, Ringwood, Victoria, Australia
Penguin Books Canada Ltd, 10 Alcorn Avenue, Toronto, Ontario, Canada, M4V 3B2
Penguin Books (NZ) Ltd, 182-190 Wairau Road, Auckland 10, New Zealand

First published 1991

Made and printed in India by Ananda Offset Pvt. Ltd., Calcutta

CONTENTS

An Elusive Dawn

This trembling light, this nightbitten dawn
This is not the Dawn we waited for so long
This is not the Dawn whose birth was sired
By so many lives, so much blood

Generations ago we started our confident march,
Our hopes were young, our goal within reach

After all there must be some limit
To the confusing constellation of stars
In the vast forest of the sky
Even the lazy languid waves
Must reach at last their appointed shore

And so we wistfully prayed
For a consummate end to our painful search.

FAIZ AHMED FAIZ

ACKNOWLEDGEMENTS

Throughout the length and breadth of Pakistan there are many people for whose help I am grateful and because of whom I have an enduring affection for the country – so many that it is not possible to mention them all.

The Arbab family, Naseem and Sehyr Saigol, Kamal Azfar, Arif Nizami, the late Brigadier Salik, Najam Sethi and Nusrat Javed were all of particular help.

Not least among those to whom I owe thanks are the many Afghan *mujaheddin* with whom I travelled into war zones and late into the night discussed the region's past and future.

Hamid Karzay, Hamid and Ishaq Gailani and Asim Nasser-Zia were particular friends, as was Commander Abdul Haq, with whom I shared a fondness for ice-cream.

Sir Nicholas Barrington, the British High Commissioner in Islamabad, also deserves a special mention for his help in trying to stop the Interior Ministry deporting me.

Thanks are owed to my colleagues at the *Financial Times* for their support, in particular to Robin Pauley and Jurek Martin for encouraging me to give up a perfectly decent job at Central TV to go out and live in Pakistan.

Professor Akbar Ahmed at Cambridge University has been an invaluable friend and sounding board.

My editor, Jon Riley, has patiently guided me through my first book.

Above all, thanks to my parents for putting up with a daughter frequently lost in the wilds and my endless battles with the word processor.

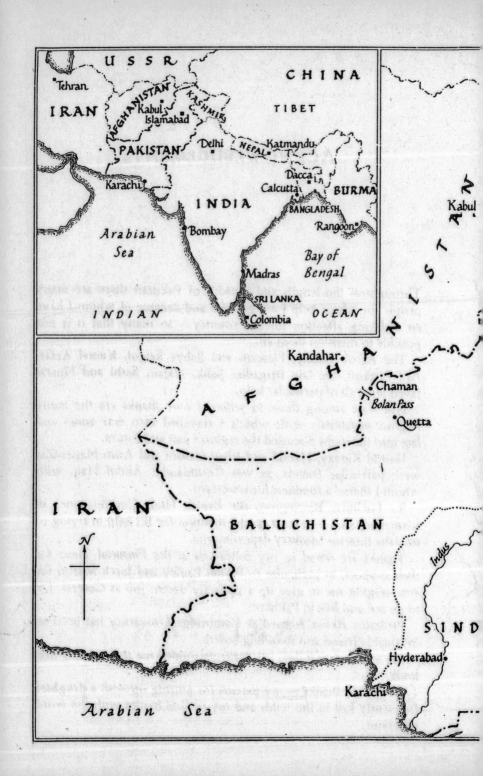

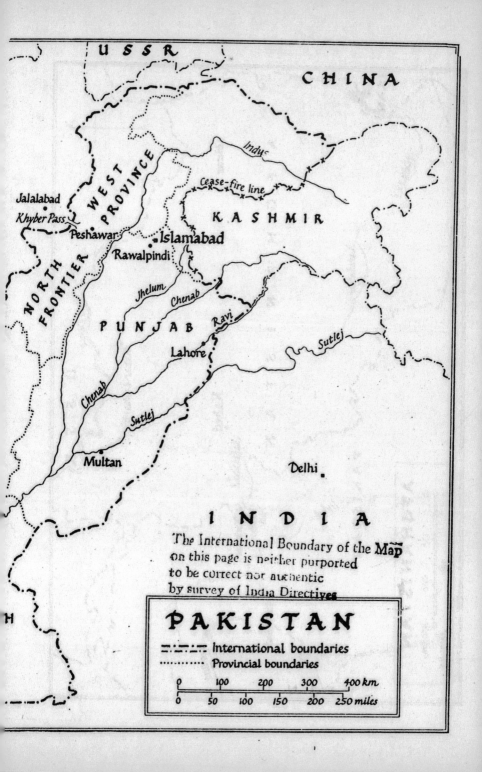

U S S R

CHINA

Indus

WEST PROVINCE

Cease-fire line

Jalalabad

Khyber Pass

K A S H M I R

Peshawar

•Islamabad

NORTH FRONTIER

Rawalpindi

Jhelum

Chenab

P U N J A B

Ravi

Chenab

Lahore

Sutlej

Sutlej

Chenab

Multan

Delhi.

I N D I A

The International Boundary of the Map
on this page is neither purported
to be correct nor authentic
by survey of India Directives

PAKISTAN

▬▬▬▬ International boundaries

••••••••• Provincial boundaries

0   100   200   300   400 km

0   50   100   150   200 250 miles

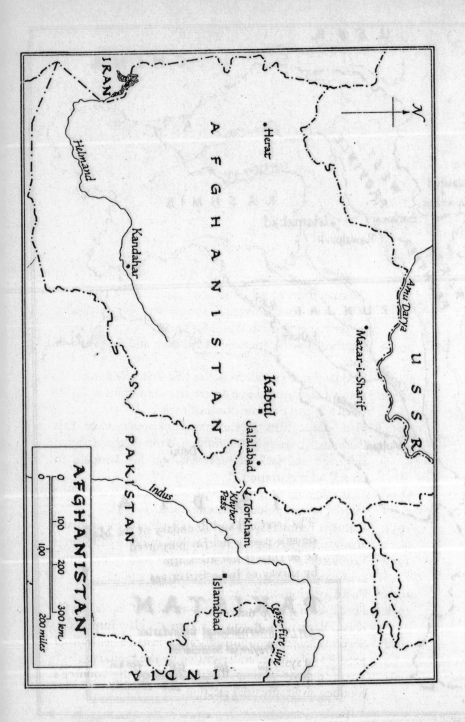

AFGHANISTAN

IRAN

Helmand

Kandahar

Herat

AFGHANISTAN

Amu Darya

U S S R

Mazar-i-Sharif

Kabul

Jalalabad

Khyber Pass

Torkham

Indus

PAKISTAN

Islamabad

Cease-fire line

INDIA

N

0   100   100
0   200   300 km
         100   200 miles

CHRONOLOGY OF PAKISTAN

1947: Independence from British Rule and formation of Pakistan from Muslim majority provinces of India.
War with India over Kashmir, the only Muslim majority province to stay in India.

1948: Death of Jinnah, founder of Pakistan and first head of state.
Liaquat Ali Khan takes over as first Prime Minister.

1951: Liaquat assassinated in mysterious circumstances.
Civil servants become dominant force.

1952: First ethnic riots in the majority province of East Pakistan, at attempts to impose Urdu as the national language and lack of representation for Bengalis in central administration.

1953: First religious riots against minority Ahmadi sect. First martial law imposed in Lahore.

1954: Pakistan joins SEATO, a US-sponsored military alliance, and US becomes principal military supplier.

1955: Provinces of West Pakistan merged into 'One Unit', causing resentment among smaller provinces.

1956: First Constitution framed.

1958: First military coup under command of General Ayub Khan. Parliament dissolved and martial law imposed.

1962: Second Constitution introduced to install a centralized presidential system underwritten by the military.

1964: Ayub 'defeats' Fatima Jinnah, sister of the country's founder, in Presidential election.

1965:   Second war with India over Kashmir. Defeat weakens Ayub's position.

1966:   Awami League, main party of East Pakistan, proposes a confederation of the two regions.

1969:   Ayub hands over to General Yahya Khan after period of unrest.

1970:   Pakistan's first free elections. Awami League sweeps East Pakistan and Z. A. Bhutto's People's Party wins majority in West Pakistan.

1971:   Army refuses to transfer power to Awami League and sends in troops to East Pakistan. India goes to aid of Bengalis who secede from Pakistan to form Bangladesh.
        Z. A. Bhutto takes over as Martial Law Administrator of remaining Pakistan.

1972:   Bhutto, now Prime Minister, devalues rupee by 131 per cent and begins nationalization campaign.

1973:   Third Constitution introduced, but this time with the support of all political parties.
        Baluchistan government dismissed and NWFP government resigns in protest. Army sent into Baluchistan to deal with insurrection.

1977:   PPP government rigs country's second parliamentary elections. Army called out to deal with resulting protest movement and martial law declared in cities.
        General Zia ul-Haq takes over in coup, promising elections within ninety days.
        Bhutto charged with murder.

1978:   Islamicization process begun in attempt to legitimize military rule.

1979:   Bhutto executed. Political activity banned.
        Soviet Union invades Afghanistan.

1980:   Afghan refugees begin pouring into Pakistan.
        US ends Pakistan's international isolation by declaring support.

1983:   Army sent into Sindh to suppress revolt against military rule.

1984:   Benazir Bhutto leaves Pakistan for London.

Zia declares himself 'elected' President after referendum on Islamicization.

1985: Zia announces Mohammad Khan Junejo Prime
Minister of Assembly elected on non-party basis to
form civilian buffer for military rule.

1986: Benazir Bhutto returns to Pakistan to largest ever
crowds for a political leader.

1987: Bhutto marries Asif Zardari, a Sindhi feudal.

1988: Soviet troops begin withdrawing from Afghanistan.
Zia dismisses his own handpicked government,
dissolves assemblies and announces elections.
Ten weeks later he is killed along with entire top brass
of the army and US ambassador in a mysterious
plane crash. PPP emerges as the largest party in
elections but not with a majority. After long delay,
Bhutto is allowed to form government.

1989: Soviet troops complete withdrawal from Afghanistan
but Pakistan-backed resistance fails to topple communist regime in Kabul.

1990: India and Pakistan on verge of fourth war after unrest
breaks out in Kashmir.
Troops once more sent into cities of Sindh to sort out
ethnic violence.
Bhutto government dismissed.
Nawaz Sharif, army-backed former protégé of
General Zia, wins election to become Prime Minister.
PPP trounced.

INTRODUCTION:
INVITATION TO THE TAMASHA

'Benazir Benazir *Wazir-e-Azam** Benazir!' Thousands upon thousands of underfed bodies crushed together in Lyari stadium in one of the poorest slums of Karachi, hanging from skeletal trees, crowded on overlooking balconies, screaming frenziedly for the young woman they believed would lift them out of their miserable poverty.

Above the excited din, flabby and sweat-stained members of the Pakistan People's Party jostled for the microphone to compete with the static in obsequious songs eulogizing their leader. As Benazir Bhutto's Japanese jeep pressed its way through crowded narrow bazaar streets to reach the feverish audience, fireworks exploded into the night sky, reflected in thousands of burning eyes. It was impossible not to share in the excitement, as the most dormant of Western senses were dizzied and assailed by the thumping discordant music and heady Eastern aroma of sweat, jasmine and rose-petals, curling hashish smoke and sizzling samosas.

It was the *tamasha* to end all *tamashas*. But Big Brother, in the form of Pakistan's military, was as always not far away. Among the pulsing throng slipped intelligence agents, sending back reports to the sterile capital of Islamabad to be fingered impatiently by the slyly grinning general who was one of the world's longest-ruling dictators.

Billed the 'People's Wedding', the public ceremony of the

---

* *Wazir-e-Azam*: Prime Minister. For other italicized words and phrases requiring explanation, see the Glossary on p. 297.

marriage of Benazir Bhutto with Asif Zardari was a barely disguised political rally. For me, a young English journalist on my first foreign assignment, the spectacle was simultaneously fascinating and repelling – what could these most marginalized of people really expect from the white-skinned feudal princess, arriving glitter-clad and attendant-surrounded on her rose-strewn stage? Yet they danced, that night in the fever of hope. In contrast, barely disguising his boredom, lounging next to Benazir in starched white on a red velvet throne, was Asif, the chain-smoking playboy who would ultimately help bring her down and himself end up behind bars.

Her every move under scrutiny by General Zia's thousand eyes, as it had been for eleven years since her father was removed from the premiership and subsequently hanged, Benazir's courage and stamina were impressive. The wedding scene was a striking contrast to the silk-lined Kensington flat where I had interviewed her for the first time four months earlier. But even then, outlining her political plans as she sat surrounded by extravagant bouquets congratulating her on her engagement, Benazir Bhutto was clearly a woman with a destiny.

On that sultry wedding night in December 1987 in downtown Karachi, it was nobody's guess that within one year Benazir would be Prime Minister. Nor would the struggle end there. In less than two more years, similar crowds would surround the colonnades of the nearby Karachi court where she stood tearfully accused of corruption, removed from power by the same generals who had reluctantly let her in. The story of her rise and fall was without doubt one of the best political sagas of the 1980s.

The morning the gold-embossed wedding invitation dropped through my letterbox in Birmingham was one of industrial shades of autumn grey. By contrast, the spidery gold Urdu script promised an exotic adventure far from my normal routine as a trainee reporter at Central TV, one of Britain's largest regional television stations.

I was not to be disappointed. From the moment the plane stopped in Dubai, to be boarded by pyjama-clad Pakistani Gulf-workers swathed in clumsy cloth and clutching high-tech ghetto-blasters, I was intrigued. So utterly illiterate were these proud-faced tribesmen that not one could decipher his seat number, stumbling clumsily while a sniffy-nosed air hostess and the Western-suited businessman next to me looked on in disgust. In the twenty months I was ultimately to spend in Pakistan, I never lost the initial sensation of how, instead of passing from one epoch to another, the centuries somehow co-existed there.

The scene on the plane and the sweaty clamour of Karachi airport, where I was tugged this way and that by insistent porters, fingered by beggars and harangued by taxi-drivers, one of whom ferried me helterskelter through the noisy traffic, was another world again from that of the elegant silk-clad ladies swishing through the cool rooms of the Bhutto house in the week-long wedding celebrations.

Followed up the road from the house by an unsubtle intelligence agent in cravat and dark glasses, I came across a group of scruffy hawkers beneath a green and white painted shrine, selling fragrant rose and jasmine garlands to the constant flow of people climbing its long flight of steps in search of health and prosperity. Taking photos, I was pursued by a man with a dancing monkey to a roadside stall where a scrawny faded green parrot told fortunes by picking out cards. An ill-tempered creature with one eye produced a card predicting that I would be back within a year. It was a safe bet. I was intrigued by the enigma of Pakistan, with its tragic history.

Back in the dreary British Midlands, I longed for the colours and sounds and realized that reporting on car crashes and knitting exhibitions would never be quite the same again. When the trusting Asia editor of the *Financial Times* gave me the opportunity to return a few months later, I set off with an oversized suitcase packed with all my worldly goods, arriving in the chaos that was the frontier town of Peshawar in the run-up to the withdrawal of Soviet troops from neighbouring Afghanistan.

Eleven years into military rule, the country was in a mess: Benazir seemed the only hope. A twentieth-century Western-educated woman as leader of a country rooted in Islam and Eastern precepts, run on a feudal social code belonging to the Middle Ages – was that really the answer?

With the benefit of foresight, perhaps the country's founder, Mohammad Ali Jinnah, would never have pushed so hard for

Pakistan. Only a year after securing its creation in 1947 he was dead, no longer able to fight off the tuberculosis that had been devouring his lungs. Looking at faded photographs showing Jinnah with Mountbatten, the British Viceroy, and Indian Congress members in the run-up to Partition. it seems incredible that they did not guess the deadly secret behind the stretched, ghostly face.

Without Jinnah's guiding ambition, it became tragically clear that religion was not enough to hold together a country with two wings 1,500 miles apart and no common language. As the cracks began surfacing, traumatic events followed in quick succession. The first Prime Minister, Liaquat Ali Khan, was gunned down in October 1951, an assassination carried out, some suspected, by the clergy who resented his secular stance. Language riots broke out among the Bengalis of East Pakistan, who, denied a fair share of jobs in the army and civil service — the two organizations which were already becoming the country's masters — felt that they had simply exchanged one set of oppressors for another. Pakistan's first martial law was declared the following year in Lahore, when *mullahs* took to the streets demanding the outlawing of the Ahmadi sect in an attempt to purge Islam and make Pakistan the 'land of the pure' to which its name translates.

Within four years of Pakistan's creation the country had been robbed of its two pre-eminent leaders, and the Muslim League, the party which had fought for Pakistan, was disintegrating. Unlike the Indian Congress Party, which had its links in all regions, the strongest roots of the Muslim League had been in Uttar Pradesh, which had remained in India. The party's decline left the way open for the civil service to run things, and in what amounted to a civil coup, a senior bureaucrat, Ghulam Mohammad, became Governor General of Pakistan.

While India was holding its first election in 1952, Pakistan was still arguing over a Constitution. There were two main obstacles. The country had been created at cross-purposes: secularists like Jinnah and Liaquat had wanted it to safeguard Muslim political and economic interests, while the clergy saw it as a new cradle of Islam, purged of modern influences. Consequently from the start they had no hope of agreeing on the role Islam should play in the running of the state. The unresolved debate over this, in particular the question of whether democracy and Islam can be compatible, was fundamental in Pakistan's failure to shake off its military shackles. But in those early years there was another, more tangible, obstacle. In a democratic system the East Pakistanis who made up 54 per cent of the population would hold sway, a situation their oppressors in West Pakistan could not abide. It took a bloody war to resolve the issue finally, with a further partition in 1971 to form Bangladesh.

The first Constitution was finally introduced in 1956, formally naming Pakistan an Islamic nation, which only a Muslim could head. But two years and three prime ministers later it was scrapped, along with all pretence of democracy. In 1958 Generals Iskandar Mirza and Ayub Khan declared martial law, stating that the Constitution was unworkable. A long cycle of military rule had begun.

Today the late Field-Marshal Ayub is looked back on as something of a hero, as a dictator who really did make the trains run on time, even if he awarded himself many medals and titles for his accomplishments. In the search for legitimacy which preoccupies so many military rulers, he introduced a scheme called 'Basic Democracy' under which the country was divided into 80,000 constituencies, each of about 1,000 people, who voted from a pre-selected list for a representative known as a 'Basic Democrat'. Basic it was, and crude too. In February 1960 the 80,000 Basic Democrats, who were rather easier to manipulate than an entire electorate, mostly answered yes to the question, 'Do you have confidence in President Ayub?' allowing him to declare himself 'elected' by a 95.6 per cent vote.

Two years later Ayub introduced a Constitution which did not recognize political parties, concentrating power in the hand of the President. It also institutionalized the power of the military and bureaucracy, as the latter selected candidates for Basic Democrats, who then chose members of the national and provincial assemblies. Article 131 was the icing on the cake, sanctioning whatever action the President might care to take that was in the 'national interest'. Such centralization of power and reliance on the Punjabi-dominated bureaucracy seriously inflamed Bengali alienation, particularly as Ayub was openly racist about what he called the 'inferior breed'.

But Ayub's green revolution and pro-business policies brought an economic boom to Pakistan. Between 1958 and 1963, industrial production grew by 72 per cent – well above the Asian average of 55 per cent. The second half of the decade saw an annual average agricultural growth of 6.3 per cent. But the benefits were concentrated among the élite, and mostly in Punjab. While the rich were getting richer the poor had got poorer, and the social sector received scant attention, beginning the illiteracy spiral. Education received less than 1 per cent of GNP. Dr Mehbub-ul Haq, the Planning Minister, argued that a widening of income inequalities was necessary in the initial stages of development, in order to provide a larger cake which eventually everyone would get more of.

But as the cake increased in size it became available to fewer consumers, and disclosures such as the fact that twenty-two families owned 66 per cent of the country's industry, 97 per cent of insurance and 80 per cent of banking could only generate unrest. Despite the consistent rise in per capita national income, the living standards of many actually fell. Between 1954 and 1967 wages of industrial workers in West Pakistan fell by 12 per cent, while the gap between per capita income in East and West Pakistan grew from 30 per cent to 61 per cent.

Failure to tackle both regional and economic distributive discrepancies could not continue ignored. While Ayub was celebrating his 'Decade of Development' the people of both East and West Pakistan were stirring. His authority over the army had been weakened by Pakistan's defeat in the 1965 war against India over Kashmir, and he never lifted the state of emergency then imposed. In fact fundamental rights remained suspended in Pakistan until March 1985. Resentment had reached a crescendo in East Pakistan, where Sheikh Mujib's Awami League led strikes and protests against West Pakistan, which, like the British colonizers, was buying Bengali jute cheaply, processing it and taking the profits from exporting it.

In West Pakistan the opportunity was seized by Zulfikar Ali Bhutto, who had been a protégé of Ayub and his Foreign Minister till he was sacked in 1967. Bhutto set up the Pakistan People's Party (PPP), using socialist rhetoric and personal charisma to win support among workers and peasants for a grand anti-Ayub movement. Ill and facing mounting pressure, on 21 February 1969

Ayub handed over power to another general, Yahya Khan, who rather surprisingly kept his promise to hold elections.

Calling for *'roti, kapra aur makan'* ('bread, clothing and shelter'), Ali Bhutto remains the only politician in Pakistan to have fought an election on economic slogans. He became its first elected Prime Minister, but his victory was marred. While Bhutto won 81 out of 138 seats in West Pakistan, the real winner of the 1970 election was Mujib, who swept the East, taking all but two of the 162 seats, giving him a countrywide majority. It was the logical outcome of the 1947 Partition, but for the Punjabi-dominated military and civil service the prospect of Bengali rule was the worst possible scenario and one they refused to accept.

Already betraying his supposed commitment to democracy, Bhutto told his party members he would 'break their legs' if they attended the Parliament, forcing Yahya to reject Mujib's compromise suggestion of a confederation with two sovereign states, two Constitutions and common defence, foreign policy and currency. The Awami League began a wave of protests across East Pakistan, bringing the capital, Dacca, to a standstill. Mujib was arrested and flown to West Pakistan and the army moved in, beginning a catalogue of atrocities against the 'bingos' as they referred to their darker-skinned, smaller Bengali countrymen.

The inevitable happened. On 23 November 1971 India invaded and the battle was soon over. While Pakistan Television was talking of glory and Bhutto was tearing up a ceasefire resolution in the UN in New York, shouting that Pakistan would fight for 'a thousand years', Dacca fell most ingloriously. Bangladesh was declared an independent country and Bhutto was sworn in as Chief Martial Law Administrator and President of what remained of Pakistan.

Despite, or perhaps even because of, the humiliating defeat, Bhutto started office in a strong position. Though the army was by no means united over the idea of a civilian government, junior officers were no longer prepared to take instructions from seniors who had surrendered up more than half the country.

The first two years under Bhutto were the closest Pakistan has ever come to democracy, culminating in the all-party signing of the country's third Constitution – the first to guarantee universal suffrage through direct elections. But even in that time periodicals were banned and editors arrested, and the impressive array of rights guaranteed by the new Constitution remained suspended throughout Bhutto's rule. Many now believe Bhutto had seized on democratic slogans only when, after falling out with Ayub, he realized that this was his only route to power, as the army would never support him for the top job.

On 14 February 1973, in a most undemocratic manner, he sacked the left-wing government of Baluchistan, accusing it of planning secession. There seems little evidence that it was doing anything more seditious than trying to improve the appalling lot of Pakistan's largest and least populous province, but Bhutto was paranoid about a repetition of Bangladesh. The ill-thought-out move sparked off an insurgency in which 10,000 people are estimated to have been killed. Bhutto was already making the mistake of using the army to clear up a civilian government's mess, and within a year the military was back in power in one province.

Obsessed by staying in power at all costs, Bhutto discarded his socialist colleagues, fearing that they were creating their own lobbies, and set up a paramilitary organization called the Federal Security Force to persecute the enemies he began to see everywhere. Forgetting his slogans, Bhutto turned to Pakistan's traditional power-brokers for support, recruiting rich *zamindars*. Too late he tried to win over the business community, but they had been alienated by his ruthless nationalization campaign and the devaluation of the rupee by 131 per cent, which had put an end to Pakistan's boom. To woo the *mullahs* and the Islamic world he banned alcohol and outlawed minority Muslim sects such as the Ahmadis. But the clergy would not forget how he had ridiculed them in his early days, when he defended his penchant for whisky by arguing that the *mullahs* drank blood.

However, the ordinary people had no one else to turn to and Bhutto could still work his magic before a crowd. Yet so paranoid was he that though he would have won the 1977 elections anyway, Bhutto felt compelled to rig the vote to secure 80 per cent of the seats. This was the final straw which convinced many that he wanted civilian dictatorship. The opposition parties, which ranged from religious groups to former PPP members, all ganged up in a grand anti-PPP movement known as the Pakistan National Alliance (PNA), backed by money from businessmen and Saudi

Arabia. Betrayed by Bhutto's repression and failure to introduce progressive government, people took to the streets all over Pakistan.

Panicking, Bhutto declared martial law in the cities of Lahore, Karachi and Hyderabad and ordered troops to fire on PNA supporters coming out of mosques. As all Pakistan's leaders have discovered in turn, using the army as a government police force is to invite disaster, and the army began refusing to fire. There was general relief when on 4 July 1977, in an operation code-named 'Fairplay', the army surrounded the houses of all PPP leaders and put Bhutto under house arrest in the hill resort of Murree.

Declaring himself interested only in being a good soldier, General Zia, the army chief who had headed the coup, promised elections within ninety days. It was the first of many such promises to be broken. When Bhutto was freed, his renewed ability to draw huge crowds made his victory seem assured. Inevitably the elections were cancelled, and Bhutto was locked up with a murder charge issued against him.

It soon became clear that the general whom Bhutto had made army chief because he thought him too unintelligent to present a threat was a master strategist. Loathing politicians, Zia relied on civil servants and a few *zamindars*. But his big mistake was to hang Bhutto, convinced that while alive he would present a threat even behind bars. What he failed to appreciate was that by executing Bhutto on an apparently trumped-up murder charge he would make him a martyr, clearing his name to make his ghost and ultimately his heir a far greater threat.

Condemned internationally for the hanging, Zia launched a stern Islamicization programme to make Pakistan a theocracy, in the start of a painful search for legitimacy for his regime. Thousands of people were arrested in the process, but luck was on his side. The Soviet invasion of neighbouring Afghanistan on 26 December 1979 suddenly made Pakistan a crucial American ally and conduit for support to the Afghan resistance. Overnight the stocky general with the comically pomaded hair became a heroic defender of the frontier of the free world. Western aid soon began pumping in. But along with the money came an influx of weaponry and drugs to add to Pakistan's already myriad social problems.

And there was another force Zia had not reckoned with. On the eve of Bhutto's execution his daughter Benazir, the young convent-educated girl who wanted to enter the foreign service, had promised her father that she would carry on his mission. Her only training on the floor of the very civilized Oxford Debating Union, the nervous twenty-six-year-old began touring the country, clutching her father's Mao cap and catching the country's imagination. In a subcontinent which thrives on political dynasties, Benazir was the obvious heir to her father's political mantle, despite the oppressed position of women in Pakistani society which meant that even at the public ceremony of her own wedding the sexes were segregated.

Zia countered with a series of prison spells and house arrests for Benazir and her mother Nusrat, co-leaders of the PPP. Finally in 1984 Benazir was driven by ill-health to London, where she remained in exile in the Barbican for two years. There she began showing that as well as inheriting some of her father's powerful charisma and the all-important Bhutto name, she had been dealt a fair share of his famous arrogance. Angered by Benazir's refusal to allow elections within the party, some of its founding members left in disgust, including Ghulam Mustafa Jatoi, who had led a movement of civil unrest in 1983 to push for elections and had twice refused offers from Zia to become Prime Minister.

Meanwhile, in 1985, under both national and American pressure, Zia began a civilian experiment based on non-party elections. Despite a PPP call for boycott, 53 per cent voted – more than in the two subsequent party-based elections – and Zia installed the unknown mango farmer Mohammad Khan Junejo as his hand-picked Prime Minister.

But Zia could not destroy the PPP, and Benazir was to dog him to the end. On 10 April 1986, apparently assured of American support, she made a triumphant return to Pakistan, inspired by watching the scenes on television of Cory Aquino's successful movement against the Marcos dictatorship in the Philippines. More than a million people came out into the streets of Lahore to shower Benazir with rose-petals, as she was driven under the shadow of the city's massive fort along the Mall, past the building in which the young Rudyard Kipling once hammered out copy for the *Lahore Civil and Military Gazette*, drawing bizarre comparisons between Pakistan's city of Arabian nights, and the Sussex Downs where he had spent his youth.

For that first month Benazir drew record audiences at meetings from the Khyber to Karachi, even in areas like the Baluchi capital of Quetta, which was usually hostile to the PPP. The large crowds drawn perhaps as much by curiosity and boredom as by genuine support, led Benazir to overestimate the party's strength. After party leaders were arrested in a crackdown in August, the 'peaceful' anti-government campaign for elections soon fizzled out, along with her hopes of simulating Cory's Peoplepower.

When Benazir's wedding took place in December of the following year, few among even her most ardent supporters believed that within a year she would be Prime Minister. It was with obviously fake bravado that on the first day of the week-long celebrations Benazir's friends sang to her future husband, 'You must agree that Benazir will serve the nation,' to which he replied, 'That's all right, I will look after the children.'

When I returned to Pakistan in April 1988 international interest was only in Afghanistan. In fact, I was with a *mujaheddin* group dodging Soviet bombs across the border when on 29 May to nation-wide shock, Zia abruptly dismissed his own government and dissolved the assemblies, again promising elections within ninety days that few believed he would hold.

Starting to feel the pressure from Pakistan's US backers, who were uncomfortable at continuing to support a dictator, Zia had begun making mistakes. Public outcry at the explosion of the Ojheri camp missile dump in Rawalpindi, killing hundreds, had brought the reputation of the army to an all-time low. When the government joined in the criticism it was dismissed. Zia had obviously never intended actually to share power.

With the country confused and fearing Zia's next move and the US angry at the termination of even a pretence of democracy, the general's sudden death in a mysterious plane crash in August was nothing if not convenient. For Benazir finally the field was open.

This book follows the intrigues to stop Benazir getting into power and to undermine her even after she had assumed office. With spies from all major powers at work in the country and Pakistan's massive military intelligence machine running its own state within a state, the situation was frequently surreal. My own personal experiences ranged from the bizarre, such as finding a lime-green dyed sheep tied up in my garden with a compliments note attached explaining it was to be sacrificed at a time deemed appropriate by the moonsighting committee (part of the yearly celebrations for the Muslim festival of Eid), to the frightening, such as being taken in and interrogated by intelligence officials, accused of acting as a liaison between British and Soviet espionage in a plot to restore the king of Afghanistan.

Throughout this time I was fortunate enough to have close access to Benazir and to army officials, including the head of the military intelligence. There is no doubt that a large section of the army did all it could to prevent elections taking place after Zia's death and then to prevent Benazir winning, often through the most sordid methods. It was with great reluctance (and heavy US pressure), after midnight negotiations among go-betweens, that they allowed her to become the first woman prime minister of an Islamic nation when she scraped through the elections with the largest number of seats, if without a majority.

But throughout my stay the military were always in control and it was obviously only a matter of time before they stepped back in. Benazir played into their hands by accepting many of their terms for taking office, then appearing more interested in power than in social and economic reform, though she would argue that the former was needed to effect the latter. Like her father, she was impatient at criticism, and kept hold of the state-controlled news-agency and papers despite election pledges to free them. Within a month the state government in Baluchistan was dismissed. Her time would be taken up with minute details such as organizing cooks and tableware for official banquets while the larger canvas of problems went ignored. Ministers openly indulged in making money, arguing that they did not expect to be in power long, while her husband's name became involved in a series of scandals. Under pressure from all those who wanted rewards for their eleven-year struggle against Zia, Benazir surrounded herself increasingly with cronies who kept her isolated from public opinion.

One of these was Aitzaz Ahsan, the diminutive and womanizing Interior Minister who, fearing for his own position, which gave him nominal authority over the military intelligence, had my visa stopped when I questioned the success of Benazir's overt efforts to woo the army. The brewing uprising I wrote of in the offending article was suppressed by the army chief, who still had some sympathy for Benazir. But within ten months the government's failure to tackle escalating ethnic violence in Sindh, and blunders in dealings with the military, allowed the hawks within the armed forces to win the day. On 6 August 1990, while the eyes of the world were on the Iraqi invasion of Kuwait, Pakistan's second elected government was dismissed by the President, citing corruption and ineptitude and claiming that it had 'wilfully undermined and impaired the working of the Constitution'. Corruption charges were laid against both Benazir and her husband, who at the time of writing remains in a Karachi jail.

With elections promised and Mr Jatoi finally Prime Minister if only as caretaker, I was suddenly allowed back to Pakistan in September. Perhaps partly because I came there from the carefree city of Rio de Janeiro, where I now live, Pakistan third time round was a sadly depressing place. I found the same conversations, the same generals and the same power-brokers — but more people asking whether the country should even exist.

Benazir, whom I visited in her new fortress-like house in Karachi, was tearful but unrepentant, refusing to believe she had made any mistakes, though conceding 'You don't dismiss an elected government to let it back.' Two weeks earlier the jovial British High Commissioner had been asked to leave her house for subtly suggesting that perhaps her husband might need taking in hand.

Given Benazir's record and her formidable array of opponents, the results of the 24 October elections were unsurprising. The PPP was trounced, winning only forty-five seats out of 217. Benazir naturally cried foul, calling the results 'an electoral *coup d'état*', but she could not deny that many people were angry, feeling that she, like her father, had cheated them of democracy.

General Zia may be chuckling in his grave, with his protégé Nawaz Sharif now ensconced as Prime Minister and backed by a safe majority and the army and civil service. But it is an unenviable job. Before the elections a crucial $600 million a year in US aid was suspended, theoretically because the White House had suddenly decided to act on long-held suspicions that Pakistan possesses a nuclear bomb. The Gulf crisis doubled the price of oil imports and cut off hard currency remittances of hundreds of thousands of expatriate Pakistani workers in the Gulf, the country's most profitable export. Once more Benazir was back lobbying for support in Washington. The curtain may have come down on several acts of her story, but the tale may not yet have ended.

Rio de Janeiro, January 1991

I

INVENTING A COUNTRY

There is a moment in the grey half-light of pre-dawn, long after the jackals have stopped screaming and just before the birds start singing, in which time seems frozen. Soon the wail of the *muezzin* calling the faithful to prayer will shatter the silence – the signal for millions of men to kneel forward, hands placed behind ears and facing Mecca, to begin the day's first call to Allah. Curfew will be lifted and the biggest squatter camp in the biggest town in the world's only Muslim homeland will throb with jangling bells, squawking horns, and the babble of multifarious subcontinental tongues.

Twelve thousand more people will be born in Pakistan this day. Two thousand will be dead within a year. More of them will learn to use a gun than to speak the national language. Medieval sports of cock-fighting and bear-baiting will provide more of their entertainment than television, and they will have no theatres or concert halls to visit. Only a third will have access to clean drinking water and only 15 per cent will have sewerage. A quarter will go to school. Many will become heroin addicts. This is a country killing its future.

As the sun sucks up the dust-cloud breaking the apricot dawn, do not fear to blink. The dream of a British-trained lawyer cum frustrated actor, Pakistan is more than mere fantasy. A vision brought to fruition by the British departure from India, it took just seven years to create yet forty-four years later has reached no consensus on its meaning. A magical land inhabited by nonsense names like the Wali of Swat, the Mir of Hunza and the Jam of

Lasbela; full of hidden valleys where people trade in buttons and
shells; mountain passes where a rugby-like version of polo is played
among the peaks, cows wandering on and off the pitch; deserts
where suspected criminals are tried by walking across burning
coals; tribal territories where the Kalashnikov is king and no Westerner has ever gone; borderlands where spies of today's superpowers play out small wars. Many of its people share neither
language nor social system nor tradition but have been gathered
together in the name of the crescent in a geographical mass that is
tangibly real, often frighteningly so.

In Orangi, an illegal settlement of more than a million people
on the outskirts of Karachi, Pakistan's largest city, curfew and
ethnic violence is such a way of life that gunfire no longer makes
people jump. During times of riot, entering it can seem like
passing through the gates of Hell. The influx of guns and drugs
from the Afghan war in an area inhabited by ethnic groups from
all across the subcontinent means killings are so frequent that
newspaper reports of massacres are relegated to a lowly inside
paragraph, just about where a British local broadsheet would note
a small theft or a forthcoming jumble sale.

After dawn prayers, Orangi life dissipates into streets ringing
with the hammering of enough tyres to supply a nation, the
chatter of grease-monkey children set to work in the more inaccessible parts of engines, the cracked strains of a haunting Pushtu
melody on an ancient transistor. Inside sweatshops, bony figures
hunch over whining sewing-machines and knock out cloth to
export to East Asia, where it will be printed with designs and sold
far more profitably. As the heat and dust of the day intensify,
inside a few of the more fortunate shacks fans lazily stir the putrid
air. They are powered by electricity stolen via an intricate network
of bare wires from overhead cables supplying power to the rich
southern suburbs.

Shapeless burqas unidentifiable as women pick their way
sparrow-like through where streets crack and denigrate into cloaca.
Like silken shuttlecocks they shuffle hurriedly to bargain for vegetables, unsure when the next outbreak of rioting will bring back
army trucks and curfew. Fleets of impossibly overcrowded and
ludicrously decorated tin buses with skirts of chains ply towards a
network of roundabouts, hurtling precariously past derelict estates

which look like relics of bombing raids. One was the drug bazaar at Sorabgoth until bulldozed by army tanks in December 1986. Another is the ladies-only market where women haggle over cheap glass bangles and musk perfume, and have intricate henna designs painted on to their hands. Eventually the desert is visible through the sprawling mass of buildings, and the black-eyed hashish-smoking Pathan drivers sulkily deposit workers at textile and pharmaceutical factories to begin their long shifts.

But in those pre-dawn hours before erupting into a maelstrom of undernourished humanity, Orangi is simmering, ever on the verge of boiling. It is in this moment in which the day has not quite decided how it will treat mankind that Pakistan is trapped. 'Islam in danger' was the cry raised to justify the necessity of dividing India and inventing a country for Indian Muslims, who feared they would be swallowed up by the large Hindu majority in a united independent India based on one man, one vote. Today in their very own homeland Muslims need safeguarding from each other and must, through half-truths and exaggerated myths of land-hungry Hindu dragons on the borders, maintain their expensive hostility to India to justify their country's existence. Pakistan's huge army, entrusted with the task of protecting the country's 'ideological frontiers' as well as its borders, has, not surprisingly, often been tempted to indulge in politics. There is a further irony. Drawn by religion and culture to the East and an earlier glory remembered only in the crumbling palaces of the great Mughal emperors, the country is both resentful of and dependent on American aid to survive. Walls are slashed with slogans against the 'Great Satan', but the deserts have not yielded the oil of neighbouring Iran that would enable Pakistan to turn its nose up, as it would dearly love to, at a $4 billion US aid package.

Created as a Promised Land for the Muslim religion by a mostly irreligious élite led by the British-trained lawyer Mohammad Ali Jinnah, Pakistan's *raison d'être* seems insufficient to hold together a disparate people speaking twenty-two languages and, rather than uniting, produces only division. The country inherited then lost by Benazir Bhutto, only its second nationally elected Prime Minister since independence, has never before been so disunited. Punjab, the biggest province, is promoting aggressive Punjabi chauvinism (the result of government by a different and hostile party to the centre), Sindh is in a state of armed insurrection, Baluchistan rejects what it sees as federal government interference in its territory, while North West Frontier Province runs wild, whole areas off limits to the government but havens for drugs and arms dealers, and the base for increasingly disillusioned guerrillas fighting in the continuing war in Afghanistan. After forty-three years of swinging between martial law and unsatisfactory democracy, Pakistan's second democratically elected government was dismissed within twenty months, once more raising uncomfortable questions as to the governability of Pakistan and whether a country based solely on religion can survive. After her abrupt removal from office in August 1990 Benazir Bhutto commented: 'The real question is can the army come to terms with an elected government?'

The lingering malaise of a country is not a pleasant sight. Born through the horror of Partition, which saw the biggest and bloodiest migration in history, millions killed and millions uprooted, neighbours turning guns and knives on each other, train doors opening to tip mutilated bodies on to platforms as they passed between India and the newly created Pakistan, its people remain in the wilderness. In the Great Migration of 1947, 15 million people crossed the new borders dividing families and beliefs, their journeys often proving fatal. The bitterness remains in those who remember, as they describe never-ending straggles of people, some in bullock-carts, others on foot, the old and crippled on backs, children in baskets often abandoned at the roadside as Muslims fled the *lathis* of Hindus in the Indian Union and Sikhs and Hindus fled the muskets of Muslims in the new Pakistan. Many died of cholera or smallpox, and the sorry refugees were preyed upon by marauders, often joined by the police, and by the blackest vultures circling overhead following the smell of blood.

The 1947 reality of the poet Mohammad Iqbal's dream in 1930 of a separate Indian Muslim state was fatally flawed. As late as 1933 the idea of Pakistan was described by Muslim leaders to the Joint Select Committee of the British Parliament as 'only a student's scheme . . . chimerical and impractical', referring to an oyster dinner held by Cambridge student Rahmat Ali at London's rather un-Islamic Waldorf hotel to propose a country for Muslims. After the 1937 elections, had the Hindu-dominated Congress Party agreed, the Muslim League would still have settled for a share of power in independent India, and before 1940 Muslim hardliners were still dismissing the idea of a separate nation for Muslims as absurd.

Even when the Muslim League adopted Iqbal's two-nation theory in the 1940 Lahore Resolution, it did not consolidate the Muslim vote in India until 1946 on the eve of Partition, and then only in the provinces where Muslims were in a minority.[1] It was a Muslim party without the support of Muslim masses, run by an élite who cried 'Islam in danger' when it was their own positions, never their religion, that was at risk. The fact that in 1946 Jinnah indicated to the Cabinet Commission Plan[2] – a last-ditch attempt by British cabinet ministers to preserve the unity of India – that he would accept a united India providing it contained two separate Constitution-making bodies of Hindu and Muslim provinces, suggested that to him at least, Pakistan was really a bargaining position. Those Muslims who really wanted Pakistan lived in the parts of India which at Partition remained Indian. Only a fraction of these could flee to Pakistan, leaving more Muslims in India than in the longed-for homeland.

Pakistan has never quite lived up to the idea. Not surprisingly, it is those who gave up most to make the hazardous cross-border transition into the new country who are most frustrated today and most often in the forefront of Karachi's ethnic violence. The whole concept was based on the hypocrisy of a few. Why was it necessary to create a country for perhaps the world's most all-encompassing religion – one surely strong enough to be practised anywhere and which had never been in any danger of being consumed? If religion determines borders, why is the Muslim Gulf divided into twelve states? And if it was so necessary for Muslims to have their own country, how could they justify a Partition which left 40 million Muslims in India?

The contradictions arise because the issue was never freedom of religion. As the Indian scholar M. J. Akbar wrote: 'Pakistan was not created by the Muslim masses; it owed its birth to a handful of "leaders" who were not content with separate beliefs – they wanted separate electorates, separate language, separate dress, separate identities and finally separate homes.'[3] Those at the forefront of making the dream happen did not do it for Islam but, like

Mohammad Ali Jinnah, a man with a weakness for a drop of whisky and a ham sandwich, to secure their own economic and political ambitions. In fact, were Jinnah alive today, he could be flogged under Pakistan's strict Islamic laws. A cold nationalist who disliked connecting religion and politics and who right up to the mid 1930s claimed he was an Indian first and Muslim second, Jinnah saw in the *mullahs'* slogans the route to safeguard both his own future and that of the Muslim landowning élite.

The stranglehold of this unholy alliance continues in Pakistan today, preventing democracy taking root and the formation of a middle class. Whether under martial law or democracy, under Zia or Bhutto, the *zamindars* have been allowed to loot the country and suffocate development which could weaken their own position. As a *quid pro quo* they tolerate religious laws they themselves ignore, but this means, for example, that every visitor to Pakistan is confronted at the airport with the immortal words, 'Have you alcohol?' To appease the *mullahs* alcohol was banned by the very secular Zulfikar Ali Bhutto, who never denied his own fondness for whisky. A few years ago some diplomats were expelled for drinking wine from a teapot in a Chinese restaurant in Islamabad, yet no house of the upper class or of senior civil servants is complete without a well-stocked bar.

Jawaharlal Nehru, who with Mahatma Gandhi spearheaded the movement for Indian independence, was not wrong when he described the Muslim League as a creation of the élite, concocting a problem which did not exist in the minds of the Muslim masses. The masses were more interested in where the next meal was coming from. In an article in 1947, Gandhi argued: 'I hold it utterly wrong to divide man from man by reason of religion. What conflict of interests can there be between Hindus and Muslims in the matters of revenue, sanitation, police and justice?' But by then the clergy and *zamindars* had whipped up Muslim feeling into such a frenzy over the idea of Pakistan that it was thought perfectly logical to have a country made up of two wings 1,500 miles apart, a hostile territory in between.

Given its roots, it is not surprising Pakistan has not found its way. But Jinnah never let contradictions hinder ambition. When he was thirty-nine he had taken as his second wife the sixteen-year-old daughter of a Parsi friend, but he denounced his own daughter when she wanted to marry a Parsi and left her in India. He declared Urdu the national language of the new Pakistan, yet he himself spoke none. With his first speech as elected President of Pakistan's Constituent Assembly in Karachi on 11 August 1947, Jinnah told the House: 'In the course of time Hindus will cease to be Hindus and Muslims will cease to be Muslims, not in a religious sense because that is the personal faith of each individual, but in the political sense as the citizens of the nation.' He was himself already contradicting the necessity for Pakistan's creation. Having got what he wanted through religion, it was, he was saying, to have no further role in politics.

What then was the guiding ideology of Pakistan? Jinnah had used the terms of a liberal democrat, but his use of the title 'Quaid-e-Azam' ('Great Leader') his declaration of himself as Pakistan's first Governor-General, concentrating powers in his hands, and his love of pomp, suggest that representative political institutions may have had little chance of developing. Over the years a myth has grown up around Jinnah as a man motivated by Islam, his numerous portraits in government buildings all repainted to show him in Islamic dress rather than the London-tailored suits he favoured, and fulsome tributes paid to him saying had he survived, Pakistan would not have fallen into today's morass. But, going on his record, this seems unlikely. Unlike Nehru, Jinnah had not fought for socio-economic justice of the people, more for plums for a small coterie. A telling comment came from Sheikh Abdullah, the popular leader of the Muslim majority state of Kashmir, whose position within India remains hotly contested by Pakistan. 'We have a religion in common with Jinnah but a dream in common with Nehru,' said the man who was to dominate Kashmiri politics for fifty years both in and out of jail.[4] But within thirteen months Jinnah had orphaned his creation, consumed by the tuberculosis which his ambition could no longer fight off. He had lived his last days with one lung totally destroyed and the other two-thirds eaten up.

The formation of Pakistan was only the start of the fight. Pakistan had generally taken over the poorer parts of the subcontinent and was not self-sufficient in any important manufactured products or fuel resource. From scratch a new capital and government had to be created. Its Foreign Office began life with just one typewriter. Islam could not provide food and shelter, and men wanted tangible benefits. Those who succeeded Jinnah may have been closer to Islam but lacked his vision and allowed the country to drift into the military rule which had dogged it for more than half its lifetime. The first coup plot was as early as 1951, and by 1958, when the first countrywide martial law was declared, dreams of democracy had evaporated, leaving Pakistanis to watch enviously India's development as a mass democracy despite beginning with the same problems of regionalism, the lack of a common language and a large influx of refugees.

India's struggle for independence had been a nationalist one on which its leaders could build, whereas Pakistan's had been the demand of a few that many did not want. Even in Pakistan today its people call themselves Sindhis, Baluch, Pathans first, Muslims second and finally Pakistanis. Until that order can be reversed, the country has no hope of developing, as no one will put the country's interest before their own – a factor which shows up in every area, from the burgeoning growth of the black economy, to the unfair distribution of inputs for agriculture (the main sector of the economy), to refusal to pay income tax, to the suppression of the peasantry by the ruling *zamindars*.

Within twenty-five years of its inception Pakistan had not only lost its way ideologically but had split in two, losing more than half its territory – the eastern wing which is now Bangladesh – and putting the last nail in the coffin of the two-nation theory. After three wars with India and another looming, two over Kashmir and the last in 1971 over the secession of East Pakistan, and long periods of martial law, Benazir Bhutto was faced with the task of putting the dream together again and finding a national identity for Pakistan. Her father, Pakistan's first elected Prime Minister, failed. While he realized that the only things which could hold the country together were democracy and greater regional autonomy, Zulfikar Ali Bhutto was a man of Napoleonic ambition and used these issues to promote his personal power and set in motion operations to crush the regional nationalities in Baluchistan and North West Frontier Province. President Zia, the most recent in the line of Pakistan's grinning military dictators, saw the problem too. His solution was to return to the basis for Pakistan's creation and purge the country, spreading orthodox

Islam through trying to impose the identity of the majority Punjabi population on the nation. He failed too – one cannot create winter simply by declaring it so when the days are still warm and the trees full of leaves – and the minority provinces resented what they saw as Punjabi colonization. Even with the generals back in the barracks and the politicians once more in control, the hurdles were immense. The power of the army and bureacracy is so entrenched that Benazir Bhutto's task was almost like being given a desk and a phone in the middle of a lawn and told: 'Right, you're Prime Minister now. Run the country.'

Partition still haunts, but on an ethnic rather than a religious basis. It is carved in the chest of a twelve-year-old boy, lying dead in a pool of blood, innocent victim of ethnic rivalries that a common religion seems increasingly unable to overcome. He is a *mohajir* – the name given to Muslim migrants from India, those who gave up most to find themselves isolated in their longed-for homeland and fighting for jobs and survival. The truth rings from Nehru's words: 'The alliance of religion and politics is a most dangerous thing and it yields the most abnormal kind of illegitimate blood.' Rivalries between Muslim groups in a country of many Islams – such rivalry that a Sindhi has taken a knife to the innocent *mohajir* boy and engraved in his taut young flesh 'Altaf is a buttsucker', referring to the leader of the *mohajir* community. In the space of forty-five years, Pakistan has gone from a nation searching for a country to a country searching for a nation.

Yet the strains of poverty and lack of representative government, a stagnant economy and failure to replace the colonial system, have not led people to question the country's basis. While the validity and viability of Pakistan are hotly debated, rather than doubt Islam they doubt themselves; or, better still, the outside world, particularly Hindu India or Jewish Israel, the world's only other religious homeland. Unable to create their own national identity in a positive sense, they define themselves negatively by being anti-India, anti-Moscow and even anti-West, though not within earshot of their US patrons when the next delivery of American fighter jets is awaited. The more fragmented the country becomes, the more aggressively its people fall back on Islam, seeing all their problems as the result of KGB intervention or the work of a mysterious Indo-Zionist lobby.

A country which is unable to organize a lunch, where appointments are never kept and the capital's airport will close on mere whims, sees conspiracies behind everything. A plane cannot simply crash in the mountains, it has to have been shot down by Indians or hijacked by Afghan secret agents. Even changes in train timetables are blamed on secret conspiracies. A front-page story in a Pakistani newspaper in autumn 1988, headed 'Scandalous Changes to Quetta Train Times', is typical: 'The Quetta 171 has been a very popular train with farmers, traders, litigants, and those from all other walks of life. Now, however, thanks to the sinister manoeuvring and machinating of the road transporters, the timetable has been collusively tampered with.'

The Afghan war and its resultant influx of intelligence agents from all over the world has increased the paranoia. The CIA has one of its biggest stations in Islamabad, admittedly partly for gathering Gulf intelligence through the many Pakistani soldiers provided to that region. In 1988, according to a US State Department report, Pakistan was the world's second heaviest victim of terrorist attacks, with 1,400 deaths or injuries from bomb attacks apparently carried out by agents of the Afghan secret police. In one city, just before the 1988 elections, the lights went off as masked men on motorbikes went on a mass killing campaign that by dawn had the gutters running in blood. There were many people within the country anxious to prevent elections going ahead, some politicians had even begged the generals to impose martial law, yet the finger as ever was pointed outside, this time at Indian agents thought to be interfering in Sindh in retaliation to Pakistan's alleged arming of Sikhs.

There often seems to be no logic in Pakistan. Set down by a military government, its planned capital, Islamabad, has an Orwellian feel with its numbered streets and houses starting at Zero Point, but in typical Pakistani fashion the numbers just add to the confusion, rarely following on in the correct order.

A frighteningly widespread religious view argues that the only solution to the country's woes is a return to earlier days when Islam was pure. This means stopping the learning of English or of modern scientific methods. A direct result is that in a country of 110 million people there are less than 500 holders of PhDs. Not for lack of talent – in the US alone there are 50,000 foreign-educated

Pakistani doctors. The more the country strives for what its religious scholars see as true Islam, the less equipped it becomes for running a twentieth-century state, and the more it is forced to watch once-lagging competitors such as South Korea, Thailand and Malaysia steam ahead. And the greatest irony of all: Bhutto is a modern, Western-educated young woman, but the country in which she is the dominant political figure almost entirely excludes women from the economy, and were she ever to have to give evidence in a Pakistani court her testimony would count as only half that of the most uneducated man.[5]

Many of those responsible for placing such laws on the statute books live just a few miles away from the squatter camp of Orangi, but in a different world and age entirely. Clifton is a place of wedding-cake finery – of wide boulevards lined with marble White House copies with plush silk interiors and gold taps, leather sofas and leopardskin bars. This is the powerhouse of Pakistan where the élite live – the zamindars, the retired generals, the drug barons, the politicians, and, in slightly more modest palaces, the senior bureaucrats. These are the people who created the country and make the laws by which the rest must live. The by no means undisputed queen of this insulated life is Benazir Bhutto, a Harvard- and Oxford-educated aristocrat, who rose to power on the votes of a rural poor who could not begin to imagine such luxuries but understood promises of food, shelter and jobs.

For her part, Bhutto could not have estimated the huge task she had undertaken in bridging this apartheid of wealth. Between the two worlds of Orangi and Clifton there is no meeting point. In Orangi the government fears to enter and provides nothing. Electricity is stolen, buses and schools have to be provided by community groups. In Clifton, wealth, which means that people have their own generators, their own water tanks, and their own security guards, shields them from the deficiencies of government. Bhutto, brought up surrounded by a coterie of servants, cannot imagine what it is like to scratch a living from an unforgiving land. Even when in exile during the last period of martial law, she stayed in London's luxurious Barbican Centre, with party faithfuls to do the shopping for her.

After just twenty months in power with no legislation but the budget, Bhutto was in the dock, charged with corruption and

maladministration, left to contemplate the impossibilities of working a system in which corruption and vested interests are so entrenched. Becoming the world's youngest Prime Minister at
thirty-five, Bhutto proved unable to take on successfully the powerful triumvirate of army, bureaucracy, and *mullahs*, many of whom
hold that a woman cannot be ruler of an Islamic state. Despite
having won elections, she was forced to make commitments to
these power-brokers, immediately undermining the legitimacy of
her rule.

Policy decisions were constrained by pledges Bhutto had to
make to the US before she could take power – the very superpower that she believes to be responsible for the removal, and by
implication the death, of her father. Bhutto never won the trust of
the business community, who find even more palm-greasing necessary under an elected government. Her own party, overwhelmingly dominated by *zamindars*, prevented her introducing either
the Thatcherite economic policies she so admires or the social
reforms she once so enthusiastically advocated on the floor of the
Oxford Union.

To understand Pakistan is to go back a few centuries to the days
when big landlords ruled through their grip over the peasants,
their ancestral lands electoral rotten boroughs. It is to understand a
culture based on a colonial past which bequeathed a centralized
system where the bureaucracy is all-powerful, the army is the only
force of stability and the Punjabis, the majority ethnic group which
dominates both these institutions, are the colonizers of today. Zia,
realizing this, tried to create a Pakistani identity based on the Punjab identity, thus alienating the other provinces. He invented a crime
– to be anti-Pakistan, which in his terms meant to be anti-Punjab,
but with its heritage rooted in Islam became a convenient stick with
which to beat opposition and one which later even Benazir's secular
government used. For in making sense of Pakistan, it is essential
above all to appreciate a religion that is not relegated to the place
of worship but is lived, breathed, walked and even dreamed.

The problem is that no consensus has been reached on what it
means to have a country based on Islam. Too much stress on
religion as a common bond provokes the unsolved argument as to
whether Pakistan should be a theocracy where Islam is used by
government to dictate all important social and individual be-

haviour, and where the benchmark for everything from education to law to the media is whether it is Islamic, or whether Islam should be kept separate from the workings of government, simply providing a broad set of guidelines for policymakers to refer to. Zia and Benazir Bhutto are the extremes of these views, with Bhutto favouring secular government but forced by fear of the religious lobby to pander to their wishes. From their crushing defeats in Pakistan's few elections it is clear that the religious parties' ideal is not shared by the majority of Pakistanis, but religion has been a powerful tool for undoing governments. Starting in 1953, with riots against the Ahmadi sect necessitating martial law in Lahore, time and again religious slogans have been used to destabilize those in power.

Islam is a very different thing in the opulent air-conditioned houses where politicians argue points over whisky and soda in cut crystal glasses from what it is in rural villages, where the *mullah* is often a man to be feared, his battery-powered megaphone the closest thing to modernization. Awareness of the destructive potential of the religious parties prevented the very twentieth-century Ms Bhutto from keeping pledges to remove medieval Islamic laws which discriminate against women to the extent that if they are raped and go to court they are liable to end up in prison themselves, where 43 per cent are raped again. To prove rape in Pakistan a woman must provide four male witnesses to the penetration. Many Islamic scholars have argued that this is based on the misreading of an incident in the Arabian desert during one of the Prophet's military campaigns, when his favourite wife Aisha disappeared one night and rejoined the caravan the next morning accompanied by a young soldier. The Prophet's companions demanded Aisha's death, but Allah told the Prophet that she was innocent and that four witnesses were needed to prove adultery.

In no major religion are word and deed so closely tied as in Islam – the Koran (Holy Book) and Hadis (sayings of the Prophet) are the word of God and the basis for social law. Salman Rushdie's controversial book *The Satanic Verses* caused an outcry because of its treatment of the Koran, a book on which life as well as faith is based. Sometimes the meaning is ambiguous and can be twisted. How can women be so repressed by a religion whose holy book states, 'to every man what he earns and to every woman what she earns'? The *mullah* is an extremely powerful figure as interpreter of this, and his word is accepted even if, as often happens, it flies in the face of progress. A student member of the fundamentalist Jamaat Islami at Lahore University told me earnestly that too much education was harmful, a view hard to connect with the glorious Mughal heritage which produced some of the world's most exquisite art and architecture, such as the Taj Mahal. Most of the time the interests of the *mullahs* and the élite coincide: neither wants power to fall into the hands of the masses, so they keep them subjugated – the élite because they fear progress will bring threats to their privileged positions, the clergy because they see democracy as incompatible with Islam. President Zia, who spearheaded Pakistan's most recent Islamicization campaign, feared the *mullahs'* power so much that he sent spies to village mosques to. find out what they were spreading at Friday prayers.

Dadu, deep in interior Sindh, is such a village, a place where death is a constant presence. Nights in Dadu are very, very black. The heat presses down and time passes like a funeral march as the evil white salt creeps across the lands, cracking open the earth until nothing will grow. Without money or crops there is no way to bribe the canal supervisor for even a little water.

Life in a Sindhi village is like a penny shove machine in which every few moments the weight comes down and pushes more pennies over the edge. It is a game of chance and not skill, and Lala, who started life in the wrong position – as a Dadu sharecropper at the opposite end to the politicians of Clifton – knows he is about to be pushed over the edge. He has searched hard for the answer and is convinced it is not Islam.

Islam is why they are all there. Lala remembers the stories his father told him when he was a child of the immense hope and excitement behind the creation of Pakistan – the Muslim promised land. He wishes he could read the Koran but, like more than three-quarters of the population, he is totally illiterate. Of course he knows the formulaic prayers Bismillah Al Rahman Al Rahim (Allah the Beneficial, the Merciful), for which he prostrates himself five times daily, but the tales his father told him of the Prophet's love and generosity are hard to reconcile with the blood and thunder with which the *mullah* regales them in the mosque. Muslim brother is killing Muslim brother in his own village, and young people talk only of breaking the country up.

There seem to be so many Islams. At the mosque on Fridays, the *mullah* rants hysterically against 'the curse of woman's rule' and calls for Islamic government and Iranian-style revolution. In the village *chaikana* (teahouse), through clouds of hashish smoke, Lala's younger friends talk enthusiastically of civil war and independence for their province. Over the ramshackle bazaar, red nationalist flags fly, marked out with menacing black axes. Things are so bad that many talk with hope of an Indian invasion, wanting to be part of the country their fathers fought to separate from.

The labourer cannot see how either option would solve his immediate problem of feeding a pregnant wife and six children, two of whom have tuberculosis. As his land turns white from the seeping salt, he is finding it increasingly hard to survive on the third of the produce he is allowed to keep. The rest goes to the feudal lord on whose land he and his ancestors have always worked, whose shirt-hem he must kiss and for whom he voted in the election. The *zamindar* was one of Bhutto's MPs, who at cocktail parties in his marble palace speaks fervently of universal education but would not dream of weakening his own unthinking peasant vote bloc by allowing schools in his own fiefdom.

In the one-room shack in which Lala's family, like most of the villagers, lives, is pinned a picture of Benazir Bhutto. Lala still believes she is their only chance. He once heard her father, Zulfikar Ali Bhutto, Pakistan's first elected Prime Minister, speak, and Lala had never been given such hope. Bhutto's words, '*roti, kapra aur makan*' (bread, clothing and shelter), seemed directed straight at him. Bhutto did not keep his promises but instead took into his government the very landlords who were oppressing Lala and his ilk. 'When he was toppled in a coup we made little protest. Army rule again.'

Lala says they felt guilty later, when Bhutto was hanged by his army chief who ousted him, General Zia ul-Haq. 'Bhutto was a Sindhi and Sindhis have always been oppressed by the majority Punjabi population, who fill the army, civil service and police. Some of us tried to make amends in 1983 when we joined the movement to protest against martial law but as usual the rest of the country did not support Sindh. The army came in tanks then. They stole cattle and raped women and shot those demanding their rights. They rounded up thousands.'

Lala fled to the forest and became a bandit. Some of his friends stayed there. They got guns – plenty were available from the Afghan war – and started kidnapping people and demanding protection money. They made a lot of money, Lala knew, 'but what kind of a life for a man, living like pigs in the dirt, in the forest, always on the run?' So he went back to the land, although he recalls that 'one year was particularly bad. There was no rain so we did not even have subsoil in which to grow crops. We had a goat but had to sell it to keep alive.'

Lala thought of going to the city: 'People used to say the streets of Karachi were paved with gold.' He also heard that they were killing Sindhis. 'But there was always hope – Zia could not last for ever and one day the army would go back to barracks.' In the meantime they would continue to pray.

Zia's plane fell out of the sky one day in August 1988. Lala was in the field, his face, running with sweat, looking far beyond his thirty years as he tried to coax crops from the parched land. He heard shouts and some friends came running. They were so excited they could hardly get the words out. 'Zia is dead! Zia is dead! Now everything will change.' Lala was sceptical. He thought the army would take over, but as they all crowded round Ghulam's cheap crackling transistor they heard there were to be elections.

That autumn was incredible. 'Every day brought new hopes. Benazir had had her baby early, tricking the generals who had thought she would be unfit to campaign. Benazir would be allowed to contest elections.' Politicians appeared in great noisy cavalcades, promising the moon and stars. Lala went to meetings and brought back lumps of goat-meat for his family, a welcome change from their usual diet of rice and *nan* (unleavened bread). '*Jeay* Bhutto [long live Bhutto], *jeay* Benazir,' he roared, until his lungs burned. No subcontinental politician could stir emotions like she did. On voting day Sindh repaid its indifference to Mr Bhutto's death with a massive majority for his daughter.

When they heard she was to be Prime Minister they danced till dawn. 'Danced! In the face of the *mullah*! Benazir would let us dance.' There would be jobs and food, and perhaps Lala's oldest son could even go to school. Already Benazir had released all political prisoners and freed trade unions. But hope fades quickly, and soon Lala had no more rice to feed his family and was thinking of rejoining his friends in the forest. 'Prices have gone up, more than doubled. There are no jobs.' Recently the old shoe-keeper at the nearby Sufi shrine had died. He used to make only a few rupees a day but people fought for the tender, which eventually went for 500 rupees.

Lala wished he had the means to go to Islamabad, to the specially created Placement Bureau through which all state jobs were controlled, but someone told him that you only got jobs if you could prove you had been in prison during Zia's rule. A Karachi jailer was offering fake prison certificates and prison numbers stamped on arms for 500 rupees, or you could get photos of yourself pretending to be whipped (apparently guaranteeing a grade 17 position in the civil service) for 2,000 rupees, but Lala had nothing. Then someone told him the Bureau had been disbanded anyway – corruption again.

'Some foreigners came and said they would build a school but the landlord laughed when we asked him. There were rumours of a clinic but it did not come. Electricity and water? Well, every politician promises those – we don't fall for that one. But we did hope for a road this time. People who went to Karachi are back. They say there are no jobs there – just curfew and killing.'

Jinnah's dream of democratic Pakistan died in 1958 with the first army rule. Whether politicians or grinning generals are on top, it is still the same coterie of élite ruling the country with no interest in the masses while the *mullahs* who have been trounced in Pakistan's three elections continue to exert control. Governments and generals alike are frightened to lay themselves open to the charge of being un-Islamic, thus undermining the whole existence of the country. Lala's wife wants to tear down the yellowing picture of Benazir, but to Lala that would be the end of all hope. He would rather die first. And so life goes on in most Pakistani villages, doing time in the struggle against ever-shrinking resources, and waiting for Allah.

2

'GANGSTERS IN BANGLES' COME TO ISLAMABAD

BENAZIR BHUTTO'S INHERITANCE

Only a few months earlier it would have been an unthinkable scene. On one side sat the generals, stiff-backed and unsmiling, about to hand over the power they had enjoyed for more than half Pakistan's existence. On the other, close friends and relations of Benazir Bhutto and leading members of her People's Party chatted and laughed. Young and brightly dressed, best hound's-tooth jackets, double-breasted blazers and wide ties out for the occasion, silk handkerchiefs in pockets, they were a different generation entirely to the poker-faced bureaucrats in grey traditional *shalwar kamiz* who lined the back rows. Roped off at one end, the Pakistani press corps was buzzing with excitement. Many of them had suffered lashes under Zia's martial law, and until recently censorship had meant that the name of Pakistan's first elected Prime Minister and founder of the PPP, Zulfikar Ali Bhutto, could not be mentioned. Today his daughter was being sworn in as Prime Minister.

In the front row Benazir's Iranian-born mother, Nusrat, dabbed her eyes, overcome by the occasion. Opposite, General Hamid Gul, the military intelligence chief, looked on disapprovingly. For eleven and a half years he and the men in khaki had seen these people as enemies of the state. They had persecuted them, arrested them, tortured them, tapped their phones. In the elections two weeks earlier, Gul had masterminded the strategy of the opposition Islamic Democratic Alliance (IDA), whose propaganda denounced the Bhutto ladies as 'gangsters in bangles'. But to no avail. The will of the people had prevailed, and Pakistan's powerbase was gathered together to witness a swearing-in ceremony which would put Benazir theoretically in charge of Gul and his cohorts.

It was a perfect December day. Sunlight fragmented on the huge golden chandeliers of the Aiwan-e-Sadr, Pakistan's excessively ornate presidential palace, nestling at the foot of the lush emerald Margalla Hills. Outside, work had resumed on the Prime Minister House next door, which people had long ceased hoping would ever be occupied by a fairly elected premier.

Just after three o'clock muttering began. Benazir was coming. The large gold doors opened, and along a red carpet the Presidential guard in starched white *shalwar kamiz* with gold *pagris* escorted the Islamic world's first female Prime Minister, accompanied by Ghulam Ishaq Khan, the dour dome-headed bureaucrat who had become President on Zia's death. Prayers were said, and then Bhutto, dressed in green silk and white *dupatta*, the colours of Islam, repeated the oath on the Constitution that her father had brought in and that Zia had later tailored to increase Presidential power. Still uneasy in Eastern dress, the woman who had once bought all her clothes from Saks Fifth Avenue adjusted her *dupatta*, pleasing the photographers, and stumbled on the words of the oath of office, which she later claimed had been deliberately read out a different way to trip her up. But as she signed her name she could barely restrain the smile amid supporters' cries of 'Long live Bhutto'.

It was a day of victory, marking the conclusion of eleven years of struggle. 'In the end good always triumphs over evil,'[1] said Benazir after the ceremony, recalling that at her last meeting with her father in his prison cell she had promised to continue the fight for democracy. At only twenty-six, she was imprisoned when her father was hanged in 1979 and was refused permission even to see the body. The five years she then spent in jail and detention was a far cry from the life she had enjoyed as a student at Oxford, driving a yellow MG littered with parking tickets and flitting between debates and Pimms parties. In 1984 ill-health eventually persuaded the military regime to allow her to live in exile in London before returning to Pakistan in 1986 to be greeted by a crowd of more than a million people packing the streets of Lahore.

On 2 December 1988 Benazir Bhutto became the world's youngest premier, but while her supporters let off fireworks and danced in the streets, she claimed she was not excited by the prospect. 'The idea of being Prime Minister has never held any glamour for me. What really excites me is the idea of fulfilling the dreams of the PPP and the people.'[2]

For her mother, who had campaigned alongside Benazir after a fight against lung cancer, the loss of her husband and of her son, Benazir's younger brother Shahnawaz, in a mysterious poisoning, it was all too emotional. Eyes glistening, she confessed, 'She looked so young and vulnerable standing there. It's beautiful, but I wish it could have happened without so much sadness and the deaths of my husband and son.'[3]

The unreality intensified after the ceremony when the band outside on the balcony struck up 'Yankee Doodle Dandy' and the guests crowded not round the new young Prime Minister but round General Aslam Beg, the apparently benign army chief whom everyone wanted to congratulate for overseeing Pakistan's first peaceful transition of power. It was impossible to scrutinize the expression behind the dark glasses of the man whom many suspected was involved in the plane crash which had killed Zia and wiped out the senior ranks of the army, leaving the scarcely known Beg in charge. Why had he decided to travel in a separate helicopter, and why had he flown straight over the wreckage instead of turning back to see if there were any survivors? These were the questions on many lips.

The tall, cold-eyed American ambassador stood aloof in the mirrored and wood-panelled room, carefully watching proceedings in which he had had a not unsubtle hand. Already starting to acquire his nickname of Viceroy of Pakistan, it was only when Ambassador Robert Oakley had called on Benazir for tea that the public really believed that she might become Prime Minister. Later he was to admit that he had deliberately blocked an FBI inquiry into the mysterious crash which had also killed his predecessor. Could Bhutto trust the superpower whose aid was so essential but whom she believed to be behind the removal, and by implication the death, of her father? She still felt a chill when she remembered Henry Kissinger, the US Secretary of State, warning her father in 1976 that if he did not drop his nuclear ambitions he would be 'made a horrible example of'.[4] Benazir was well aware that she did not have the majority political support her father had enjoyed to enable her to go against the wishes of both superpowers. But she had had a hard time stopping her supporters burning US flags in the election run-up.

Bhutto, sipping sweet tea and nibbling gaudy sweetmeats, looked momentarily bemused. Suddenly she was in control of those who had for eleven and a half years seen her as enemy number one. Intelligence agents devoted to monitoring her movements, who had tortured and rounded up her supporters, were now pledged to protect her. A thousand and one questions went through her mind. Five of the nine corps commanders were thought to be Zia supporters – would they let her govern?

More worryingly, General Hamid Gul had been behind the propaganda campaign of the right-wing opposition, creating the IDA which, in an attempt to denounce her Western background, air-dropped leaflets showing her dancing in a Paris nightclub and her mother clad in sequinned Western evening dress waltzing with President Ford as evidence of their 'anti-Islamic' behaviour. Newspaper advertisements claimed she would ship babies to Paris and let Americans into Pakistan's controversial nuclear plant. In a rare break in her hectic election campaign just outside Lahore in November she had confided to me, 'Every time I pick up the paper there is a new sleaze factor.' It was more sinister than mere rhetoric. Bhutto had claimed that they plotted to kill her: 'God must be on our side. I fell ill during the campaign and missed a scheduled stop, then later found they had been planning to kill me there.'

Could she now trust the brain behind the IDA to head the country's most sophisticated intelligence agency, the ISI? Moreover, Gul was a committed Islamicist who had brought tears to the eyes of Pakistan's previous civil-military government with the eloquence of his plea for a military solution to the Afghan crisis. Would he really accept the orders of a woman who had always favoured negotiations and an end to the conflict in which she had little interest? Already the *mullahs* were beginning their battle of the *fatewas*, denouncing woman's rule as un-Islamic – would they accept a young Westernized woman, even if she did wear a *dupatta*?

Bhutto knew her party could find no support in the Senate. Eighty of the eighty-seven members were against her, and could block any legislation her party tried to pass. With so much to do, that was not an encouraging thought.

President Ghulam Ishaq, chairman of the Senate until Zia's death completed his phenomenal rise to the top, wiped samosa from his lips and muttered a few words of congratulation. During the elections Benazir was convinced he was not neutral. It was he, after all, who as her father's Defence Secretary had apparently tipped off Zia that Bhutto was thinking of removing him, prompting the army chief to make the move which later led to Bhutto's death. Could she really work with this man?

Behind those thick-lensed glasses, Ishaq was shrewd – he had to be. Now seventy-three, he had risen from clerk to President and served in every administration, civil or military, since 1961. It was said he was a man who went by the book, but would power go to his head? Would he try to take advantage of Zia's Eighth Amendment, an addition to the Constitution which gave him as President sweeping powers to dissolve the Parliament? During the election campaign he had issued the decree that all voters must show identity cards, a move that Benazir believed had cost her many votes among rural supporters unable to obtain cards and been the cause of the low turnout of only 40 per cent. Even after her party had emerged from the elections as clearly the largest, it had taken him fifteen days to nominate Bhutto Prime Minister. In return she had had to pledge her party's support to his forthcoming election as President. 'Who is going to be the real power, the President or the Prime Minister?' Catching them together, I asked the question in her mind. 'The Constitution,' Ishaq replied obliquely before turning away. It was prayer time. Bhutto asked if she could pray with him in the mosque. The President's reply was brusque. 'It's for men only,' he said. 'But you can watch,' he added, as an avuncular afterthought.

And what of his constituency – the huge unwieldy bureaucracy which chugged on as a hangover of colonial days and which under military rule had become a major power, without whose co-operation nothing could be achieved? Bhutto had promised there would be no purges, but they were Zia's men as she had already discovered. Phone calls were being misdirected, files going missing, her own servants blackmailed by General Hamid Gul's ISI. That very day, senior civil servants had given permission for a hijacked Soviet plane to land in Pakistan without consulting her.

Benazir claimed there would be no vengeance, but not all her party felt the same. Some of them there had suffered indescribable tortures, and many of her ministers-to-be had lost relations, business, and endured lashings and electric shocks while kept among disease and their own excreta in beetle- and rat-infested suffocating cells in the notorious Lahore Fort. They joked that it was the only cabinet in the world where every member's curriculum vitae would include prison records, but would not some of them be tempted to settle old scores? Already some were predicting that they would not be allowed to stay in power long so should make the most of it. Benazir was pledged to stamp out corruption but would her ministers, even her own family, be able to resist the temptation of swinging a licence here, a lucrative contract there, jobs to friends, bringing them back to the same cycle of previous regimes?

How would the army feel when the Bhutto name, for so long banned from state media, reappeared everywhere? Zia had inexplicably allowed the Zulfikar Ali Bhutto traffic kiosk at a roundabout in Karachi to remain, but now there would be Zulfikar Foundations, Bhutto buildings and his photographs everywhere. At Benazir's first press conference as premier, a huge portrait of Bhutto was erected and the required picture of Jinnah was forgotten and had to be hurriedly summoned, though it was unfortunately dwarfed by that of her father. This provoked an outcry, as had the retitling of Ali Bhutto as *shaheed* or martyr. Army officers and IDA members were calling for Zia to be recognized as *shaheed* for his services. Hearing the man who murdered her father spoken of as a martyr was going to be hard to swallow, but she knew she might have to if these men in khaki who had governed the country for twenty-four out of the last forty-three years were really going to stand back. In June, just after Zia had announced the elections, she had told me, 'The army is a very powerful institution – much more so than eleven years ago. Anyone thinking that after elections the power of the army will automatically wane is being unrealistic.'[5]

But coups in Pakistan had always been from the top, and she was confident of the new army chief, General Beg. As a *mohajir*, he had no real constituency in the predominantly Punjabi army and was anxious to re-establish the army reputation. The four months since Zia's death had already seen a remarkable transformation.

Only six months earlier a group of army officers had been beaten up in broad daylight in the garrison town of Rawalpindi, showing just how discredited army uniform had become.

Zia had brought the army into such disrepute with his refusal to return it to the barracks that even his own handpicked Prime Minister, Mohammad Khan Junejo, a hitherto unknown mango farmer from Sindh, had dared to challenge him. First they had clashed over Zia's refusal to sign the Geneva Accords that would pave the way for a withdrawal of Soviet forces from Afghanistan. Junejo had organized a round table conference of opposition leaders to get his way. Then he had challenged the appointment of two generals, including Pir Dad in Mangla – Zia had got his way over that one. The last straw had been the government report on an explosion at the Ojheri camp arms dump, in which thousands of rockets had rained down over Islamabad, killing hundreds. The report had blamed General Akhtar Rehman, Zia's most powerful ally, and rumours were spread that the dump, which served as a store for US-supplied arms for the Afghan *mujaheddin*, had been blown up deliberately just before the arrival of a US defence audit team, to cover up the fact that some Stinger missiles had been sold off to Iran.

When Zia had nominated Junejo as Prime Minister and introduced a civilian government in 1985 it was meant to be nothing but a convenient front to take the blame while the army wielded real power. On 29 May 1988 he had brought the experiment to an abrupt end. Just as Junejo ended an official tour in the Philippines proclaiming that democracy had taken root in Pakistan, Zia called a hasty press conference to announce that he had dismissed his handpicked government, accusing it of corruption and failure to implement Islamicization – something that with all his sweeping military powers he himself had done on no more than a cosmetic level. 'Zia never intended to transfer power, or really even share it,' his military secretary Brigadier Siddique Salik had told me in July 1988, when we were discussing how much longer Zia could hold on to the reins. Consequently no one really believed that Zia would hold the party-based elections he had promised within ninety days.

It was, after all, a familiar promise. He had said the same on 4 July 1977, when he took over in a then widely welcomed intervention. 'I want to make it absolutely clear that neither I have any political ambitions nor does the army want to be taken away from its profession of soldiering,' he had stated. It took the small man with sunken panda eyes and huge teeth ninety months to honour that promise in a very limited manner with non-party elections, which produced a Parliament allowed to discuss little more than whether trousers were Islamic.

In June, after dismissing Junejo, Zia had already started backtracking on his promise of party-based elections. In that very same grand salon in the Aiwan-e-Sadr he stated, with no explanation, that the elections would take place after six months and that parties would not be allowed to contest. There was no protest from the Pakistani journalists. Dictators are expected to break promises. And Zia did it with such aplomb that in the same month a Gallup poll found that 75 per cent of the population said he was the leader they most admired for his honesty.

In a subsequent interview with Zia just before his death, I found his barefaced lying combined with utter charm and humility disarming. In a pantomime-like situation he denied that he had ever said elections would be party-based, leaving me to make futile protests that I had it on tape, at which he smiled sympathetically and poured me tea. Whipping out a copy of the British *Economist* magazine, he explained that in fact a British political scientist had explained that parties were not representative. 'Besides, these are not parties,' he said with obvious distaste. 'They are just pressure groups. To allow them to run things would jeopardize the democratic process.'[6] To Zia parties were not Islamic – he favoured a presidential system with himself as Amir – but his problem was achieving legitimacy. The Soviet invasion of Afghanistan had turned him in the eyes of the West from a hangman into a defender of the frontiers of the free world, but at home he would always be a dictator. Brigadier Salik explained: 'His biggest mistake was hanging Bhutto. A man can be forgotten but a martyr will always haunt you.'

When Zia dismissed Junejo, who later remarked truthfully, 'He could find no more obliging government than mine,' no one believed elections would happen. The risk that Benazir Bhutto would win was too great. If elections were to happen he would ban her or her party – perhaps decree that a woman could not head the state, as he had said before in interviews. Islam was always useful for justifying his decrees. A deeply-pious man who wept in the holy Kaaba in Makkah, and the grandson of a *mullah*, Zia saw it as his mission to Islamicize Pakistan, saying, 'I have been kept in power so long by the grace of Allah who has appointed me to carry out his task of making Pakistan a truly Islamic country.' During his rule Zia had introduced many Islamic penalties on to the statute books, such as amputation of hands for stealing and stoning to death for adultery. But his mission was unpopular, and though many had been imprisoned under the Islamic laws, the penalties were rarely implemented. Benazir inherited jails full of petty thieves waiting for a surgeon to cut off the offending hand.

By 1988 Zia, the polite dictator cum master tactician, had been starting to make mistakes and Benazir had even managed to outsmart him. Zia had deliberately set the date of the elections as November, to coincide with the expected birth of her first child. Bhutto's doctor had substituted the records with others, so that when the military intelligence checked they would see the baby was expected in early December; in fact it was due in September, leaving her time to get fit for campaigning.

But Zia had known how to play the press all right – that man whom her father had appointed because he seemed harmless, loyal and 'somewhat stupid'. Instead he had kept everyone guessing and become, said Brigadier Salik, 'his own best PR man'. While lying over the form of elections he had promised, at his press conference in June 1988 Zia had raised a laugh by admitting to Western journalists with a tolerant grin, 'I don't have a good record but I hope I've improved.'

And it seemed that his successor, General Beg, shared that ability, chatting now about politics to foreign journalists. Benazir knew he read all the foreign papers, something she no longer had time for. But she had a lot to thank Beg, for. On the night of Zia's crash the world expected martial law to descend once more on Pakistan. The politicians allied to Zia were clamouring for it but Beg resisted, insisting he would go by the Constitution even if this was partly because of his own lack of support within the army.

Beg kept his stance throughout those critical autumn months, despite pressure to stop elections because of heavy floods which rendered thousands in Punjab homeless, a cold-blooded massacre in Hyderabad, riots in Sindh and bomb blasts in Islamabad and Lahore. There were persistent rumours that martial law was to be declared but Beg never faltered, though he did turn a blind eye to the activities of those army officers busily putting their weight behind the right-wing IDA.

The Supreme Court ruled that elections would be party-based, the baby was born and elections went ahead. The results were disappointing – the PPP had emerged as the largest party with ninety-three seats, almost twice that of the IDA, but Benazir had not won a majority. She claimed that many PPP supporters had been disenfranchised by the ruling that ID cards were needed to vote, and that her great opponent Nawaz Sharif had rigged the elections through having the administration on his side. It would be some months later before she would admit that 'there is a substantial Zia lobby' among the public.[7]

The strain of the fifteen days Ghulam Ishaq had kept her waiting in a dentist's house after the elections before nominating her Prime Minister had put Bhutto in her place. Ghulam the Grim, as the PPP leaders referred to him, had met all the political leaders in that time, and the army had suggested a Grand Alliance of both sides even though Bhutto's party was clearly the largest. Bhutto and Sharif had both claimed that they could form a government, and undoubtedly could, as whoever was nominated premier would soon find MPs flocking to their side. Benazir sat in the sitting-room of Dr Niazi, the kindly dentist who had treated her father in jail, and received journalists and diplomats, holding press conferences under a marquee in the garden, reassuring the vested interests on her stance on Afghanistan, India, defence and the economy, and occasionally issuing threats of what would happen if the wishes of the electorate were ignored.

After her long struggle there was no way Benazir was going to accept power-sharing in the broad-based government of national consensus that Beg and Ishaq recommended. Some PPP leaders advised sitting in opposition, but given Pakistan's coup-ridden history she did not believe they could rely on the prospect of future elections. Gradually her emissaries' offers to the large numbers of independent MPs elected paid off and she drew nearer the magic 109 needed for a majority. One night her legal adviser Aitzaz Ahsan put the dentist's constantly engaged phone down triumphantly. An agreement had been reached with the MQM, a party representing Indian migrants in Sindh that had swept the cities and won thirteen crucial seats, making it the third largest. The price was high but less than expected — a fifty-two-point Karachi Accord of demands and some ministries. These things could always be backed down on later — what mattered was winning the numbers game now.

The next day official security replaced the PPP students who had been manning the dentist's gate. Bhutto was quick to point out the irony, saying, 'When we were in opposition this house used to be raided and surrounded all the time. Now we're surrounded again but this time to protect us rather than hunt us down.' She had dinner with Beg, a meeting with Gul, and tea with the US ambassador, saying the right thing each time. The West stepped up its pressure — she made the front cover of *Time* magazine (an ambition her father had never achieved), and editorials of leading international papers warned that she must be allowed to take over. Ultimately, perhaps, it was the fear of the volatile province of Sindh erupting and leading to the further break-up of the country which was crucial in persuading the army to accept her.

There were fireworks in the streets the night the President announced Bhutto's appointment. But as Jehangir Badr, her loyal lieutenant in Punjab, said, 'The hard part is just beginning.' The news of the hijacking showed she was to have no honeymoon period. Could she govern under the commitments she had been forced to make? Parallels had often been drawn between her and Cory Aquino, whose popular movement in the Philippines had inspired Bhutto to return to Pakistan. Would she too ultimately find herself suffering from the Aquino syndrome — perceived as well-intentioned but indecisive, surrounded by corruption and cronyism and unable to act against the entrenched power lobbies?

'I will not be a rubber stamp like Junejo,' Benazir insisted, but the wait before she was given office and the promises she had had to make had only served to confirm the public perception that rulers in Pakistan did not come to power through popular will but because powerful institutions decide that they will. Even her father, who had swept the polls in 1970, had been resisted by some factions of the army and had only been allowed to assume office in

1971 because the military was demoralized by its third defeat against India, resulting in the loss of Bangladesh; and junior officers were refusing to accept orders from seniors who had surrendered so disgracefully.

Benazir had taken over after a similar crisis in the army when almost the entire top command were killed in a mysterious air crash. But she was to have less of a free hand than her father. She had reassured the US that foreign policy would not change when all she wanted was for the Afghan war to be over and the refugees to go home. She had agreed to keep on Beg for three years, and General Gul and Sahabzada Yaqub Khan, Zia's Foreign Minister, until the Afghan conflict was resolved. She had resolved to take tough action on the drug barons who supply more than half the West's heroin, and had agreed to keep to the terms of a tough and politically difficult agreement just negotiated with the IMF for a much needed $1.3 billion package. She had stood firm against retaining Dr Mehbub-ul Haq as Finance Minister, though she had kept on Wasim Jaffarey as Economic Adviser. The army was to have a say in the choice of Defence Minister, a portfolio she ended up nominally retaining, and the large chunk of budget given to defence would be maintained. Contrary to all her rhetoric, the lucrative land and scholarships given to army personnel and their offspring, as well as plum jobs heading public sector corporations on their retirement, would continue.

Where was the money going to come from? Benazir was already discovering the extent of the government's bankruptcy. Zia had borrowed money at crazy interest rates just to pay government wages. The Foreign Ministry owed millions of dollars to PIA, the state airline. That morning she had been informed of a wheat shortage and had had to ring round embassies like a charity co-ordinator asking for help. How would she fund all that needed doing? Everyone wanted something. She was already receiving 60,000 applications a day for jobs. Political exiles were returning; her mother wanted her brother Murtaza back from his exile in Syria, but he was wanted in Pakistan for a hijacking. She had promised ministries to people to persuade them to join and now had to pay up. Her own people were too inexperienced, all the PPP old guard and managers whom her father had worked with were gone. She was determined that there would be no lobbies or factions created in her party, and thus dominant personalities who she knew referred to her as 'a silly young girl' had been purged.

The provincial election results had been disastrous, leaving Bhutto with no government in the largest province. Punjab, home to 60 per cent of the population, was to be governed by Nawaz Sharif, the protégé of Zia, who had never had to struggle for his position. He was already saying that he would prevent her from governing. The deal she had struck with the MQM to make up her majority at the centre was causing violent complaints from Sindhi nationalists in her party. Overtures to the Senate had won over only a few independents, such as Javed Jabbar, who had to be given ministries. Her father had said that to succeed in politics 'one must have light and flexible fingers to insinuate them under the bird sitting on its eggs in the nest and take away the eggs. One by one. Without the bird realizing it.'[8] Was she wily and light-touched enough? As she made her way outside, Bhutto saw a cluster of supporters shouting '*Jeay* Bhutto' and her heart lifted. The people were with her. But she wished she had not caught sight out of the corner of her eye of the general, who she was convinced was laughing at her.

3

TICKETS TO
THE MASKED BALL

DEMOCRACY – PAKISTAN STYLE

Martial Law Order No. 48, 1979: 'All political parties with all
their groups, branches and factions . . . shall cease to exist.'

'Democracy for Sale' read the graffiti slashed across the imposing
wall of the fort, built more than four centuries earlier by the great
Mughal emperor Akbar, which towers above the old city of
Lahore. In the shadow of the city's Bhati Gate, hundreds of pilgrims were flocking around a tinsel-bedecked shrine to praise the
Sufi saint Syed Ali Halvery. The name of the shrine is Data Ganj
Baksh, which means 'one who gives generously'. Further along
the narrow lane, lined with tiny shops selling everything from
paper-money garlands for weddings to rat-traps, a man in an electrical shop was giving very generously indeed. An agent for IDA
leader Nawaz Sharif, he was buying MPs.

The ambiguous results of the 1988 elections, in which neither
of the main parties had won a majority, had meant that independent MPs had become a very highly priced commodity,
well worth the £100,000 investment it had generally cost them
to get elected. Money, ministries, licences, jobs for relatives, all
were on offer. As soon as the results had come in, the PPP and
IDA had engaged in a battle of purse-strings, first to secure their
majorities in the national and Punjab assemblies respectively, and
then to try and destroy each other's cobbled-together majorities.
It was fitting that the action should be centred in Lahore, where
rival potential Mughal emperors had once played out succession
battles; though neither leader went to the extremes of Emperor

Jehangir, who once had claimants to the throne sewn up inside the skins of a freshly slaughtered ox and ass and paraded round the city in the heat of the day until the skins dried out and the victims suffocated.

Sharif had been quicker off the mark than Bhutto. While PPP members were celebrating their own personal victories, his lieutenants were already out seducing anyone who might be persuaded to help him reach the magic number of 109 MPs in the national Parliament and 131 in the Punjab assembly. Businessmen, drug barons, smugglers, anyone who feared a PPP government as the end to their field days, all were tapped for funds. Assignations were arranged in dark car parks or anonymous hotel rooms, to win over independents or PPP members of suspect loyalty. Sympathetic local police or deputy commissioners were called upon to twist arms. Entertainment was laid on in Hira Mandi, the diamond market, home of the Lahore dancing girls, to help persuade the weak of will to switch allegiance to the party of Islam.

Once the Punjab PPP leadership had stopped strutting around like the ministers they were convinced they soon would be and realized what was happening, frantic calls were put in to Larkana, where Benazir was receiving congratulations at her family home of Al Murtaza. The phone in the remote town was constantly engaged and crucial hours were lost, members of the very centralized PPP anxious to do nothing without their leader's instructions. By the time they had entered the game Sharif had already secured himself a majority in the Punjab assembly, holing up provincial MPs who had been won over at a camp in the forest of Changa Manga, just outside Lahore, where no one could reach them to change their minds.

But for the National Assembly, where the PPP had won a thirty-eight-seat advantage over the IDA, Bhutto's troops soon got their act together and fled to the capital, where independent MPs were already arriving in Islamabad's only two hotels. It was a farcical situation.

In room 308 at the Holiday Inn in Islamabad, Farid Jadoon's phone would not stop ringing. Every time he picked it up a wheedling voice would offer him a house, a car, a plot of land, a ministry. Occasionally there would be threats — to stop the licence for his textile mill or to sack one of his relatives in government service.

Mr Jadoon was a wanted man. To leave the hotel required the complicity of the management to smuggle him out so that he could avoid the men in white shirts in the lobby. He had done nothing wrong but, like thirty-seven others, had been elected on an independent ticket in the national elections and become a crucial player in deciding which of the two main parties would form the government.

Mr Jadoon was a successful businessman who did not need the money. New to politics, and shocked by this mercenary introduction, he opted for the PPP, who had promised to develop his backward constituency, Hazara. He commented wryly, 'If they give me even a tenth of what they've promised me, Hazara will be the model state of Pakistan.'

In fact, politics being a rich man's game in Pakistan, none of those elected needed the money, but many of them were to be swayed by large sums or the lure of ministries. Pakistan's return to party politics was already turning into a fiasco. Suddenly being a politician had become a far more profitable enterprise than traditional growth industries of cotton export or sugar mills. The stakes had been raised vastly by Pakistan's new *nouveau riche* of drug barons and arms smugglers, anxious to ensure that they had the support of whoever was in government in order to continue their trade unharassed.

But the unseemly spectacle of MPs for sale was not purely a consequence of the unclear election results. The selling out had begun long before the November elections. Once the Supreme Court had given the go-ahead for party-based elections in early October there was a clamour for PPP tickets. In a country with such a low rate of literacy – Benazir has put the figure at 8 per cent though officially it stands at 26 per cent – party symbols are all-important in elections. But that was not enough. 1988 was not going to be a repeat of 1971, when even unknowns swept the polls purely on the basis of the PPP name. This time PPP leaders estimated that the party name commanded between 15 and 20 per cent of the vote, perhaps more if Benazir visited the constituency – the rest depended on the individual. In rural areas – and 70 per cent of the population is rural – the society is feudal, and successful candidates needed to be large landowners with plenty of money and vote blocs from their peasant workers or tribal clans.

'We need winners,' Benazir told a crucial meeting of the party hierarchy. 'We have to be sure of victory.' Party workers who had struggled and suffered for the fight to restore democracy over the last eleven and a half years would be denied tickets in favour of big names who were prepared to join the party even if they had formerly allied with Zia. Rana Naaem, Junejo's Defence Minister, Tariq Rahim, a member of Zia's Majlis Shoora which had ruled for the first eight years of martial law, Yusuf Raza Gilani, a provincial minister under Zia, and Zafar Ali Shah, a former federal minister, were just a few of those welcomed in, the past apparently forgotten in the rush for power. A third of those nominated had joined the party in the last three months. Party faithfuls such as Rao Rashid, a former adviser to Benazir's father, were thought unable to command enough support and denied tickets. At one point the committee set up to contact disillusioned Muslim Leaguers had even approached Jamaat Islami,[1] the right-wing religious party which had long been the PPP's most vicious enemy and had distributed sweets on the announcement of Bhutto's hanging.

Benazir had become cynical about Pakistan's politicians yet seemed to be going the same way. In June I had been to see her in 70 Clifton, the high-walled Karachi house that still bears the plaque 'Zulfikar Ali Bhutto, Barrister-at-Law'. The last time I had visited the Bhutto residence was for Benazir's wedding to a polo-loving feudal the previous December. Then it had been filled with lights and colour and had enchanted with its glitter and oriental aromas. Later I had been taken to Orangi and the slums of Lyari to see the contrast, and in Bhutto's library had seen the books on Napoleon, Sukarno, Stalin, the heroes of a man fascinated by power. Now I wondered if his daughter, who had seemed so charming with frank admissions such as her obsession for peppermint ice-cream, was going the same way as she scented the first chinks in Zia's armour.

In the glass conservatory, amid constantly ringing phones, I waited for the lady who was receiving politicians from a stage under a purple and red *shamiana* constructed in the garden. It did not look very democratic, more like a tableau of Queen Elizabeth I receiving her subjects. Eventually I was summoned into the drawing room where, sitting posed and pensive under a large portrait of her father, Benazir told me: 'In 1977 Zia said I only have to snap my fingers and the politicians will come running like dogs. I didn't believe him then, but now I'm more realistic and accept there is this political opportunism.'[2]

In the run-up to the elections, as a disappointed Pakistan witnessed proceedings emanating from this new realism, many senior PPP members were unhappy. 'I'm not sure if power is worth it on this basis,' confided Jehangir Badr one night in Lahore. 'We don't know what we represent any more.' How could they convince the electorate of Bhutto's assertion that 'the PPP is the only party of the poor and downtrodden' when in the biggest province, Punjab, ninety-three out of 115 national tickets had been given to leading feudal figures? Some suspected that the new converts were in fact army agents sent to split the party.

Bhutto's belief that powerful vote-catchers, even former associates of Zia, should be allocated tickets dealt the last blow to the Movement for Restoration of Democracy or MRD, the nine-party alliance of which the PPP was by far the biggest, set up in 1981 to fight for the end of martial law. A loose and unlikely alliance comprising socialist parties and right-wing religious parties, it had often seemed on the verge of breaking up, and leaders of the smaller parties complained that Bhutto behaved arrogantly at meetings, frequently did not turn up and made statements without consulting them. Mairaj Mohammad Khan, former union leader and head of the small QMA party, whose bid to be Secretary-General of the MRD had been vetoed by Bhutto, said, 'Ever since Bhutto returned she's been following policies unilaterally without consulting the MRD. On 3 June after Zia announced elections she said the PPP would participate in any polls before we'd even discussed it. Benazir has lots of reservations about the MRD and we have many about her.'[3] Later Bhutto was to make a telling comparison between the MRD and the seven-party Afghan resistance alliance, whose leaders have on occasion even drawn guns on each other.[4]

Bhutto was eager for her party not to campaign on MRD tickets, wanting victory alone, and believing loyalty to the MRD would drag the whole party down. In a strategy meeting in October, MRD leaders offered to back PPP candidates if in twenty-one constituencies the PPP backed them. Bhutto refused, initially offering to back the leaders and no more, but later she withdrew even that and the alliance was finished. The PPP and MRD had fought hard together and the collapse left a sour taste in many mouths on both sides.

Mumtaz Bhutto, Benazir's uncle and founding member of the PPP, who had been thrown out of the party in 1985 and set up the Sindh Baluch Pushtoon Front, complained that PPP members were also treated with little respect. 'Benazir wants everyone in the MRD to believe they're breathing because of the PPP and everyone in the PPP to believe they owe their political existence to her.'[5] Her father too had often said, 'I am the Party,' and had not always been kind to his friends. His specially set-up paramilitary organization, the Federal Security Force, was used against former allies of the left such as Mairaj Mohammad Khan, who, having taught Bhutto his skill in oratory and Urdu, was later discarded, accused of involvement in a conspiracy. He was imprisoned for four years and beaten so badly that he lost much of his sight. Mairaj winced when, not aware of the background, I like so many people likened his impressive oratory to that of Ali Bhutto. He seemed almost in tears as, from his cramped Karachi apartment far from the grandeur of the Bhutto house, he admitted, 'Bhutto was a great man . . . but could be cruel.'[6]

For a leader who claims to prize loyalty above all else, Benazir's desertion of her former allies showed her desperation to win the elections, only Pakistan's third since coming into existence. Even before the split, MRD leaders were openly critical of her policy of accepting turncoats and newcomers rather than those with whom they had suffered lashings during martial law. Rasul Bux Palejo, Secretary-General of the left-wing Awami National Party, argued, 'Getting a majority through such people will be a bogus majority. Benazir's father, Zulfikar Ali Bhutto, did not die for the cause of bringing back the men who hanged him.'[7]

Such men were present in plenty the balmy October night in Karachi when Bhutto, barely recovered from the Caesarian delivery of her first child and suffering a kidney infection, stayed up all night making the crucial decision about who would represent the PPP. Numerous people gathered inside and outside the new black glass house overlooking the sea in Karachi's Beach Basin, which is nothing like the play and holiday paradise the name suggests. Instead it is an area of desert and scrub with few luxury houses scattered, of which the Bhutto residence stands out like a Foreign Legion fort with its high walls, green, red and black PPP flag and constant comings and goings.

That night was a revelation in pragmatic politics. Politicians of all shades had filled the suites of Karachi's best hotels, and with the PPP's chances apparently on the up since the Supreme Court ruling in favour of party-based elections were offering as much as 3 million rupees (approximately £100,000) a time for one of the party's 700 national and provincial candidatures. According to Benazir, she had received more than 18,000 applications. It did not seem to matter what the candidates' past was or what views they held – that night it was definitely money and local standing that counted. Her father's advice that 'consistency is a virtue of small minds'[8] was being taken to extremes.

Sardar Shehbaz Mazari, head of the powerful Mazari clan, explained, however, that there was no point in giving tickets to those with no money. Shaking his head sadly, he told me: 'In 1985 it cost 10–11 million rupees to win a national seat. Now there is a new class of *nouveau riche* who have grown fat from smuggling, arms sales and drugs, pushing the stakes up even higher. To the poor man in the street he has no reason for faith in any politicians, and when the chips are down, whoever hands him 100 rupees he will vote for.'[9]

Though no one dared challenge it, Benazir's realist stance upset the few remaining old guard of the PPP (she had purged anyone she perceived as a threat). But the 'party of democracy' had not practised what it preached and, as Zia liked to point out, had never had internal elections. The issuing of tickets to newcomers meant the election of many who owed Benazir nothing and from whom she could not expect the same unquestioning loyalty. Much later, a Sindhi MP told me of a row he had had with her when she rebuked him with 'You're only here because of me,' to which he replied, 'No I'm here because of who I am.' This was hardly a good basis for restoring democracy, and combined with the commitments Bhutto later made to become Prime Minister, did much to squander the legitimacy she gained through coming to power through a democratic process.

The money also caused suspicion. Provincial party bosses held much influence, and as Benazir had rarely lived in the country, she was dependent on their views for assessing who was most popular in each district. People began asking questions about how leading figures, particularly of the Punjab party, were affording suites in the Sheraton Hotel, appearing in new suits and sporting flashy watches. Old splits within the Punjab PPP seemed to be re-emerging. Tickets were given to one candidate and then, under the influence of another Punjab lobby, taken back and given to another candidate. Asif Zardari, Bhutto's feudal husband, showed that he was not content to remain in the background as a Denis Thatcher figure; he stepped in with his own suggestions, backed by his father Hakim Ali, who had just left the ANP to join the PPP and of course was greeted with a ticket.

It was not just old faithfuls who were being forgotten. Policies were going by the board too. The party founded on Marxist principles had dropped its street socialism in favour of advocating free market economics and Thatcherite privatization. Ali Bhutto would not have recognized his party. Suddenly Benazir, who had previously demanded a negotiated end to the war in neighbouring Afghanistan, was going out of her way to talk of her support for positive symmetry by which the arms flow, and thus the conflict, would continue, and spoke in glowing terms of the army most PPP supporters regarded as their main enemy. PPP workers who not long before had burned American flags at rallies were forced to listen to praise for the country's main benefactor. Bhutto's challenge was to present the illusion of change to the people while reassuring the army, civil service, business community and important Western allies that if the party were to win power it would not upset the status quo. The US ambassador had already been quoted in the press, warning against radical economic policies. Mairaj Mohammad Khan was not fooled. 'The PPP has retracted from all their popular positions and slogans — power of the people, anti-imperialism, socialism, and openly declared support for the feudals responsible for crushing the poor ... How many times must her father be turning in his grave?'

It was not just the PPP that was shedding principles like autumn leaves — in Lahore a similar process was occurring as the right wing desperately tried to get its act together in a grand anti-Bhutto coalition. It was a hard task. Bhutto's main opposition, the Muslim League, the party credited with the creation of Pakistan, had since formally split at least nine times. It had become the ruling party in 1985 as a result of Zia's partyless elections when, having picked Junejo as Prime Minister, he asked him to form a party which, as .the king's party, attracted large numbers of MPs eager for cabinet posts. Zia later admitted that this had been a mistake, as creating the party out of government rather than vice versa meant it had no grassroots support.[10]

Zia's dismissal of Junejo's Muslim League government on 29 May brought all these organizational weaknesses to the fore, exacerbated by the reinduction into the caretaker cabinet of many of those who had been ousted as targets of Zia's diatribe against corrupt and inefficient ministers. The whole move seemed aimed at removing only a handful, and created a division between the haves and the have-nots. There were large-scale desertions, but Junejo's refusal to hand over the Muslim League and his objection to his party men taking positions in Zia's caretaker government forced the party to split once more. Junejo issued notices demanding that Nawaz Sharif and General Fazle Haq, caretaker Chief Ministers of Punjab and the Frontier and both close to Zia, should either quit their government positions or resign their posts as party provincial chiefs. Sharif and Haq, only too aware of the value of having the administration at one's disposal in a forthcoming election, refused.

On 13 August, just four days before Zia's fatal plane crash, the Muslim League Central Executive met in Islamabad Hotel to elect senior officers. As Junejo tried to get himself re-elected President, Sharif's men stormed the meeting, which broke up in disarray, Muslim Leaguers hurling chairs and china at each other. Shortly after Zia's death the party formally split into pro- and anti-Zia factions. Junejo told me: 'We will come back – we're not scared of these Chief Ministers.' He added his voice to the growing demand that the new President Ishaq sack the caretaker cabinet. 'They will most definitely rig the elections;' he said. 'You can see this from the high-handed manner in which they used official machinery to try and capture the party elections. If a neutral government is formed, Sharif and Co. could not exist for a moment – their policy is power.' Harsh words; but within two months Junejo and Sharif would be back contesting on the same platform.

For the next few .weeks new political alliances grouped and regrouped so often that one despaired of reporting developments

which would almost inevitably have changed by the time the
paper came to print. As Junejo announced the formation of one
unlikely alliance, with Asghar Khan's socialist intellectual Tehrik
Istiqlal and the conservative religious JUP of Maulana Noorani,
Naseem Aheer, former Interior Minister, was briefing the press on
the creation of the IDA or Islami Jamhoori Ittehad – a combination
of eight parties including the pro-Zia Muslim League. Over milky
tea and sinewy chicken legs in the house of Dr Safraz, we discovered just how little the eight had in common, other than a
hatred of Bhutto. Even more ironic, the compromise leader was to
be Ghulam Mustafa Jatoi, a former PPP leader whom Benazir
called uncle and whose own party, the National People's Party
(NPP) could win only a few seats. Jatoi was a likeable man, who
had twice turned down the premiership offered him by Zia in
1981 and 1984 in an attempt to weaken the PPP, which Jatoi was
organizer of while Benazir was in exile. On her return they fell
out, partly over Bhutto's refusal to hold internal party elections,
and Jatoi left to form his own party. Today he had despaired of
principles and just wanted to be Prime Minister, saying, 'A mad
dog must have bitten me the day I refused Zia's offer.'[11] So here
he was, leading a party comprised mostly of his former enemies
and the main platform of which was Islam, he a man with a
weakness for pretty girls and whisky at breakfast. It was no secret
that Sharif coveted the office himself, but at only thirty-eight, the
army considered him immature; Jatoi was the man most acceptable
to both military and bureaucracy.

Sharif claimed that their effort was backed by the army, and
along with General Haq made frequent veiled references to suggest
that if the PPP won the elections they would never be allowed to
govern. Many analysts believed this to be pure propaganda, but
General Gul, the powerful military intelligence chief, later claimed
credit for the formation of the IDA and was heavily involved in persuading Jamaat Islami to join; its student workers were invaluable
for organizing the campaign. Jamaat joined when Sharif agreed
that some of their student workers, who had been imprisoned
by Punjab police for inciting violence in Lahore University,
would be released. Gul was apparently even present in Karachi
when Sharif flew in to try to persuade the MQM, a party representing migrants from India, to sign an electoral pact, threatening to

release harmful information the military intelligence (ISI) had on them if they refused.

As the 15 October deadline for filing nominations approached, the PPP was appearing stronger and the wave of departures from the Muslim League persuaded the army to step in behind the scenes. It was 'suggested' that the right's only hope was to unite completely, and from a room in the old British Falettis Hotel in Lahore strategy was co-ordinated. Brigadier Imtiaz, from the domestic politics section of Gul's ISI, directed operations, as for five days and nights frantic negotiations went on between the two branches of the Muslim League. Sharif in his Model Town home, advised by his father; General Gilani, the creator of ISI, and calls from General Gul, whom he describes as 'a sincere friend', with Shujaat Hussein, the former Industry Minister, acting as go-between, finally persuaded Junejo in his suite in the Avari Hotel at the eleventh hour that Bhutto was the greater evil, whom they could defeat only by uniting against. Junejo, an honest but unintelligent man, had tried to be principled, but ultimately the promise that he could remain President of the reunited Muslim League won him over. He had been conned – it was no secret that Sharif would run the show whoever held the titles, and the IDA had already allocated tickets, leaving only a handful for the Junejo faction. In disgust some Junejo supporters left and contested as independents, splitting the right-wing vote. Later, some of those from Junejo's faction given IDA tickets, such as Shujaat Hussein, complained that Sharif had used local government machinery against them in their campaigns to ensure that only his own men won.

The right was united, but now had at least three people who thought they were the leaders and who wanted to be Prime Minister. On the last night before nominations, as the PPP was squabbling in Karachi, in the smoke-filled living-room of Hamid Nasir Chatta, the former Speaker, in Lahore, tempers among the now nine-party IDA were high. In both places it was money that counted. The Muslim League Secretary-General was poor by the standards of Pakistan's feudal politicians, and thus was not allowed to contest. Tickets were going to the highest bidder wherever the money came from – rich sponsors in the form of drug barons, businessmen or personal incomes. People drifted in and out of the nerve-centre, muttering about how Sharif was asking which of the hopefuls for each seat had most cash. Sitting outside, Brigadier Asghar, Finance Secretary of the Muslim League, complained, 'We politicians in Pakistan know no such thing as principles.'

The elections seemed to be turning into a costume ball whereby only the masks would change while the faces behind them remained the same. It was no wonder, then, that in a national survey just before the elections, almost half those asked said the nation's leaders were not dependable. General Beg had stated baldly, 'It is now up to the politicians to make the polls a success,' and they seemed about to squander it. Instead of campaigning, both sides were preoccupied with infighting over the allocation of seats.

The unsavoury events of October 1988 revealed much of the nature of Pakistani politics – no one wants to sit in opposition or, worse still, be defeated. An elected politician in Pakistan enjoys almost deified status, able to allocate land plots and development licences to those he favours; a politician out of power becomes at best a marginal drawing-room celebrity.

To retain the local influence necessary for the survival of feudal families, it is crucial for them to have someone in a position of political power. Political activity had become a prerequisite of economic activity. Hence, all over Pakistan, brothers and cousins were standing against each other.

Rana Naaem's family had always been Muslim Leaguers and, though unhappy about his defection to the People's Party, it meant they could not lose – his cousin was standing against him on the IDA ticket (and ultimately won). Shahzada Sultan-i-Rum, brother of the last Wali of Swat, whose family was fielding several opposing candidates for each of the four seats in Swat, explained: 'That way we make sure we win. It's just like backing all the horses in a race.'

In a room just off Peshawar's manic Khyber Road, Arbab Jehangir Khan, former Chief Minister of the Frontier and head of the Arbab clan, was holding a *jirga* (tribal council) to decide with which party he should contest. He would win the family seat regardless, but till late into the night the men argued over the pros and cons of being with each party, while in the kitchen the women cooked interminable amounts of curry. Ideology was never mentioned. Jehangir was reluctant to join the IDA because he was with the Junejo faction of the Muslim League, and his long-standing rivalry with Fazle Haq meant that the IDA would only offer him a national ticket, as Haq was trying to eliminate any rival contenders for the provincial post of Chief Minister of the Frontier. Besides, when Haq had become caretaker Chief Minister, the post Jehangir had held until the Junejo government's dismissal, he had sacked many Arbab relations such as Arbab Tariq, the Mayor of Peshawar, and Dost Mohammad, who had headed the NWFP Sports Directorate.

On the other hand, Jehangir had already been Chief Minister – perhaps he would like to be a federal minister? But if so, with which party? Or perhaps he should contest the provincial seat as an independent, and the national with one of the two main parties, and decide later? But that might confuse the voters, as well as being extremely expensive. Eventually, just before dawn, Arbab decided he would go it alone. Two other members of the family would join the PPP, however, for family security. The move paid off. After the elections, when the PPP took power in NWFP, leaving Jehangir in opposition, Tariq, who had joined the PPP, was reinstated as Mayor.

Even Pakistan's leading politicians were hedging their bets by contesting large numbers of seats. Benazir and her mother fought five national seats between them. Nawaz Sharif contested four national and five provincial seats, while General Fazle Haq was a candidate for two national and three provincial ones.

It was beginning to look at though Zia had been right that Pakistan's political parties were 'too immature to govern',[12] particularly when in August 1990, after twenty months of horse-trading, the elected government was removed and the sorry merry-go-round of bribery and infighting began once more. The lack of a middle class and the country's long history of martial law had prevented political parties taking root. In both 1988 and 1990 the party elections might as well have been non-party. No one mentioned issues; in every constituency the battle was being fought between personalities. But it did not take too much to draw the connection between the politicians' behaviour and Zia's banning of political parties on 16 October 1979, when he imposed fourteen years imprisonment and twenty-five lashes for anyone even calling

himself a member of a party. A few years later his specially
formed Islamic Ideology Council had declared political parties un-
Islamic, and just before his death he reiterated, 'I believe political
parties are nothing but a source of division.'[13] If today political
parties were immature, Zia must be much to blame. The fact that
politicians could be bought by the highest bidder said much about
the state of the society Zia had both inherited and left behind.

4

THE SUPERPATRONAGE ROADSHOW

FEUDAL POLITICS

In Multan in October 1988, political parties seemed very much alive. A small town in southern Punjab, overlooked by a bump of a hill on which only the delicately turquoise and white tiled tombs surrounded by wailing women and irreverent pigeons suggest its former glory as a Mughal capital, where emperors once strolled and their offspring plotted out succession battles, Multan today is noted in the tourist literature mainly for its preponderance of heat, dust, beggars and tombs (they missed out pigeons). The usual highlight of the day for the walnut-skinned children who live on the streets was to run after old Mr Gardezi, one of the town's most prominent residents, in his horse and trap on his nightly promenade at the exact time the falling dusk meets the tangerine dust-cloud permanently suspended just above Multan's terracotta roofs.

Suddenly, with the announcement of elections, the politicians had moved in. Denied radio or television access, their message had to be carried on whistle-stop flesh-pressing tours where people long frustrated by Islamic strictures banning many forms of entertainment got a chance to publicly sing, dance, release balloons, and let their hair down in a way that would normally end in arrest.

For the children of Multan the election campaign was the best thing that had happened to their small lives. They would run between rallies of rival candidates, swapping party flags and stickers *en route* to earn a few rupees. To contest the election one had to be rich, and many workers saw the campaign as their way to effect the redistribution of wealth that they had little hope of the politicians bringing in. So while the official limit on spending was 500,000 rupees (about $25,000), many candidates were spending more than that each day – much slipping into the pockets of everyone from the man distributing the posters to the rickshaw driver and cigarette vendor paid to display them. Chaudry Shu-jaat's house in Gujrat, the headquarters for the family's election campaign of four seats, resembled the feeding of the five thousand throughout the thirty-eight-day campaign, with huge marquees erected in the garden to serve up unimaginable quantities of lentil curry and rice.

In Multan the election fight was close, the town's leading families doing battle, with Nawaz Sharif one of the contenders to add to the excitement. Flags were hung all over town, loudspeakers competing above the hubbub of traffic through streets so narrow that sunlight could not penetrate. For the first time he could remember, Mr Gardezi was forced to stay at home solemnly regarding the worn black leather and scratched brass fittings of the once grand trap that had originally belonged to the British colonial administrator. The nightly rides through streets crammed with people, goats, pigeons and bicycles reminded him of his ancestor riding into Punjab from Afghanistan, as legend has it, on the back of a tiger using live snakes as whips. To avoid the crush of the rallies, Mr Gardezi, once a politician himself, resorted to riding through the wide avenues of the neat military cantonment with its square white bungalows, manicured lawns and cultured English roses. In Multan, as in every other town, the British had set down a cantonment to insulate themselves from Pakistan, constructing a church, clubs, schools and railway stations in often perfect copies of the originals back home. One day even that was crowded, as with both Nawaz Sharif and Nusrat Bhutto coming to town for rival rallies, party workers tried to outdo each other bussing into town bemused villagers, each of whom collected a welcome ten rupees. The show demonstrated no more than who could raise the most money – Sharif probably won, through the PPP cheated by gathering in narrow streets where their numbers looked greater. Children borrowed spindly bikes and raced from one rally to the other, changing the party banners on their handlebars to pick up a few rupees. Older residents were at it too. One man told me, with some justification, 'it's our once in a decade chance to cash in.

Who knows when we'll have elections again, so we're making what we can from these.'

Consequently the crowds meant nothing. People had come out of curiosity, boredom with the traditional pastimes of cock-fighting, bear-baiting or playing conkers with hard-boiled eggs, or simply because they were paid. They were there for the *tamasha*, the gobshop and the snacks. The largest and most enthusiastic group of spectators I saw were those in Arifwala, where the former Defence Minister, Rana Naaem, was contesting. Yet he lost badly.

Since her triumphant return from London exile in April 1986, Benazir Bhutto had attracted the biggest crowds on the subcontinent. Following in her father's populist footsteps, her campaign was conducted from a train (first class, as her opponents gleefully pointed out), travelling on the Khyber Mail from Karachi to Lahore then to Rawalpindi. Still fighting a kidney infection, she lost her voice but it did not matter – people had come to see and be in the presence of Ali Bhutto's daughter, not hear what she had to say. Many of them could not understand her, and there was no question of stirring speeches or complex political or economic ideals. The widespread illiteracy and lack of any other diversions made it easy to incite the masses with simple slogans. They danced on top of the carriages, shouting '*Wazir-e-Azam Benazir*' ('Prime Minister Benazir'), while inside she held discussions with local party leaders, stopping at platforms, to induce the people to vote for the arrow – '*zalem o ke dil may teer*' – the arrow in the heart of the tyrants. The Election Commission had disallowed the party's traditional symbol of a sword.

That was not Bhutto's only grievance against the caretaker administration. The President had passed a decree according to which all voters would have to show National Identity cards to vote. Bhutto described the move as 'an unconstitutional attempt to disqualify and disenfranchise our supporters'. In answer to PPP protests, the administration claimed intriguingly that 103 per cent of Pakistani voters already had cards. It was Ali Bhutto who made the cards compulsory in 1973, but his daughter claimed that among rural voters only 5 per cent of women and 30 per cent of men had cards, and there was no way that enough could be processed in time. She complained that 'While under Zia political candidates were disqualified, now his henchmen are disqualifying voters.'[1]

The party once more turned to the courts, and a week before the election the Lahore High Court struck down the Interior Ministry requirement, pointing out that in one constituency in Lahore the number of ID cards officially in circulation was twice the number of registered voters. Those issued to women bore no photograph, leaving them open to fraud, and stories abounded of candidates printing their own cards. But the government appealed to the Supreme Court, and just four days before the election the condition was restored.

There seemed some truth to Bhutto's claims. The day before the elections I visited the Lahore registration office, a British colonial building just opposite Zanzama, the mighty gun on which Kim played in Rudyard Kipling's novel, and behind the museum where Kipling's father was curator. The office was swarming with angry people, some paying their tenth visit to obtain a card without success. The Punjab registration director found the procedure apparently so complicated to explain that he advised me to fly to Islamabad to obtain a manual. Several IDA workers were present in the office, and when I later challenged Sharif he denied the PPP's allegations. 'We have no such designs,' he said. 'They are making these charges to put the blame for their defeat on us.'2

In the face of disappointing results, Bhutto did indeed claim that the polls had been rigged. It is hard to assess how much effect the ID card condition had. Although the turnout was surprisingly low (only 44 per cent) in the first free and fair elections in eighteen years, this may have reflected disillusionment with the politicians rather than non-possession of ID cards. Moreover, on coming into government the PPP dropped its case. Aitzaz Ahsan, who as Benazir's legal adviser had put the case, found it to be the first document on his desk on becoming Interior Minister. As he was now both prosecutor and defence, he decided to drop it, admitting that in future elections the ID card condition could be in the party's favour.

In the frontier town of Peshawar the break-up of the MRD was causing problems for the local PPP, which was facing a strong challenge from the leftist ANP. Aftab Sherpao, the PPP President and former army major who had entered politics after his brother was assassinated, allegedly by Afghan agents, was under pressure in his own constituency. He claimed that the caretaker government had redrawn constituency lines to 'mutilate those of opposition leaders'. His traditional seat in Charsadda had been made part of the adjoining constituency to be contested by Wali Khan, the ANP leader. Sherpao decided to fight Peshawar Town, where his opponent was the millionaire deputy leader of the ANP, Haji Bilour.

In Sherpao's election office in Peshawar's cantonment area, hundreds of workers were making banners with cheap Russian cotton smuggled over the border from Afghanistan. Perhaps not the most patriotic idea, but for once there seemed to be genuine dedication not motivated by financial gain. Sherpao had reorganized the party in the Frontier, keeping the central leadership out of it as much as possible and winning genuine respect for himself. The Frontier is Pakistan's most conservative area, where having a woman as leader is not necessarily something to make much of.

While Sherpao was campaigning late into the night among the sizzling kebab shops and *paan* stalls of the bazaars of Peshawar, similar rallies were continuing across the country. Among Sharif and Bhutto it became a battle to see who could take the longest to reach their destination and arrive showered with the most rose-petals. Both wooed the Western press. One night I had returned to my hotel in Lahore from a rally in Sharif's Lahore city constituency. The crowds were disappointing and I slipped away, unnoticed I thought. Some time later there was a knock at my door. It was one of Sharif's assistants, to say the Chief Minister had seen me at his rally and wanted me to come back because 'it was now much bigger'. Reluctantly I went with him and he was right, far more people had appeared. However, I could not help imagining Sharif's men desperately rounding up innocent residents to appear before a Western journalist.

But generally with his guidance from the military intelligence (ISI), Sharif's PR machine was more subtle and sophisticated than that. In a master-stroke he had secured the help of one of Pakistan's brightest journalists, Hussain Haqqani, who wrote for the *Far Eastern Economic Review*, to go through lists of journalists arriving in the hotels and give them a rundown of the political situation from an apparently independent and very plausible viewpoint. Many fell for it, plagiarizing almost word for word the analysis of the man who at the same time was also writing Sharif's speeches and thinking up electoral ruses. Whenever Bhutto was expected to hold a huge rally, on Haqqani's advice Sharif's Punjab government or the IDA would take out large adverts on the front page of the country's newspapers to squeeze out coverage of the event.

With the provincial government machinery at his disposal, Sharif had many other advantages. Equipped with the chief ministerial helicopter and Cessna plane, he could cover far more ground, sustained by the whole chickens he would devour for breakfast. Chubby and petulant, Sharif told me once that he fancied himself as a Mughal king, but with his balding head and short stature he resembled more a little Buddha. The protégé of Zia, an industrialist who had been plucked from nowhere to be made Punjab Finance Secretary then Chief Minister in 1984, getting much richer in the process, Sharif had none of the charisma of Bhutto, and, a wooden speaker, was uneasy on a platform or with journalists.

But he was a good manager and had patronage politics off to a tee. I flew with him to a place called Mianwalli just outside Multan, flying over badly flooded land, then fields brown and scorched. 'This is Pakistan's real problem,' he gestured – a line intended for my notebook. I pointed out that he had had four years as Chief Minister of the province to do something about it if he really cared. Sulkily he went back to his notes. We landed in a muddy field and were whisked into a brightly coloured tent in which two men on tatty orange hobby-horses and an impassioned Urdu poet were warming up the crowd. In the 45°C heat the tent was steamy, all fans directed at the Chief Minister. The amplifier was shrieking, obscuring his words, which mattered little because everyone knew it was an elaborate game in which he would make promises he would never keep. After pledging a road and hospital amid rousing cheers, a rosy-cheeked old man in a sloppy white turban leapt up and demanded for the school in the area to be upgraded. Momentarily flummoxed, Sharif agreed, only to find the restless audience erupting in a wave of demands. The stage began to wobble and Sharif's assistants smuggled him hurriedly back to the helicopter, leaving me running behind laughing. Safely back on board, Sharif demonstrated his panache by filling in certificates to send to the village stating what he had promised, though it was not clear that he felt any more obliged to keep his word. He lost that constituency but the strategy worked in other areas.

The Superpatronage Roadshow was in action again shortly after the elections at a horse and cattle show in Gujrat, a Punjabi town less remarkable than Multan, famous for heat, dust, footwear and electric fans. I was taken aback when the editor of a local newspaper told me solemnly, 'People kill each other over the best buffalo contest.' But he was right. The show had far more to do with political rivalries than bovine quality.

Every year come April, the nation's shoe industry would shudder to a halt and local teashops creak under the weight of conspirators planning how to sway the judges and ensure the success of their chosen candidate. 'It's like a mafia operation,' grumbled Butt, a local farmer who had been persuaded by what he described as 'security considerations' to withdraw his prime beast. As in the elections, lines were drawn on the basis of biradaris or clans. Gujrat has three main biradaris – Gujas, Jats and Kashmiris – each of which would field a candidate selected by practised 'spotters'.

As the day of the show approached, the peaceful fields around Gujrat were transformed into scenes of heinous crimes as rival groups went to extraordinary lengths to seek victory. 'It's a matter of honour,' explained the editor of the local newspaper. 'They start with trade-offs or bribes. If that fails they resort to grievously wounding the owner or his relations. In a close year it can be a fight to the death.' A local police officer confirmed that the crime rate rockets. The beasts themselves are rarely touched, surprisingly, though one year a wolf was let loose upon a particularly fine specimen.

Camel dancing and best sheep contests apparently never evoke such emotions. 'They are usually settled by a few wife abductions,' said the editor dismissively. He spoke of the show as an incentive for development, but to the onlooker it represented the worst excesses of Pakistan's feudal society. Leading landlords lounged in cushioned chairs on a rose-bedecked stage, protected from the sun by colourful awnings. Waiters in crumpled, sweat-stained white jackets and slipping bow-ties scurried among them obsequiously, bearing tea in china cups and sandwiches on silver platters.

As the teams of the major feudals trotted past on powerful white chargers, their riders resplendent in bright silks and jewelled turbans, the lesser landlords clapped limply, apparently oblivious to the surging sea of faces below, kept back by the lathis of the riot police. For the crowds it was perhaps the only annual entertainment, TV being unaffordable even if they were lucky enough to have electricity, and dancing forbidden. For bonded labourers it was almost certainly their only day off. The highlight of events was, judging by the roar of the crowd, tent-pegging, a horseback game similar to jousting. As expected, the biggest landlord emerged victorious, his Herculean mount far superior to the scrawny creatures of his lesser colleagues.

As with most events in Pakistan, the show had a political dimension. Local bigwigs as always took the opportunity to make turgid speeches, eulogizing their role in upholding Islam. Using wealth and tribal connections, Gujrat's leading Jat family won all four seats contested in the elections.

They had scored a further coup by attracting as chief guest Nawaz Sharif, enjoying the attention in his role as high priest of patronage, verbally doling out schools and hospitals and other vote-winning goodies. An old man with the audacity to mount the stage was rewarded with a road to his village. A police officer was upgraded for his outstanding performance in an utterly indecipherable game of tag-wrestling, played by skinny men in Speedo trunks.

By the end of the day the Chief Minister's secretary was laden with sheafs of applications from people demanding postings, transfers and project approvals. Outside Sharif's private house in Lahore, a mini-secretariat had been built to accommodate the floods of people who arrive daily asking for help in resolving domestic disputes or minor problems that seem baffling to most of Pakistan's population. One woman I met there told me tearfully that her father had married her off to a dwarf in exchange for money to pay off a debt to the landlord, and she had fled out of the window on their wedding night. I never found out how Mr Sharif resolved that one. One needed to go to the top for everything, and the man at the top would not willingly relinquish the powers of patronage that enabled him to remain there.

The PPP leadership was condescending of this system but in power found themselves expected to make use of it, while many members saw government as their turn to get rich. Perhaps they were no different to their predecessors but, judging from comments by Western bankers, diplomats and businessmen, they were more blatant. Economic success in Pakistan had little to do with talent or hard work and everything to do with political access and who one knew. Nepotism and using connections was seen not as corruption but as a right. A friend of mine returned from Johns Hopkins University imbued with Western values, to take up a job as manager of the Agricultural Development Bank in Mardan, a position with both jobs and much credit at his disposal. Daily he was besieged by relations, friends of aunts, acquaintances of cousins, sons of colleagues of his father, and others claiming even more tenuous connections, asking for positions or loans. Amjad refused to treat their cases any differently from other applications he received from those with no connections. Eventually he found he could get no work done because of the constant stream of people touting family or tribal links. So he shut his door and put a notice on it asking people to make appointments with his secretary. There was outrage.

Relations, however distant, are supposed to be accessible, and from bank managers to ministers, travel agents to police superintendents, it seemed that no one was supposed to do any actual work in offices. Life for those some step up the hierarchy involved a constant round of samosas and cloying tea with visitors. Spending hours chatting in the offices of senior civil servants, I often imagined that somewhere in the depths of buildings there must be armies of faceless people scurrying around, mole-like, producing the vast quantities of files that occasionally surfaced. Amjad, for his attempts at efficiency which had his branch whizzing up the league table of credit reimbursement, was censured by the family for his behaviour. Nepotism was expected – if you have contacts you use them. Not to participate was seen as 'not cricket' – friends or acquaintances would constantly ask me to get them a visa or to ask a favour for their son, brother or cousin when I met a minister. My refusal and explanation that it would compromise my position was never understood.

When Bhutto became Prime Minister she found that everywhere she went she was mobbed by supporters waving petitions, demanding recompense for their sacrifices during martial law. Ministries in Islamabad would be under daily siege by people waving green, red and black party cards and demanding entry to see their 'People's Minister'. A senior official from the Development

Finance Institute told me, 'corruption will be far worse under a political government – now they have not just friends and relations but also constituents and party workers to provide for.' Under eleven and a half years of dictatorship an awful lot of people had suffered for the PPP, and with the Treasury coffers empty Bhutto could satisfy few of them.

Committed to cutting development expenditure but the victim of promises made to lure people into the party, Bhutto appointed the biggest cabinet in Pakistan's history and an entire battalion of advisers – more than seventy in all. According to press reports and diplomatic chitchat, loans, sanctions and contracts were given to friends and relations with gay abandon, in what one general later described as 'the rape of a nation'.

This was apparently not patronage politics. In the PPP's terminology, it was people's politics. When ministers spent all day arranging jobs for voters and licences for their patrons, this was not corruption – it was people's government. Using the same ploy, the party renamed many of the country's schools People's Schools, then claimed to have created thousands of new schools.

For once there was a price to pay. On 6 August 1990 Bhutto's government was abruptly dismissed by President Ishaq, accused of corruption and maladministration. Less than two years from assuming office, Bhutto was in the dock on four charges, the penalty for which was seven years' disqualification from public office.[3] Also charged were several ministers and her husband Asif Zardari, of whom even Bhutto's closest colleagues said that he had been running a parallel government and that his nod had been essential for projects to be agreed. His frequent presence at cabinet meetings infuriated the President, who sent Bhutto notes saying, 'I don't remember swearing in a Mr Zardari as minister.'

Mr Roedad Khan, the retired civil servant who was heading the inquiry said, 'We have concrete evidence – I'm sure several people will be disqualified.'[4] He added, 'Even if not, the important thing is the accountability process has started and will warn politicians to behave in future.' Ms Bhutto, emotional after the first court appearance in Karachi for charges of selling cotton at a cheap price to a British company, claimed that the whole process was a political vendetta. Face blotchy and voice one note from hysteria, she said, 'I'm outraged. I'm the only Prime Minister whose relatives did not take an industrial unit, who did not have loans written off, yet those who looted the country go scot-free and dare to point their fingers at me.'[5] But she admitted, 'Pakistan is a third world country. I'm sure if you can have scandals in America with 200 years of democracy you can have them in Pakistan.'

Certainly in Pakistan's complicated social system it could be difficult to position the fine line between corruption and patronage. 'Pakistan is a country of superpatronage,'[6] explained Fakr Imam, the Clifton-College-educated former Parliamentary Speaker who had lost his Multan seat in the election. I had wanted to see his village and had gone to visit him by train, a complicated process. The tourist office had condemned the idea, the bored director who would rather be an artist telling me in the most disparaging of tones that there was 'nothing to see but Islamic architecture' and suggesting a trip to the mountains. The railway director was even less help, telling me vaguely that there was a train, 'some time in eveningtime'. Eventually a timetable from British days was produced, and a train located (the Shalimar Express — the fastest in Pakistan and interminably slow), only for me to be told that it is always full and seats cannot be reserved unless one knows a 'high-up'.

Going to Multan by train seemed so complicated that it became an obsession, and eventually I was forced to fall in with the system and find a 'high-up' who sent some of his servants to the station with me, brandishing a piece of paper on which was scrawled VVIP in very big red letters. An entire family was shoved from their seats to make room so that I could get on, and then compounded my guilt by pressing on me some of their small flask of cold curry and *nan* bread wrapped in newspaper.

In honour of my visit, Fakr Imam took me and his sister to the town's one Chinese restaurant. With its red flock décor and grubby fish-tank, it could have been anywhere in the world except that there was no alcohol on the menu. Fakr picked at his sweet and sour with obvious discomfort, anxious that he would be spotted by people wanting favours. His sister, as round and jolly as he was tall and uneasy, was thrilled by this unexpected outing and talked with enthusiasm of her project in their village to protect local arts and crafts from dying out. Fascinated, I expressed a desire to visit. Fakr, the Western-educated intellectual, was mortified. 'They're just dead skills,' he said. Instead he wanted me to visit his milk factory, where he is employing Western techniques. I was less enthusiastic.

Breakfast next morning at their house, after Fakr had returned from his daily jog – thirteen times round the house so that he does not have to meet favour-demanding constituents on the streets – was a complete performance. Served by white-jacketed bearers, fluttering silently with dishes laden with curry, *puri* bread, congealing eggs and fruit, it seemed to require a knowledge of oriental food combinations that I did not possess. Fakr winced as I got it wrong and mixed apparently incompatible dishes.

Further embarrassment was caused by my insistence on visiting the village – Fakr had a duty to his guest but was unwilling to expose what he saw as the primitive side of his home. I played mercilessly on the former, and eventually a compromise was reached. I would visit the milk plant and see the scientific methods of wheat-growing, and he would show me the crafts project.

A large Japanese-made jeep was arranged and we set off with a security man armed with guns, which seemed incongruous as we drove through rolling, almost Hardyesque countryside. The lane through the fields to the village was remarkably good – Fakr was once a provincial minister and used his considerable patronage wisely, though it pains him to admit that he too took advantage of the system he so despises – he with his English public-school background of which he is so proud. We discussed the merits of universal education and social equality with all the vehemence of forgotten college summers.

We passed through rows of mud huts and stopped in a walled courtyard in front of a huge sugar-candy-pink mansion, reminding me of a mock Georgian dolls'-house I once owned. Fakr, smoothing his crisp white *shalwar kamiz*, stepped into the heat. Immediately he was surrounded by men falling on their knees to kiss the hem of his shirt. I was shocked – I felt as though the two-hour ride had taken me back two centuries.

This man too, for all his Western principles, advocated so strongly *en route*, much debated in drawing-rooms in Islamabad and London, was master and beneficiary of the feudal system he so condemned. His villagers were tied labourers who would vote blindly for him and in return were kept from starvation, though often only just. Thus it was throughout Pakistan's rural areas.

Only a quarter of those employed actually earned money, the rest being paid with a share of produce. There are few schools which might lead peasants to question such devotion. Their illiteracy meant that landlords like Fakr were their only link with administration and the legal system, and all the serfs have problems, usually involving women, goats and land encroachment, over which he must advise and mediate.

While Fakr sorted out his business, dealing with abductions, stealings, arranging weddings and gun permits, I was kept with lurid yellow cakes and greasy samosas in an oppressive sitting-room decorated with plastic flowers, watched by a painfully hunched old woman grinning toothlessly. The exquisite lacquerwork crafts were brought to me – Fakr did not want me to venture outside and make the inevitable comparison with the villagers' huts, though I slipped out to see men weaving over huge looms and smoking hookahs while women worked in the fields, a strange sight after the towns, where women are rarely visible.

Afterwards I asked about voting, and Fakr explained that the village was a solid vote-bloc because of all he did for the inhabitants. Hence of the 237 MPs elected in 1988, more than 230 were major landlords or tribal chiefs and thus presumably beneficiaries of the feudal bloc vote. Fakr lost that time because he did not secure the support of another big landed family – his estate alone was not sufficient.

What the November 1988 election results showed was that it was important for an MP actually to use the patronage at his disposal for the good of his constituents, not just to further the family's wealth and standing. For many of the country's leading political families, 16 November was a day to forget as big names like the Soomros, the Jatois, the Mengals and the Marris were swept off the political map. Former Prime Minister Junejo lost too, despite the hiring of a trendy advertising agency which called him MK as if he was a hip gold-medallion-swinging pop star rather than a sheepish mango farmer from a backwater of Sindh who had been propelled from nowhere and back again without ever really understanding that his government had been a façade for Zia, shattered as soon as he stood up to his master.

The most striking example was the defeat suffered by the Pir of Pagaro, the greatest of all Sindhi spiritual figures and feudal lords,

commanding a private army of 10,000 Hurs and the princemaker
of successive regimes. In the past, not only had he no need to
campaign but any candidate he named would be automatically
elected. This time the Pir was forced to campaign himself and still
lost badly to a much smaller *pir*. Yet wherever he went, thousands
would crush forward to kiss his hand and millions puzzle over his
obscure statements to newspapers in which, for example, he
referred to martial law as 'family planning', which to me sounded
like gibberish. So while the homage continued, in Sindh at least, it
did not always extend to the ballot-box.

- Shortly after arriving in Pakistan, I had been surprised to find
myself in a vociferous argument with a hotel manager in Nathya-
gali, a pine-clad hill resort where the feudals retain summer houses
that British officers once owned. *A propos* of nothing, this rather
fat man licked his bulbous lips and began haranguing me on
Western attempts to force Pakistan to copy their electoral systems.
'You have to realize most people in this country cannot read,' he
shouted. 'They're far too stupid to vote. You might as well burn
their ballot-papers. We need a system where only those who have
matriculated [about a sixth of the population] can vote.' I think
the November 1988 elections proved him wrong. For a society
with such feudal constraints, people voted remarkably intelli-
gently.

The majority of successful candidates were feudal lords, but in
most cases the people had voted for the lesser feudal, or, in the few
places they could, the self-made man. Few sitting members were
re-elected – in most areas people voted for change. Nine federal
ministers lost their seats. But unlike 1970, change this time did not
necessarily mean the PPP. In fact the PPP were not really offering
change, their socialist manifesto having been replaced by a vaguely
capitalist document almost indiscernible from that of their opponents, and instead of radical student and union leaders their candidates were for the most part feudals. Many of those who had
changed their allegiance at the eleventh hour were defeated,
prompting a surprised Rao Rashid to say, 'Money and family
position are no longer enough – integrity matters too.'[7]

Integrity could not save Fakr Imam, who stoically remained as
an independent resisting all offers until 1990, when he became a
federal minister in Nawaz Sharif's cabinet. And his integrity was

doubtful. The desire for power was such that even he had been a minister in Zia's martial law cabinet. He was, however, one of the few politicians I had met with a plan for Pakistan. The problem is that the way he would like to change things did not, it seemed, appeal to the voters. He wanted to turn Pakistan into a copy of England and believed his milk factory was a step there. Inside, the rancid smell was overpowering and the floor was stacked high with cartons of fast-curdling milk. The electricity had broken down and the temperature was 40°C. Despite all the Western management techniques and scientific calculations he had employed, Fakr was puzzled and hurt that the plant was losing money. 'We may have to revert to the old ways of delivering untreated milk in churns,' he said, 'and I don't know why. Such plants work in your country. Perhaps you could send me a textbook?' But I suspected Pakistan's political and social problems needed more than Western textbooks.

5

A SUBCONTINENTAL DYNASTY

THE WHITE QUEEN AND THE EVIL DICTATOR

Two men and then their ghosts have stalked Pakistani politics for nearly half the country's lifetime. One a military dictator with perfect manners; the other an inspired autocrat in civilian garb. Both met violent deaths which their offspring swore to avenge. It was one of the best political stories of the 1980s, one which Hollywood could hardly have scripted better. The heroine was Benazir Bhutto, the beautiful woman who in 1979 had devoted her youth to avenging the hanging of her Prime Minister father by the man he had chosen to be his army chief, ironically because he seemed to be no threat. Nearly ten years later, as the general and self-styled President had started making mistakes, a mysterious plane crash wiped him off the face of the earth along with the top ranks of his army, leaving his son to enter politics to seek vengeance.

Looking pale and serious on Western television, Benazir called the crash 'divine retribution' and set about campaigning in the ensuing elections. For a while it seemed as though Zia's death had changed the political landscape. With the removal of both him and Benazir's father, who had ruled as chief martial law administrator and then Prime Minister, perhaps parties would forget about personalities and finally start fighting on issues. Some believed the People's Party would lose its thrust, no longer having an evil dictator to battle against.

But by mid October 1988, with the formation of the right-wing pro-Zia anti-Bhutto alliance, the battle lines had once more been drawn as if the two men were still alive. As far as the political leaders were concerned, it would be a fight between two ghosts – those of General Zia ul-Haq and Zulfikar Ali Bhutto. The two men could not have been more different. Bhutto, the feudal aristocrat and flamboyant jester; Zia, the cold, calculating and very middle-class general with deep-set eyes, like the villain in a silent movie, whom the Pakistani academic Akbar Ahmed compares to Aurangzeb, the last of the Mughal emperors who wanted to purge Islam.[1]

Neither had particularly good records, and society had become polarized between the two, as I was reminded vividly when visiting Colony Mills just outside Multan, where I met workers who had been beaten and arrested under both leaders. So many people have friends or relations who suffered either physically or economically under one or the other leader that it is almost impossible to get an unbiased picture of either of them.

Bhutto is credited with being Pakistan's first popularly elected leader, who brought in the first Constitution to guarantee fundamental rights. Yet he governed with the help of emergency laws which had been in force since the Indo-Pakistan war of 1971, and throughout his rule fundamental rights remained suspended. Even his accession to power was controversial. In fact the rightful Prime Minister should have been Sheikh Mujib, whose Awami League in what was then East Pakistan had won 160 seats compared to the PPP's eighty-one out of a total 270. Although this was the logical outcome of Partition, which had left the majority population in East Pakistan, West Pakistan was not prepared to accept Bengali rule, having run East Pakistan almost as its own colony since Indian Independence had granted the strange arrangement. Bhutto ordered his party members to boycott the Parliament, threatening to 'break their legs' if they disobeyed, and advised the then ruler, General Yahya Khan, not to accept Mujib's suggestion of turning the country into a confederation of two sovereign states each with separate Constitutions and control of internal affairs.

The Awami League organized strikes throughout East Pakistan and the army was sent in, indulging in horrific brutality against their countrymen which was censured worldwide. Defending an area 1,500 miles away is not easy, and when the Indian army moved in on 23 November 1971 West Pakistan had little chance. As TV broadcasts back home continued to insist that Pakistan was winning, Dacca fell. Consequently the public was stunned when the news came on 16 December that Pakistan had surrendered, and the world press carried pictures of a Pakistani general being stripped of his badges at Dacca racecourse. With junior officers refusing to accept the authority of senior military men, whom they blamed for their humiliation, continued army rule was out of the question. Bhutto was sworn in as chief martial law administrator and President of a demoralized and dismembered country. Though he was the first person seen to come to power through popular will in thirty years, Bhutto's accession was tainted by the fact that it had been made possible only through the denial of the basic tenet of democracy to the Bengalis and the discrediting of the army hierarchy.

Bhutto, the showman, began his first official broadcast to the public by saying 'I am no magician,' and pledging that he would move 'not a step' without their approval. The people loved him, but he could not abide others sharing in the glory. He wanted all power to spring from himself, with the party as his maidservant, and constantly reminded senior PPP members, 'I am the party and you are all my creatures.' Anxious to prevent lobbies developing in the party, he got through four Chief Ministers of Punjab in as many years. In his attempt to destroy his enemies, Bhutto nationalized their industries, and his specially created paramilitary Federal Security Force made large numbers of arrests of his political rivals and of trade union leaders who had been his supporters. Some, such as Mairaj Mohammad Khan, had even been in his cabinet. The FSF was notorious — if they could not find the person who was wanted they would take in their families. Bhutto was convinced there were enemies everywhere. In 1973 in a memo to Mustafa Khar, then Governor of Punjab, he wrote, 'There are pistols to the right of us, pistols to the left of us, pistols all around us. This seems to be the motto of the party.'

Suspicions that Bhutto's commitment to democracy may have extended only so far as it helped him obtain power began to surface in 1973, when he sacked the Baluchistan government, run by the pro-Soviet National Awami Party (NAP), on the pretext that arms discovered at the Iraqi embassy had been intended for the Baluchistan government in a Soviet-backed plot to break up Pakistan and Iran. Ghous Bux Bizenjo, the Baluch Chief Minister at the time, always denied this, and claimed that the story was fabricated by Pakistani and Iranian intelligence as a pretext for removing him, pointing out that an Iranian delegation headed by the Shah's sister had arrived in Pakistan the previous day. The NWFP government which was also headed by NAP resigned in protest. Their leaders were imprisoned and the party banned.

Bhutto was Pakistan's only Prime Minister to have come to power on economic slogans, but it soon seemed that they had been no more than a device to ensure a share of power for himself and his *zamindar* cronies. Showmanship could not feed people, and the needs of the poor, whom Bhutto had so inspired with his rhetoric of '*roti, kapra aur makan*' (food, clothing and shelter), were forgotten as in his desire for absolute power, having discarded the left, he brought into the party the very feudal interests causing the oppression. Only seven months after taking office he had police fire on trade union demonstrations, and eleven workers were killed in Karachi protesting against lockouts by employers. Later, trying to woo the religious lobby whom he had earlier made fun of, Bhutto took extraordinary steps such as banning alcohol and gambling (despite having built a casino), and declaring the Ahmadi sect non-Muslims. His arrogance turned Parliament into a rubber-stamp and led to insurrection in Baluchistan, necessitating army action in which 10,000 people are thought to have been killed. Yet right to the end Bhutto, who wanted to become a myth in his own lifetime, aroused great passions with his populist rhetoric of the supremacy of the people. He would tell audiences, 'There are two Bhuttos – one in my body and one residing in every one of you.' But his socialist revolution never emerged, prices spiralling as a result of bad harvests and the oil price hike which he could not control, and nationalizations and often incoherent economic decision-making which he could. By 1977 a third of the population was still living below the poverty line. Ironically it took a military dictator to improve living standards, people generally becoming better off under Zia through trickle-down from money coming into the burgeoning unofficial economy, good harvests and remittances from those working in the Gulf States.

Internationally Bhutto, whose skills in diplomacy had brought China and Pakistan close together, was censured for his arrogance. In 1972 he said in an interview, 'I'm the only leader in the Third World in power despite the opposition of two great powers.'[2] He made no secret of wanting to be bigger than Pakistan, and thus determined that Pakistan would have the first 'Islamic bomb', declaring, 'We will eat grass if necessary to pay for it.' But it was the poor, not the landed élite, who would be doing so. After Bhutto signed an agreement with France for nuclear reprocessing technology, America cut off aid. In 1976 the US Secretary of State, Henry Kissinger, warned him to reconsider the agreement or 'be made a horrible example of',[3] a comment which led Benazir to suspect US involvement in his downfall.

Within only two years of taking office, keeping power had become the rationale behind all Bhutto's actions. The civil service was made lateral entry, and guaranteed life tenure was abolished in a widely welcomed move, but instead of bringing in people on merit Bhutto used this for political patronage, particularly after his widespread nationalizations made access to the state the primary avenue for amassing private fortunes. Privileges to senior military personnel continued, and defence spending increased from 4.8 per cent of GNP in 1970 to 6.3 per cent in 1975, the strength of the armed forces increasing from 370,000 to 502,000 despite the loss of territory.[4] In both services loyalty to Bhutto became the prime qualification for success, ironically leading to the promotion of the apparently faithful Zia above the heads of six generals to become his army chief.

By the time of the 1977 elections, the man who had swept to power in the country's first ever elections in 1971 resorted to rigging to guarantee himself a two-thirds majority that he would probably have got anyway. The opposition parties, among which were many of his former supporters, had campaigned as one – the Pakistan National Alliance (PNA backed with money from angry businessmen whose banks and industries had been nationalized, and from the Saudis, who disliked his half-baked Islamic reforms which were so obviously intended to outmanoeuvre the religious opposition. The PNA rejected the results and demanded Bhutto's resignation and re-elections. When he refused, a country-wide agitation began prompting him to declare martial law in Karachi, Lahore and Hyderabad on 21 April and put the PNA leaders under house arrest. Mr Jatoi, then Chief Minister of Sindh, said Bhutto had not even consulted him over the decision to send the army into the province's cities. In his anxiety to hold on to

power, Bhutto had forgotten his own warning five years earlier
that 'once the armed forces intervene they play the game according
to their own rules. It is necessary for a civilian government to
avoid seeking the assistance of the armed forces in dealing with its
responsibilities and problems . . .'[5]

The game Bhutto was asking the military to play seemed to
have no rules. Western journalists in Lahore at the time recall with
horror how protesters coming out of the mosques after Friday
prayers would be shot down. The army, under Zia, disliked enforc-
ing law for the politicians and eventually began refusing to crush
the demonstrations. Begged by leading PNA members to impose
martial law,[6] on the night of 4 July 1977 troops surrounded the
houses of PPP leaders and put Bhutto under detention in Murree,
promising elections that October. The game was once more being
umpired by the military. A Pakistani editor, Mir Jumil Rahman,
who was later arrested under Zia, maintained, 'It is a matter of
record that there was a general sigh of relief when the army finally
moved in.'

The account in Benazir Bhutto's autobiography is very different.
The biggest reservation many Pakistanis had about her was that
she is her father's daughter, and when the Baluchistan government
was dismissed within two weeks of her office and troops were sent
into Karachi and Hyderabad within eighteen months, it seemed
she might not have learned any lessons from Ali Bhutto's downfall.
Bhutto had done much damage to people's faith in democracy,
and the fact that in most of Pakistan there was very little public
outcry at his arrest and even at his hanging two years later was not
simply due to fear of the martial law authorities. A product of
the feudal classes, Bhutto was a drawing-room liberal but at his
own estate would make villagers wait hours, even days, to see
him. A man who in other circumstances may have been brilliant,
Pakistan had not developed the stable institutions needed to rein
him in.

Such institutions would not be allowed to develop under Zia,
who soon changed his mind about the elections he had promised
on seizing power. Although Bhutto had alienated all the political
leaders and vested interests, the people had no one else to turn to,
and when he was freed the size of the crowds signalled that he
would still win elections. If he did so he could condemn Zia to

death for high treason under the 1973 Constitution. Convinced that while Bhutto was alive he would remain a threat, Zia imprisoned him and set about having him convicted for the murder of a political opponent. The trial was a farce, the political murder in question said to be one of the few Bhutto had had no hand in. And hanging Bhutto did not free Zia — instead he was always haunted by his ghost and by the physical presence of Bhutto's daughter, Benazir.

In Bhutto's cell the night before his execution the twenty-four-year-old Benazir made the promise which would change her life and ensure the continuation of a subcontinental dynasty *par excellence*. Her ambitions to join the foreign service discarded, she pledged to continue her father's mission for a New Pakistan. It was a tough choice. Instead of parties in Oxford, shopping in New York, devouring ice-cream in Baskins and Robbins, she would spend the next seven years in jail and under house arrest until finally leaving the country in 1984 when, suffering from ill health, she moved into a flat in London's Barbican.

From that night all her actions were governed by her hatred of Zia and her struggle to remove him. He had not got off to an impressive start. Many shared Bhutto's view that he was unintelligent, and few expected him to last. In her autobiography, Benazir describes her first meeting with him on 5 January 1977 at her father's birthday celebrations: '[he] was a short nervous ineffectual-looking man whose p...aded hair was parted in the middle and lacquered to his head. He looked more like an English cartoon villain than an inspiring military leader.'[7]

But Zia was a shrewd tactician, a chess-player in a nation of cricketers. And he had luck on his side. Not only did good harvests keep people fed while he was banning all political activity and arresting several thousand PPP leaders, but on Christmas Eve 1979 Soviet tanks rolled into Kabul, the capital of neighbouring Afghanistan, guaranteeing Pakistan's importance to the superpowers. Zia, who was said to have described the invasion as 'Brezhnev's Christmas present' and prayed in thanks, pledged Pakistan's support to their brother Afghans in their fight for freedom and was overnight transformed on leader pages across the world from an evil dictator to the defender of the frontiers of the free world, single-handedly stopping the flow of communism. He genuinely believed in the cause, but was well aware of the international legitimacy it brought his regime and confident enough to reject President Carter's initial offer in March 1980 of $400 million of US military and economic aid as 'peanuts'. The US, eager for revenge for humiliation in Vietnam, rethought, and under the more responsive Reagan administration a six-year $3.2 billion aid package was negotiated, making Pakistan the third largest recipient of US aid after Israel and Egypt. Zia need have no more worries about money – aid flowed in from all sides.

Martial law intensified as Zia, resorting to total press censorship, was unable to achieve legitimacy for his rule at home. He turned to Islam as its justification, claiming that he had been given a mission by Allah and rewriting history to portray Jinnah as devout and favouring a theocratic state. Knowing this stance did not endear him to the West, Zia joked at press conferences, 'I'm not a bigoted *mullah* who wants everyone to grow beards and lock up their women.'[8] But he did ban women from appearing in athletics contests, tell people how to pray and enforce the month-long Ramazan fast through gunpoint. In an interview just before his death, Zia maintained: 'Education, agriculture, industrialization, there are 101 important issues but the fundamental issue is that this country must have the spirit of Islam.'[9] The country, he said, had lost its way, it was based on faith, there was an inherent contradiction between Islam and democracy, and therefore to enable it to survive it had to be made Islamic. Thus in 1980 he had set up a parallel Islamic legal system of Shariat courts, and repressive Islamic laws were introduced such as the Hudood and Zina Ordinances, with penalties of amputation of hands for stealing and stoning to death for sex outside marriage. They were cosmetic gestures. Although many were sentenced under these laws, the punishments seem never to have been carried out. The jails became increasingly overcrowded as surgeons refused to cut off hands, so those convicted of stealing items as small as an onion languished in jails waiting. Betraying his lack of confidence that the public wanted a theocracy, Zia wrote in a ten-year time lapse before the Shariat would have complete authority over all walks of life, which was due to be voted on in June 1990.

Despite widespread scepticism among the élite and the peasantry, by using Islam as a political tool Zia had begun to build himself a

constituency among the Punjabi urban lower-middle class whose
interests he promoted and from which he tried to create an identity
for Pakistan. But by doing so he alienated the other provinces and
increased ethnicity, particularly among Sindhis, who, first feeling
struck by the 'judicial murder' of a Sindhi Prime Minister, now
resented the imposition of an orthodox Punjabi Islam which they
saw as trying to smother their traditional worship of Sufi saints
and pirs. Zia might have been more successful if his abhorrence of
politicians had not prevented him bringing in at the start some big
names to legitimize his rule, as he attempted to do later.

The greatest threat to Zia came in 1983, when the PPP-led
Movement for Restoration of Democracy (MRD) launched a
movement to topple him. With Benazir in London, it was headed by
Ghulam Mustafa Jatoi, who later became her opponent. Started in
Bhutto's home province of Sindh, the rest of the country did not rally
to its support, intensifying the alienation from the other provinces that
Sindhis feel today. The army, mostly Punjabi, was sent into rural
Sindh to crush the campaign ruthlessly. They arrested more than
20,000 people and exacerbated the alienation. Almost every village in
Sindh has tales of women being raped, houses burned and cattle stolen.
When Benazir took power she found that the jails still held more than
2,000 political prisoners, the majority of whom were Sindhi.

Most of the MRD members had previously belonged to the
PNA movement which had helped propel Zia to power, and he
was jolted by its initial success. Realizing he needed more than
force to stay on top, Zia held a bizarre referendum in December
1984 on the lines of 'Do you approve of the Islamicization programme? If yes then I will remain President until 1990.' To vote
No would be to vote against Islam, so most people did not vote at
all. Some analysts put the turnout as low as 2 per cent. But Zia
took it as a vote of confidence in himself anyway.

The referendum was followed by elections in 1985 in which
parties could not participate. The MRD called for a boycott after
bitter internal rows and were ignored, 53 per cent of the electorate
voting to get their local representative in place so that he could
dispense patronage to them, which is what it was all about. The PPP
later admitted that the boycott was a mistake, and when Zia
announced elections again in 1988, Benazir was quick to announce
their participation on whatever basis.

Zia picked Mohammad Khan Junejo as Prime Minister in the civilian experiment of 1985, seeing him as a man with no constituency who could not become a challenge. Ilahi Bux Soomro, who had been the favourite contender, said, 'Junejo was so unknown we had to be taught how to pronounce his name.' Zia was thus surprised, according to his press secretary Brigadier Salik, when Junejo demanded the lifting of martial law.[10] Zia agreed, but only as *quid pro quo* for the passing of the Eighth Amendment, a revision of the Constitution legalizing all his martial law orders, giving him *carte blanche* to dismiss the assemblies and ensuring the supremacy of his own appointed Governors over the elected provincial Chief Ministers.

Zia now had a Constitution so tailored to his own requirements that it had his name in it, and a government with no real power but which gave a handy democratic image of the country and could take the blame for domestic problems. Gorbachev had come to power in Moscow that year and was speaking of withdrawing Soviet troops from Afghanistan. If that happened, Zia knew that internationally his standing would drop and his US backers would find it harder to be seen to be so generously supporting a dictator.

That was the theory. But everyone knew that the army was still pulling the strings, and as people wearied of military rule the khaki uniforms became objects of derision. Political parties were legalized within strict limits, and Junejo took over the Muslim League in 1986. A small Parliamentary opposition was formed, from which Fakr Imam was elected Speaker, but he was soon removed. It was all an intricate game, a façade with no power. The Parliament did little, spending hours debating trouser length, but what it did apparently angered Zia, who abruptly dismissed it on 29 May 1988 after dinner with the US ambassador.

According to a close confidante of Zia, ever since Benazir's triumphant return to Pakistan in 1986 the general had felt the Americans were trying to oust him. Just as Bhutto was prepared to take over from Ayub and he himself had been primed to take over from Bhutto, he now saw the same process happening against himself. The US no longer wanted to be seen as supporting a dictator, and Zia's mock assembly fooled no one. Benazir had been lobbying in Washington, where she had developed powerful backers and was getting herself prime coverage in the Western press. Her well publicized marriage to a feudal in December 1987 was designed to win the respectability thought to be needed if she was to rule this conservative Muslim country. By August 1988, said the confidante, 'Zia was a desperate man. He knew his time was up but had no idea how to extricate himself honourably.'

No one really knows what would have happened had he lived. 'Zia always had cards up his sleeves,' according to General Fazle Haq, one of his closest friends. He had consulted legal and constitutional experts on ruling that a woman cannot head an Islamic state; he had frequently spoken of his ideal of running a Presidential system. Some army officers had suggested that the PPP should be allowed to win elections but in such a hamstrung way that they would not be able to carry out any reforms and thus be defeated by the people, the Bhutto myth dispelled for ever. But Zia would not have risked allowing his great foe to govern – she would want revenge for her father's death. Others proposed that rather than rule directly, the army put themselves behind a party, but this time one properly elected (perhaps with some help) rather than created out of Parliament. Zia had never hidden his dislike for political parties, so this would seem unlikely, but he did want desperately to gain legitimacy before retiring to 'play more golf' as he said he was eager to do. He also had plans, not just for victory for the fundamentalists in Afghanistan but for an Islamic confederacy comprising Pakistan, Afghanistan, Iran, Turkey and even some of the Soviet Central Asian republics that are now experiencing unrest.

It was perhaps this ambition that led to his death. At 3.51 p.m. on 17 August 1988, villagers just outside Multan saw a plane lurching like an out-of-control rollercoaster before smashing into the desert and exploding in a ball of fire. On board were Zia, his number two, Akhtar Rehman, and fifteen other generals as well as the US ambassador, Arnold Raphel, and the Defence Attaché. They had been reviewing American Abrams tanks in the desert near Bahawalpur. The tank missed its target, and after routine security checks the party left.

Raphel, who was supposed to fly down to Karachi to meet his wife, was persuaded by Zia to accompany him back because he had something urgent to discuss. Rehman, the Chairman of Joint Chiefs of Staff, should not have been on the trip at all, but a friend of his at ISI had warned him that Zia was planning a shake-up of the high command and, as Rehman's name had been much connected with the Ojheri camp ammunition explosion, suggested that a word in the President's ear might be wise. Ironically, however, General Beg, the Vice Chief, who should have been sitting next to Zia in the VIP capsule, had pleaded urgent business elsewhere and boarded his own small turbo-jet to take off after Pak One. He was the only top general in the chain of command not on board.

Within four minutes the control tower had lost contact with Zia's handpicked pilot, Commander Mash'hood Hassan. Pak One had crashed, killing all thirty-one people aboard. Beg's plane circled over the wreckage then flew on to Islamabad where, coolly and to the amazement of most of the population, he sent military units to cordon off strategic locations in the capital, met with the other service chiefs and Ishaq Khan who, as Senate Chairman, became President, and announced the formation of an Emergency Council which would oversee the forthcoming elections.

Instead of the expected chaos which in the past had accompanied major crises in Pakistan, there was an almost palpable sense of relief. Everyone had sensed that Zia was boxing himself in and might have taken draconian measures to stay on top, and suddenly the block to democracy seemed to have been removed, enabling Pakistan to have its first ever peaceful transition of power while Zia had the honourable exit he so wanted. He had died in uniform, some said because of his unswerving support for the Afghan *mujaheddin*, and could be mourned a hero by those who wished. Benazir, trying to look serious and statesmanlike as she spoke to Western press, said, 'Zia's death has removed the shadow under which myself and all those dedicated to democracy have been living.'[11]

The sense of unreality continued at Zia's funeral. Naseem Aheer, the tall brooding Interior Minister who liked listening to the music of Richard Clayderman, was insisting that the plane crash had definitely been caused by sabotage and that Pakistan was in the midst of a destabilization campaign by 'vested interests'. Yet security for the ceremony, which around half a million people, including heads of state, attended, was remarkably lax.

Saturday 20 August was a sweltering summer's day. The futuristic white King Faisal mosque, paid for by Saudi money, seemed to shimmer in the heat. Like ants, thousands of men crawled on to its roof around the gold crescent and up the minarets, waiting for the motorcade bearing the coffin to appear. For a Westerner used to associating black with death, the rows of white shirts and the coloured tinsel hung everywhere suggested pleasure rather than pain. I almost expected to be sold candyfloss.

The holiday atmosphere contrasted strongly with the sombre suits of the ranks of foreign dignitaries, who included the British Foreign Secretary, Geoffrey Howe, and the US Secretary of State, George Schultz. The most emotional delegation were the Afghan refugees, who cried 'Man of Truth, Man of Islam' as the flag-draped coffin was borne aloft by members of the Baluch regiment for a twenty-one gun salute. The Afghan resistance leaders had a more pragmatic reason for their presence, admitting that they feared Zia's death had left them 'orphaned'. Gulbuddin Hekmatyar, the closest to Zia and thus the most worried of them all, took the opportunity to block Schultz in his path and express his anxieties. He was assured nothing would change. Nawaz Sharif and General Fazle Haq, the two Chief Ministers closest to Zia and perhaps the most fearful for their survival under a new regime, walked off with arms around each other. An odd couple, the young awkward businessman and the blunt outspoken Strong Man of the Frontier, they had been drawn together by a combination of shared emotion and political intrigue. So unsure were they of their place in any future set-up that they were to go to General Beg and plead for the imposition of martial law.

Most countries in which the entire top military leadership had apparently been assassinated would be worried about follow-up attacks. But in Pakistan, where conspiracy theories normally abound, few questions were asked. The words on everyone's lips were that disaffected members of the army must have been involved, as they were the only ones to have had the necessary access. Odd theories were raised about a bomb placed in a box of mangoes, Zia's favourite fruit, put on board at the last minute, or the Shia pilot deliberately crashing the plane in retaliation for the assassination of a Shia leader, Arif Hussaini, on the steps of a Peshawar mosque a few weeks earlier, which some claimed Zia had organized. Naseem Aheer insisted that the crash was connected to Zia's activist Afghan policy, the main proponents of which, such as Rehman, were with him on board Pak One.

A half-hearted inquiry was begun, but no autopsies were carried out on crew members, and the hospital was ordered to return the plastic bags containing the remains the day after the crash. There was no questioning of personnel at Bahawalpur airbase. Despite the death of the US ambassador, George Schultz recommended that there be no FBI inquiry, and the US sent just six airforce investigators. They established that the plane was intact when it hit the ground and, working through a process of elimination, ruled out as causes a missile, engine failure, bomb or fire; and the single autopsy carried out showed that the passengers had died before, not after, the crash. The Pakistan air force report concluded that the crash had been caused by the 'occurrence of a criminal act or sabotage leading to loss of aircraft control', and revealed that traces of a chemical had been found which could have been part of a poison gas used to incapacitate the pilots. It recommended a full investigation. But at that point the inquiry was stopped, and there has never been a criminal investigation. In December 1989 the State Department admitted that there had been a cover-up, saying that they had not wanted to rock the boat in an unstable political situation. Almost a year after the crash an FBI team was finally sent to Islamabad, but admitted in conversation that they were not there to find anything out but just to 'placate Congressmen pursuing the issue'.

No one knew who had done it and few seemed to care. Zia's death was just too convenient. The Americans had started to say he was a liability, distrusting his talk of an Islamic Confederation and his unswerving support for the fundamentalists among the Afghan *mujaheddin*. The Soviets were eager to stop his support for the *mujaheddin* and felt Bhutto would favour a negotiated settlement and an early end to the conflict. The Soviet ambassador had reportedly warned Zia that they intended to teach him a lesson for what they saw as Pakistan's violation of the Geneva Accords and its part in a sabotage campaign in Kabul. For the past eighteen months Pakistan had suffered a wave of bombing attacks thought to be the work of the Afghan intelligence service, KHAD. A State Department report released the week of the crash accused Afghan intelligence of killing or wounding 1,400 people in Pakistan that year, the world's second highest number of terrorist victims after Beirut. The Indians had accused Zia of sending arms to Sikh and Kashmiri terrorists. Domestic opponents including Bhutto's exiled brother, Murtaza, who had tried several times to assassinate Zia, were eager to see him out. Al Zulfilkar (the Sword), the anti-Zia terrorist organization masterminded by Murtaza from Syria, initially claimed credit for the destruction of Pak One. Six years before, they had tried to shoot the same plane down with a surface to air missile. But they retracted the claim after it was announced that the US ambassador was on board. Even Zia's natural constituency, the army, had been starting to show signs of unease, feeling that civilians had lost respect for the uniform after a group of officers were beaten up in broad daylight in Rawalpindi, the heart of army land.

Zia's death left a lot of unanswered questions and has neither ended the dynasty nor the Zia–Bhutto rivalry and axis of politics. His son Ejaz, a swarthy businessman just a year older than Benazir, abandoned a successful career as a banker in Bahrain to pursue the facts behind the mysterious death of his father. Along with Humayun Khan, the son of General Akhtar, Ejaz began a crusade in 1989 to open an independent inquiry. The two scoured the country for clues, interviewing thousands of people, and claimed not only to have uncovered fresh evidence but also to have found glaring inconsistencies in the initial, hastily written investigation. According to Humayun, records of calls made to Zia and Rehman before the crash were destroyed, while intelligence files on Murtaza disappeared, and military personnel who were at Bahawalpur at the time were transferred. Ejaz alleged that the Multan police superintendent had identified as involved some PPP members who moved into Bawahalpur just before the crash, but was stopped from investigating. Brigadier Salik's son, who visited the area in March 1990 to interview witnesses, had his luggage stolen and was followed everywhere. 'Someone at a very high level is trying to stop any inquiries,' Humayun insisted, in conspiratorial tones more suited to a clandestine meeting in Peshawar than the tea-room of London's Hyde Park Intercontinental Hotel.[12]

Both sons told me that they had received so many threats to drop the investigation that they could no longer travel without arms and guards. They had no doubt that there had been a deliberate cover-up both by Pakistan and by its US backers. Their findings, including signed depositions from intelligence and army officers, suggest that Al Zulfilkar, masterminded by Murtaza Bhutto, had a hand in what they call 'the worst crime of the century'. The majority of Pakistanis I spoke to about the crash were remarkably indifferent, but Ejaz insisted: 'Everyone believes that General Beg and Al Zulfilkar were involved but no one dares speak out. We're just waiting for the right time to release the information.'[13] The hatred between the two families had been made complete.

With Benazir becoming Prime Minister, the Jacobean vengeance tragedy grew murkier and the parallels between her and Ejaz strengthened. In their separate struggles to venerate their fathers' names, the two became as deadly political foes as their fathers before them, locked in a battle for the future leadership of Pakistan. As Benazir Bhutto's government got increasingly mired in worsening ethnic violence and allegations of corruption, Ejaz ul Haq emerged on to the scene, hoping to assume centre stage – through the ballot-box backed by the IDA, however, not by the bullet like his military father. His nationwide political campaign, begun early in 1990, attracted large crowds waving Zia posters. After elections were announced in August, however, and political infighting increased, it seemed his ambition would help Benazir by splitting the right, which Nawaz Sharif regards as his territory. Ultimately he was persuaded by the army to join Nawaz and was later. rewarded with a ministry in his government.

Benazir and Ejaz had a considerable amount in common. Both in their mid to late thirties with two children, neither wanted to enter politics until the death of their fathers. It could have been Benazir talking when Ejaz described how the crowds pushed him into politics: 'I had no intention of going into politics until I came back and saw so much love and affection among the people for my father and realized I could not disappoint the people.'[14]

Both were charismatic personalities, both educated in the West, and were more comfortable wearing Western dress and speaking English rather than their native tongue. Bhutto studied at Harvard and Oxford, while Ejaz went to the University of Illinois then worked abroad, more he said to keep in the background and avoid the scandals that had dogged sons of previous military dictators. Neither of them seemed entirely at ease in Pakistan's strict Islamic society, though Ejaz, whose greatgrandfather was a *mullah*, had the dubious advantage, being the inheritor of Zia's Islamicization campaign and his support of the Kashmir and Afghanistan *jihad*, while no photos have yet been produced of him dancing in Paris nightclubs.

As skilled in populism as Bhutto, Ejaz, speaking in the unblinking manner of his father, had hoped to lead a united right into the next election, which he said would 'undoubtedly be fought over the ghosts of Zia and Bhutto'. He resented comparisons between the two. 'Her father was convicted and hanged, mine died in uniform serving the nation. She was born into the family of a feudal landlord. She went to the best schools abroad and has always been surrounded by servants. How can she know the problems of the masses?'[15]

Both Bhutto and Ejaz repeatedly claimed to be unmotivated by vengeance, but somehow their protests rang hollow and hatred between the two families made it hard for either to mention the other by name. Bhutto and her supporters suffered badly under the Zia regime, and Ejaz's allegations that in power she carried out a deliberate vendetta against his family could only pale in comparison to the jail and detention PPP leaders endured. He told me angrily: 'We're being treated as badly as we could be. My mother, as widow of an army general, was forced out of the house, given no pension, insulin supplies for her diabetes stopped and had income tax notices served on her.'[16] However, clumsy attempts by Bhutto supporters to smear Zia in the press failed to take hold Many of the incidents they cited seemed absurd - I was given documents supposedly proving that Zia was smuggling drugs in lampshades on state visits to Turkey and secretly securing large numbers of bungalows in Islamabad.

In fact, if Zia wanted to siphon off money he had every opportunity through the US covert arms supplies to the Afghan *mujaheddin*, all of which were distributed through ISI with no paperwork. While no concrete evidence emerged to suggest that he was personally corrupt, and he seemed to have left his family little inheritance, Zia certainly turned a blind eye to the doings of some of his generals who made millions during his rule. However, PPP members maintain that Zia himself was making money and, continuing their attempts to smear both his name and those of generals close to him, in late 1989 the Bhutto government launched a wide-ranging investigation into arms contracts signed in November 1986 with ISC Technologies, the American company at the centre of an alleged £215 million fraud which had disabled Ferranti International, its British parent. An apparently bogus contract, codenamed Khyber Pass, to supply missile technology to Pakistan was disguised within genuine ISCT contracts to provide Pakistan with components for cluster bombs. It was this contract with KP Industries that had attracted Ferranti to buy ISCT in 1987. James Guerin, the founder of ISCT whom Ferranti sued, had met Zia on several occasions, and it has been alleged that Zia personally agreed the Khyber Pass contract in return for substantial pay-offs. According to Ferranti, KP Industries, which had not been traced, was described on contract documents as representing 'the President of the Islamic Republic of Pakistan'.[17]

And so the battle continued, but with a new twist. After Zia's death his family set up a charity called the Zia Foundation, ostensibly to provide dowry money and help the disabled, like Zia's own daughter. One year on, it had 350,000 members and obviously political functions, organizing rallies and compiling data. Ejaz admitted that 'it has many political members', adding that one of its functions was 'research into the current situation in the country'.

But there was an irony involved: while it was Zia who usurped power and ruled illegally for eleven years, and was dependent on the support of vested interests, it was Benazir who captured the hearts and votes of the poor. But by early 1990, as her administration was increasingly coming under fire because she had failed to pass a single significant piece of legislation, and because she was therefore losing her place as the white queen of the slums, people started to speak wistfully of the Zia days just as in his time they had spoken of Bhutto and Ayub before him. Ejaz, seeing the opportunity just as Ali Bhutto once had, began presenting himself as the populist, telling rallies, 'We'll bring change for the common man.'

Zia ul-Haq found that the execution of Zulfikar Ali Bhutto could not raze his ghost but instead created a martyr on which Benazir built her political base. In the same way, Benazir discovered that the death of Zia, which cleared the way for her rise to power, was to make his ghost a powerful political rival, more

popular in death than in life. However, her Joan of Arc image was
to be given another airing. Showing that nothing had been learned
from history, the army's lack of political feel was evident once
more when they prevailed upon President Ishaq to dismiss Benazir's government, in the mistaken conviction that her incompetence in power had discredited her and that the People's Party
would crumble; General Zia had once wrongly believed the same
would result from removing Benazir's father. Corruption charges
initiated against Benazir, which could result in disqualification,
enabled the PPP to cry vendetta. Iqbal Haider, the party's Information Secretary, said gleefully, 'Whatever our sins, they have been
washed away by our unfair dismissal.'[18] Once more the men in
khaki had created a living martyr – the role Benazir Bhutto
played best.

6

'BUT MINISTER . . .'

WHO RULES PAKISTAN?

'I wish I'd trained as a commando, not a lawyer,' confided a
harassed Tariq Rahim, the Minister for Parliamentary Affairs, as
he fielded at least four calls at once from his room in the WAPDA
guesthouse. 'Send three helicopters from Multan,' he barked into
one phone, in between negotiating for seven jeeps from another. It
could have been the operations room for a major offensive, and in
a way it was, but of a political not a military nature. Mr Rahim
was frantically trying to round up all the PPP's MPs and supporting independents and get them to the mountain valley of Swat,
away from the temptations of the chequebook of Nawaz Sharif,
who was mounting a vote of no confidence against Benazir in
November 1989, less than a year after she had taken office.

Surrounded by the audience of hangers-on, assistants and constituents who are a permanent fixture around Pakistan's political
personages, Mr Rahim was arranging helicopters, jeeps and plane
seats to locate missing MPs. Sharif had his supporters holed up in
the old British hill resort of Murree, where they were being wined
and dined in style. He had already scored a major coup by securing
the support of the thirteen MPs of the MQM, the party whose
backing had initially helped Bhutto take power, and of one of
Bhutto's ministers, Tariq Magsi. It was all rather ironic. Rahim, a
chubby lawyer with a weakness for exaggeration, alcohol and
women, had until a few months earlier been on the other side
himself. But with his ministerial experience, which most of the
cabinet lacked, his contacts in the opposition and his eagerness for
power, he had quickly made himself indispensable to Bhutto, who

was frequently dragging him off his beloved tennis courts in pursuit of some mission or another. The no-confidence vote was his greatest challenge. But Rahim moved fast and knew how to play the dirty tricks game too, and Bhutto clung on, if somewhat shaken by her severely dented majority.

The exercise had cost both sides many millions in rupees and did nothing for the reputation of democracy. Bhutto's cabinet had had to resign, to leave her free to lure waverers with the offer of ministries. Right up until her dismissal in August 1990 she carried their resignations in her pocket, knowing that the moment she reappointed a cabinet she would have few goodies left to retain the support of unsuccessful aspirants. The attempted no-confidence vote was just the latest round in a battle between the centre and Punjab, which for the first time in Pakistan's history were ruled by different (and hostile) parties.

War had been declared the moment Bhutto took office, claiming that Sharif had rigged the elections in Punjab and would not last two months. He in turn had said that she would not be allowed to govern. They had gone to such lengths to avoid each other that when Bhutto flew to Lahore for a visit, Sharif left for Karachi. Shortly after the national polls, Sharif had demonstrated his support by IDA victories in by-elections in seven of the nine Punjab seats, including the Lahore seat Benazir herself had held. In retaliation, Farooq Leghari, one of Bhutto's key ministers, who himself hoped to be Punjab Chief Minister, called foreign journalists together to reveal that Sharif was 'stealing electricity'[1] and had got bank loans of several millions under false pretences. These were allegations he had no evidence for other than Sharif's increase in wealth since beginning his political career, which had made his family business one of the richest in Pakistan. 'He's running the Punjab like his own personal company,' announced Salman Taseer, another PPP hopeful for Sharif's position, and the only Pakistani I knew with gold buttons on his *shalwar kamiz*. Egged on by her over-enthusiastic ministers, Bhutto had unwisely let some of them loose on Punjab in March 1989 in a clumsy attempt to remove the man whom Taseer described as 'the last vestige of martial law'.

Their efforts backfired and Sharif actually increased his majority, helped by a timely warning from General Beg that 'politicians should respect the election results'. But neither side would give up their efforts to remove the other. The return of democracy brought with it a remarkable campaign of blackmail, bribery and arrests. Anyone visiting Pakistan in the autumn of 1989 could have been forgiven for thinking an election campaign was underway, as both parties held frequent rallies to demonstrate their support, using public money to commandeer buses to bring in participants eager for the few rupees they would earn for attending. Feelings were running so high that Sharif told a rally that he would 'dump the Bhuttos' remains in the Arabian sea', while Bhutto confided over lunch at the Shandur Pass that her men had discovered an IDA plot to blow up Zia's grave and blame it on her.

What Bhutto had initially under-estimated and later was to admit was that Zia had created a constituency. She called it 'a constituency of drug dealers, smugglers and corrupt elements in society', but in fact he had won considerable support not just among the *nouveau riche* (many of whom may well be smugglers), but also among the urban lower middle classes of Punjab, which in the early 1970s provided the backbone of PPP support. Lurid posters of an eerily grinning Zia, often depicted rising from a burning C130 plane, had become a frequent sight in the small shops of Punjabi bazaars, and in the 1988 elections the PPP lost heavily in the towns of Sialkot and Rawalpindi, which they had swept in the seventies. This support was strengthened by an outbreak of aggressive Punjabi chauvinism, manipulated by Sharif's claims that Punjab was not getting a fair deal from the federal government. Bhutto's ill-judged attempts to remove him, and her refusal to allow the convening of the Council of Provincial Interests to sort out provincial grievances, played straight into Sharif's hands. Perfectly reasonable Punjabis began talking of the invasion of the Sindhis into Islamabad as though referring to creatures from Mars, and started displaying car stickers proclaiming 'Sindhis Out' in the baldest terms.

The danger for Benazir in this was more than an exacerbation of ethnic tensions. What both Zia and Nawaz Sharif realized was that it is not politicians or even generals who run the country. Bhutto herself acknowledged this during the fifteen-day wait before she was named premier, which she claimed was a deliberate delay to 'give long rope to unscrupulous elements to continue using police superintendents, deputy commissioners and other official machinery to coerce independents into joining the IDA'.[2] The real rulers were the bureaucrats, those strange alien creatures *bazaaris* and analysts alike refer to as the 'civil-military bureau-cracy', 80 per cent of whom were Punjabis. By being perceived as attacking Punjab, Bhutto was further alienating an already sus-picious army and civil service.

Throughout Bhutto's twenty months of government, whenever General Beg met journalists the first question would always be when did the army intend to move in. It was no surprise, except perhaps to Bhutto herself when, under military pressure, the Presi-dent dissolved the assemblies. But the question of who rules Pakis-tan had little to do with the outcome of the battle between the white queen and the generals, nor was it between her and Sharif. The real power in Pakistan comes from the number of people one commands and the amount of patronage at one's disposal. The politicians may be seen to dispense patronage but it is to the bureaucrats they turn to arrange it. Even when the military was running the country, they relied on civil servants to carry on the workings of government. And most powerful of all these are the twenty District Commissioners and their deputies.

These are the people with seat reservations on every plane from their district, who decide whether or not a demonstration can be held, if a road can be built, which villages will receive electricity, and the kind of reception a visiting dignitary will receive. They are the local head of police, they collect taxes, issue permits for anything from guns to newspapers to collecting shoes at the mosque, and even decide civil court cases. These are the people with power, not the politicians with roomfuls of phones and large numbers of people on their lawns. And they make it to the top, too – President Ghulam Ishaq Khan being the prime example. He had served in every administration since 1961 and probably had greater influence on the nation's economy than anyone else in the country.

Pakistan's bureaucracy is legendary – the British are always blamed for its creation but they simply improved upon the net-works of collectors installed by the Mughul Emperors, making the system more hierarchical and linking success more to merit than star-sign. After the untimely death of Pakistan's founder, Mohammad Ali Jinnah, leaving the country without a strong

central leader, the bureaucrats soon found themselves holding
sway, along with the army, as the only stable institution, making
decisions as well as executing policy.

I once walked round the old city of Lahore with its genial
commissioner Shahid Rafi and his aides. It was like being part of
an emperor's entourage. As we pushed our way through narrow
streets piled high with enticing gold like Aladdin's cave, and sticky
mounds of colourful sweetmeats speckled with flies, sizzling kebabs
and old men making bread, slapping the dough together with
great vigour, we were besieged by people asking for jobs, licences,
water supply, complaining about neighbours or of being wrong-
fully cited in cases. Bottles of fizzy drink were proffered, trays of
cakes appeared from nowhere, until eventually we ended up in the
office of the Bazaar President, which was over a cinema apparently
owned by a big drug dealer and with huge garish pictures daringly
showing a woman's ankle. I went to such a cinema once in Peshawar – it was full of heavily breathing Pathans, hashish smoke and
happy cockroaches. Whenever a woman's ankle was revealed the
audience gasped with satisfaction and there was a mass exit to the
toilets.

The occasion for the Commissioner's visit to Kim's city was the
run-up to Moharrum, perhaps the world's bloodiest religious festival, when Shias re-enact the martyrdom of Imam Hussain and
Hassan, the Prophet's grandsons, whom they believe to have been
the Fifth Caliphs. It is often a cause of tension – in British days
between Hindus and Muslims, later between Shia and Sunni sects.
The Bazaar President was expressing his fears to the Commissioner
over possible violence and bottlenecks as the highly charged parade
came through the bazaar, wild-eyed men in black beating themselves to vivid scarlet with bunches of knives or chains of razor-
blades. The DC rose to the occasion, producing a many-coloured
coded map showing where the different parades would go,
possible trouble spots, deployment of police and exits. The bazaar
officials nodded sagely, not understanding but satisfied there was a
plan.

Spending Moharrum in the DC's office and with his men in the
streets really demonstrated the power of the man. Police units,
army, intelligence all reported to him in a multi-faceted operation.
But Shahid Rafi was on top. He had set up peace committees

beforehand and had asked leading *mullahs* to tone down their closing rhetoric to preach peace and harmony, however much blood and gore they had railed before. Those involved were issued huge 100-page documents marked 'Confidential' to increase their sense of self-importance. These detailed the more than 400 processions of at least 50,000 people to co-ordinate, the positions of the 7,000 police, and factors which might cause tension. Blood transfusion units were placed in strategic locations. For twenty-four hours Mr Rafi stayed in his office, surrounded by ringing phones and buzzing wireless sets, reports coming in enabling him to tick off each of the twenty-one potential trouble-spots marked on the map as it was passed.

Fighting through the narrow streets with some of his officers disguised as 'beaters', among crowds of wailing women and men and boys streaming with blood, trying to touch the riderless white horse which represents the martyred Hussain, it was easy to imagine the horror of Partition and the riots in July 1947 when the first train of refugees arrived in Lahore full of dead Muslim bodies. The Walled City, one of Asia's most populated areas, became a seething cauldron of heat, dust, fighting and burning, Hindus and Sikhs trapped in their homes behind Muslim barricades, dying of thirst because the water supply had been cut. Those who ventured out were butchered by Muslim mobs, the gutters literally running red with blood. Today less than 1,000 of the 600,000 Hindus and Sikhs who once lived in the old city remain, but with tensions at a peak between the centre and Punjab government, Mr Rafi feared that Muslims might fall upon each other as they had in 1986. But his elaborate precautions paid off, and afterwards he admitted great relief that it had all passed over smoothly. 'A peaceful Moharrum means a good year,' he said.

. Whoever finally won the battle between Bhutto and the generals or Bhutto and Sharif, it would ultimately make little difference to the running of the country for the majority of Pakistanis. When both Rahim and Sharif were rounding up support, it was to the bureaucrats that they went to arrange jeeps and favours. When politicians pledge to deal with the numerous petitions constantly waved at them, it is to the Commissioner they refer. It is the DC whom they rely on to obtain the patronage on which their votes depend. Whether or not a candidate will command a person's vote depends mostly on his relations with the bureaucracy.

The politician's strength in rural areas is that literacy is so low that the peasants need the politician to fill in the numerous forms and circumvent the bureaucratic morass of the DC's office. Pakistan, as well as being a country of superpatronage, is also a country of peons and it is to bypass these that politicians are necessary. Peons jealously guard their position and have immense nuisance value. A friend of mine once lost a watchman who had been 'promoted to a peon'. He would be earning less money but in a hierarchical society would have a 'position'. Unfortunately, peons seem to regard their duty as creating obstacles to the public rather than serving them, announcing with a smug no-nonsense smile that 'boss is out of station' or 'not in his seat', quaint phrases which suggested urgent missions but generally meant, 'He's here. He probably would like to see you but I'm not letting you near.' Often they would add grudgingly, 'You can wait.' Sometimes I would, fascinated to try and discern the mystery of who actually does the work in government offices, producing the endless stream of files. I would join a band of people all resigned to sitting blankly. Usually a cup of tea with a nasty brown skin would be brought, sometimes hard yellow cake. People would run in and out with files, which the peons would stamp with the rubber stamps most peons seem to have. I never saw any of the documents being read – they were no doubt more licences for friends.

If one did not know a 'high-up', it could take a day even to reach the stenographer in the outermost room who would process the form to pass to the assistant to the secretary to the assistant to the deputy to the person one wanted to see. It was quite possible to get lost in the web, and money was frequently required to ease the route. I once met a Pakistani who had been born in Britain and had made a fortune selling electrical goods and building shopping centres in Leicester. He had gone to Islamabad to invest some of this precious foreign exchange in a biscuit factory. It took him five years to get the permits, a process he described as 'like watching grass grow'. Most people did not have his perseverance and would drop out to invest in Singapore or the Gulf, where they could be producing the merchandise in less time than it required to obtain permission to apply for permission for the project in Pakistan. His problem had been lack of contacts, and only when he had got to know the Industry Minister could his perfectly good project be approved.

By keeping the DC or police superintendent or federal secretary supplied in jeeps, alcohol, women or whatever he required, the politician could walk straight in. Senior bureaucrats are invited to all the best weddings and are frequent receivers of brown paper packages containing precious alcohol. In what has been described as a skimocracy, the better the party or gift the greater the favour the politician could command. Thus Johnny Walker Black Label would get one further than Red Label, while local Murree brew was guaranteed neither to make friends nor to influence people.

Politicians would use bureaucrats not just to help their relatives, friends or constituents but also for the less savoury task of improving their chances of election. Throughout my travels I never met a DC who had not been approached by politicians to help in the election, almost as if he was part of a party machine. This help could take the form of the DC disqualifying rival candidates from standing on the basis that they are 'not of good character' or are 'prejudicial to the cause of Islam'; providing jeeps and information; twisting voters' arms; kidnapping or arresting opponents; or providing a judicious spot of electrification to constituents. Sharif was a master of this reward system and it paid off. But he was not the first. Ali Bhutto, who had won support for his campaign against the 'mandarins', ultimately found them rather useful, and in 1977 members of the civil service actively participated in the rigging of elections, even arranging for the abduction of candidates.

With my British sense of 'doing things properly' I long resisted using 'high-ups'. Consequently I would constantly find myself as if trapped in an Escher maze as I tried to get permits through official channels, drinking endless cups of tea in dusty offices and being stared at by countless Pakistanis, just sitting and waiting in a way they seem to have perfected. My biggest nightmare was encounters with the state-run telephone department, 'T&T', known locally as 'Torment and Terror'. Phone connections were impossible to obtain without help, and people made fortunes as phone-brokers, registering as clinics to obtain priority connections then claiming to have moved and selling off the number.

Having got mine installed through a judicious word by a 'high-up', the phone started breaking down frequently in the way only Pakistani phones know how. The first time it happened I went to a neighbour and called the operator, who immediately asked me if

I could get him a UK visa. I told him I was press and desperately needed the line restored. After he had given me his entire family history, I was given the number for reporting faults – the supervisor's number, so I would not need to wait. The supervisor was friendly and told me he would send a man immediately. Within a few hours, the man not having arrived, the supervisor and I would barely be speaking, as he repeated with an extremely annoying level of measured patience: 'WAIT in your house, Madam – the man is on his way.'

After a day of waiting I would go to the Divisional Engineer, obtaining permits and fighting my way through barricades of peons. He would order me tea, smile sympathetically, and say, 'This is Pakistan, Madam. These phones are made in Pakistan. We are a poor country. Some people would say we should never be. What can you expect?' I was to spend many hours in the office of this stooped man, with his unbearably sad smile, as if all the problems of the world were on his shoulders, seated beneath a huge wooden board on which his predecessors' names were painted in gold. Some had lasted only a few weeks. I got to know his opinions on everything from US foreign policy to cricket, but he never fixed my phone. Eventually I learnt through necessity, and resorted to asking ministers to intervene. Then it would be resolved almost immediately, my house besieged by skinny men on bikes wielding screwdrivers, anxious to 'expedite'. Similarly, to ensure seat reservations on the domestic airline, I got to know its directors, name-dropping with abandon. Sometimes I would have it done back to me – I would be asked for visas or jobs in England, and it was no use explaining that things were different back home.

Ironically, the power of the bureaucracy increased drastically under Zulfikar Ali Bhutto, who loathed the species, referring to them as a 'class of brahmins or mandarins unrivalled in its snobbery and arrogance, insulated from the life of the people and incapable of identifying with them'. It was more than rhetoric to capitalize on public resentment of the increased powers of civil servants under General Ayub. Bhutto sacked 1,300 civil servants in 1972 and introduced a system of lateral entry, enabling people from other fields to enter high-level jobs. But his wide-scale nationalization suddenly meant an increase in their empire and capacity to extend patronage, running banks, textile mills, cotton ginning plants, petrol companies, not usually with great success. Like previous regimes, Ali Bhutto's brought in a host of new regulations; permissions were required for the slightest act, each of which meant going to the appropriate civil servant, some of whom made fortunes from auctioning off everything from cigarette concessions, to rickshaw licences, to permits for setting up a newspaper.

The biggest moneyspinner and dinosaur of all bureaucratic institutions was WAPDA, the Water and Power Development Authority, the mere mention of which would cause skin to crawl and lips to curl. With around 140,000 employees, it was one of the world's largest public sector corporations, eating up nearly half Pakistan's development budget, often, it seemed, to little effect. 'People steal electricity,' a despairing Akram Khan, the Adviser on Water and Power, complained to me, admitting that a third of electricity 'goes missing' between generation and transmission. It was easy to see why — jungles of wires are run off from poles in every town. The WAPDA inspectors could be persuaded not to notice for a small fee.

Some people had a more sophisticated way of avoiding paying. Through arrangement with a WAPDA contact, usually involving money, one's electricity could be put on someone else's bill — preferably a large industrialist who would not notice — while the actual user paid a small percentage direct to the WAPDA contact. A Karachi Chamber of Commerce official once admitted to me that he had been approached by a WAPDA official who said, 'Your electricity bill is 6,000 rupees a month. I can arrange for you to be charged only 1,000 rupees if you give me 1,500 rupees.' Initially the businessman was shocked, but then he said, 'I thought about it and realized that the system is corrupt anyway; why should I be the mug who tries to play fair? — I'll probably end up paying everyone else's bill.' This was a common racket, one which the T&T were at too. Several times the international operator gave me the option of paying him a small amount directly and having my call billed to someone else. I think I was probably one of the unlucky heavy users who paid for others' calls.

Zia and the bureaucracy developed a good understanding. His only real interference in the workings of their empire can be seen by going into any government department around 1 p.m. Coming out of the lift at this time, one has to be careful not to trip over

the rows of prostrate civil servants on straw mats. Zia declared
that they must all pray in a certain way, as well as ordering them
to wear *shalwar kamiz* instead of Western dress. Ross Massood, a
senior bureaucrat, explained to me: 'Civil servants like military
rule because the two organizations have a lot in common. The
army are military bureaucrats but they don't know the system so
need us to guide them.'

The bureaucracy was less sure of political government. Before
the elections a friend from the Development Finance Institute,
which with large grants at its disposal was much sought after,
admitted, 'We are very worried that when the politicians move in
they'll have constant favours to grant to keep in with their constituents. Zia never had any constituents to worry about so we could
get on as we liked.' One senior civil servant confessed, 'We hold
politicians in utter contempt. We get round them by playing an
elaborate version of "Yes Minister" we call "But Minister". We
say yes minister and then back it up with 150 buts. "But minister
the rules do not permit this" or "Have you considered the implications of regulation 1241?" etc., etc. It is by the number of buts that
one can tell who is gaining the upper hand.'[3]

If the civil servants could not have military rule then they
favoured weak government. Ross Massood explained, 'Inexperienced politicians do not know how things are done, so are at our
mercy.' They thought they had got what they wanted with the
1988 results − a fragile government, held back by so many checks
that it was unclear whether they would be able to do anything,
and a Prime Minister who complained, 'I am in office but not in
power.'[4] Both President Ishaq and General Beg had thought that
Sharif controlling the largest province would provide a useful
balance to Bhutto at the centre, which would leave the bureaucracy
to go on running things. Some senior PPP leaders such as Jehangir
Badr even expressed relief: 'If we had won a thumping majority
we would have no excuse for action but we don't have the experience. And it would have been hard to resist the temptation for
vengeance. Now we can barely take a step without seeking com-
promises.'

The bureaucrats certainly seemed to have the upper hand.
Initially there was scepticism in their ranks, and ears pricked
when Benazir referred to them as 'Zia's bureaucracy'. The

Communications Secretary told the new minister bluntly, 'You can build roads or make money, what is it to be?' The minister returned to Karachi and reputedly began giving out phone connections to air hostesses, infuriating his civil servants. But others thought that with a new young government this was a chance to get long-delayed projects moving. However, their worst fears were soon confirmed. The Petroleum Secretary was removed after he refused to issue a licence to a family which supported the PPP. The Communications Secretary was shifted to Religious Affairs after insisting that a licence to operate mobile phones should go to one of the two big British companies that had come out top of the ratings system. After his removal it was given to a company whose Pakistani partner allegedly had Bhutto's husband as a director. Within a short space of time around seventy senior bureaucrats had been made Officer on Special Duty (OSD), a quaint way of saying put out to pasture. Bhutto favourites like Mohibullah Shah were promoted over the heads of hundreds of others, a move guaranteed to cause unrest in the ranks of such a rigidly hierarchical system.

But they had ways of getting their own back. Early into Benazir's administration they adopted a strategy of simply giving no advice, often causing paralysis and landing ministers in awkward situations. 'Let them dig their own graves,' one of the highest-grade bureaucrats told me smugly. The damage the civil service could cause was shown vividly when the PPP presented their first budget in June 1989. The documents had been prepared by the bureaucracy, and the Minister of State for Finance, handed the speech just before entering Parliament, had little idea what he was saying, stumbling on passages and announcing sales tax on twenty items without detailing what they were. Later, at the traditional post-budget press conference, the minister, Ehsan ul Piracha, was faced by a barrage of hostile journalists not unreasonably demanding to know exactly what items were to be taxed. Piracha plainly had no idea; he turned to the bureaucrats accompanying him, who looked aside, leaving him to flounder and the journalists to storm out.

Initially Bhutto was hopeful that she could win over those against her, and argued, 'The system may be loaded against us but we feel we can still make a contribution.'[5] But six months on, she admitted the problems in an interview: 'When I met Mrs Aquino in Tokyo she said the first months and years are difficult because all those people don't want you to get power. I soon realized what she meant.'[6]

Yet rather than appease them, Bhutto increased the bureaucracy's hostility by what they saw as her anti-Punjab stance. Of the seventy-four bureaucrats made OSD, all but two were Punjabis. Punjab is Pakistan's Prussia, from which more than three-quarters of the army and bureaucracy hail, and was not to be messed with. Both organizations had a hard core of lower-middle-class Punjabis made good, who more than anyone corresponded to the identity that Zia was creating for Pakistan, essentially a Punjabi identity.

I first got an insight into what Zia had done when I met a clean-cut army officer, with the name 'Javaid' pinned on his crisp khaki shirt, who had come to meet a political personage I too was waiting to see. I had been put in an upstairs room, away from male eyes, and was pondering why anyone needed three phones in a rarely used room and why rich Pakistanis always spoil exquisitely decorated rooms with vases of tacky plastic flowers. Just as I had decided it was a show of power and importance, Javaid walked in. Army officers are not supposed to talk to foreigners, particularly not journalists and most certainly not of the female variety, but Javaid was curious and easily persuaded to stay.

The lower-middle-class son of a Punjabi shopkeeper, Javaid was articulate, well educated, and, I soon realized, far more aware of the problems of the ordinary Pakistani than any politician I had met. He symbolized exactly the constituency and ideology Zia had been trying to promote. In a cool, well-reasoned argument, almost as if we were discussing some far-off country, he challenged why the West thought democracy was so necessary for Pakistan. I replied, somewhat pompously, that we felt the people of Pakistan should be given a chance to choose whom they wanted to govern. Javaid laughed; he pointed out that the army was far more representative of the people than the politicians, who were all feudals who had never had to work and exploited the system. 'It's time we stopped messing around with these politicians and got on with running the country,' he declared. It was a potent argument, but one hard to equate with my black and white 'democracy good and army rule bad' viewpoint.

Initially a supporter of Ali Bhutto, Javaid felt that Bhutto had sold out to the feudals; Zia, on the other hand, had promoted the interests of people like him and brought people into power on their merit rather than because of their families, though admittedly he had had to appease a few of the landed interests by offering them jobs or returning nationalized industries. Javaid cited for example Dr Mehbub ul Haq, Zia's Finance Minister, and Sartaj Asis, Adviser on Agriculture, among others he had brought in who were not from rich families. Zia, he declared, had begun to give Pakistanis an identity and imprisoned those who were 'anti-Pakistan'.

Intrigued, I asked him what it was to be Pakistani. What did he have in common with the gun-toting wild Pathans of the Frontier, the Baluchis who think nothing of striking out the eyes of enemies, or the romantic Sindhis dancing at Sufi shrines and worshipping warrior saints? His reply was a collection of buzzwords – Islam, Urdu, pro-Afghan *mujaheddin*, anti-India, pro-US and anti-USSR. This was no Pakistani identity, but exactly the Punjabi identity that Zia had been attempting to impose on the rest of the country. No wonder the country was in a mess. Anyone from the other three provinces, asked the same question, would have insisted that they were first Sindhi, Baluch or Pathan, then Muslim and then Pakistani.

But just as repainting the pictures of Pakistan's founder, Jinnah, to depict him in Islamic dress rather than the Western suits he favoured could not make the country more Islamic, neither could imposing Punjabi causes as national causes bring the country together. Instead, at the same time denied any form of political expression, people turned increasingly to their ethnic or tribal identity, causing outbreaks of violence which Zia could use to divide and rule.

Holding democratic elections, far from lessening this politics of ethnicity, had exacerbated the divisions because of results which had led to Punjab being ruled by a different party to that at the centre. The more the centre seemed to be picking on Nawaz Sharif, an embodiment of Zia's Punjabi identity, the more Punjabi chauvinism emerged to horrifying levels. As Sharif was sworn in as Chief Minister, Punjabis outside the Lahore assembly yelled, 'We will not be governed by a Sindhi.' What the Pakistani academic Akbar

Ahmed refers to as the 'Punjab yuppie set', who had prospered under Zia, have, he says, in between jogging in Racecourse Park, become vociferous and unreasonable in anti-Bhutto rhetoric.[7]

For to some degree Zia had succeeded in persuading people to identify with his view. Not only did IDA candidates spouting Ziaism win unexpectedly in parts of urban Punjab, but in many ways the whole political debate had shifted on to an agenda based on Javaid's buzzwords which had been made into sticks to beat the opposition with, almost, a power of veto. Susceptible to charges of being anti-*mujaheddin*, Benazir had to allow the continuation of a war she had no interest in, ensuring the presence of millions of refugees the country could not afford. Accusations that she was soft on India forced her into a 180-degree swing, from trying to reach peace with Pakistan's large neighbour to taking a hawkish posture on India, challenging Indian premier V. P. Singh over Kashmir, the Muslim state that Pakistan claims is hers, bringing the two nations to the verge of war. The whisky-drinking party-loving brigade of the PPP even started trying to be more Islamic than their opponents, accusing Nawab Bugti, the outspoken Chief Minister of Baluchistan, of offending Islam in his remarks to a British journalist on the nature of the young boys in Paradise.

Close colleagues of the President say that when he opted for Bhutto in Islamabad and Sharif in Punjab he thought this would provide a government of consensus. This shows how little political feel the bureaucrats had, however politicized the institution may have become. Instead of compromise there was paralysis, Bhutto's government unable to pass a single significant piece of legislation while the battle against Sharif raged on.

Like her father, Benazir's first act was to commute death sentences and free political prisoners. Well aware of the fragility of her position, in her first address she struck a sombre note. 'You have bestowed a great honour on your sister and placed a heavy responsibility on her shoulders. We are standing on the brink of disaster but a whole generation is ready to launch constructive efforts to save the country. We will bring an end to hunger and degradation. We will provide shelter over the heads of the homeless.'

But such worthy aims were to come a poor second to attempts

to remove Sharif, or 'consolidate democracy' as her ministers preferred to call it. The PPP could not stomach their greatest rival in power in the largest province and were determined to oust him. Salman Taseer insisted: 'He represents all we've been fighting against – of course we cannot work with him.' Just four days after taking office, Bhutto told me. 'He will not last two months.'

Sharif alleged that she had tried to stop his oath of office, a claim substantiated by the Punjab Chief Secretary, the top civil servant in the province. He soon retaliated, refusing to accept federal officials posted to Punjab and reassessing the cases of political prisoners released by the centre. Exacerbated by Sharif's by-election victories, the buying and selling of MPs began in earnest, the ban on floor-crossing ignored as always, with the party in power able to use it to its advantage. Some MPs seemed to have made changing parties into a career making millions, causing the President to liken Pakistan's democracy to a stock exchange.

Emboldened by his survival of the PPP's attempt to remove him, Sharif became more assertive. He started a campaign of destabilization in the Frontier province, until the Frontier Chief Minister Sherpao had some of his agents, such as Senator Vardag, expelled from the province. To retain power, however, Sherpao was forced to make almost everyone on his side a minister – at the last count he had twenty-four, and fourteen advisers, in an assembly of eighty. Bhutto claimed that the Islamabad riots in February 1989, supposedly in protest against Salman Rushdie's *Satanic Verses*, which sparked off worldwide reaction, were manufactured by Sharif to destabilize her government while she was away in China. Sharif was also thought to have organized the series of religious conferences across the country declaring that a woman cannot head an Islamic state. One of Bhutto's press spokesmen, Bashir Riaz, even claimed that Sharif was sending agents to poetry symposiums around the world to quote verse against her, an intriguingly subtle ploy.

Playing on Punjabi chauvinism, Sharif began declaring Punjab's own foreign policy, criticizing the centre for being weak on India through Bhutto's attempts to forge peace with Rajiv Gandhi. A Punjab Bank was set up, and plans drawn up for a separate Punjab power network and TV station, ironically making use of the provisions in Ali Bhutto's Constitution for autonomy for the provinces. Benazir, who had been an avid supporter of more autonomy, found herself trying to limit it and accused Sharif of a 'virtual declaration of independence . . . trying to run a state within a state.' Sharif also blocked efforts to launch the party's development drive — the People's Programme — in Punjab, a way of spreading patronage through PPP MPs, but on this he had to be careful as he could not afford to be seen as depriving his constituents of anything.

For both sides no method was too low, and usually involved dragging in the bureaucracy. Rival intelligence agencies were used to tap each other's phones and shadow movements. Police were dragged in for arrests of opponents. In August 1989 the government arrested General Fazle Haq, Sharif's close ally, implicated in arranging the murder of a Shia leader, Arif Hussaini. Nationalized banks were instructed not to provide credit to Sharif's family company, Ittefaq, and state railways refused to provide carriages to transport steel scrap from Karachi to his foundry near Lahore. Eating lunch in a café on a hill overlooking Islamabad, the walrus-like Rao Rashid, an adviser to Benazir and himself a former police chief whom Mr Bhutto had used on occasion to quieten political opponents, argued, 'We've taken away his privileges not his rights.'

Sharif fought back, using Punjab police to break into a Lahore courtroom and arrest Salman Taseer, whom he disliked intensely and who had just been granted bail for making an anti-army speech. An arrest warrant was issued against Mukhtar Awan, the minister for manpower, on a murder charge. Rao Rashid, who, given his background should have known better, said angrily, 'He is using Punjab police like his personal henchmen.'

As the situation deteriorated further in summer 1989, officers from the Federal Investigation Agency (FIA) raided a Pepsi Cola bottling plant owned by some close allies of Sharif including the Punjab Education Minister and the sons of General Akhtar Rehman, who had died with Zia in the crash. At midnight the next night two FIA officers were arrested by Punjab police and cases of murder and kidnapping were registered against them. The Interior Ministry accused the Punjab government of treason, issuing a statement in which it said that the Punjab government was guilty of 'rebellion against the centre' and listed a chargesheet of

'illegal steps ... aimed at subverting the constitution'. Further
embroiling the bureaucracy, the centre recalled four senior civil
servants posted in Punjab, including the police chief. Sharif, who
had always kept a tight hold on the Punjab administration, instructed them to stay. Eventually the Interior Ministry was prevailed upon to withdraw the statement, the FIA officials were
freed, and the cases were dropped by both sides.

But the battle continued in the streets. Having passed through
the first stage of peaceful transition of power, no one, it seemed,
had told the politicians that after elections they were supposed to
stop electioneering and get on with governing. By September
1989 every conceivable religious day or national anniversary was
being used as an excuse for politicians to demonstrate their political
manliness, causing some unease among the IMF delegation then
visiting the country to assess efforts to get the economy in shape.

Defence Day, Iqbal Day, Pakistan Day, Jinnah's death anniversary, Jinnah's birthday, Zia's death anniversary, Bhutto's
death anniversary – all were chances for national rallies 'to boost
morale'. They were expensive exercises which meant little, politicians trying to outdo even those within the same party by bringing
the largest procession, all of whom had to be transported, paid and
fed. On rally days there was not a bus to be had, all having been
seized by provincial governments to move supporters. The government could barely afford to pay its own wages, yet ministers
estimated it cost more than 300 rupees (or two weeks' average
wage) per head attending, on top of which they had to pay for the
stage and sound system, seating, security, medical facilities, banners,
newspaper adverts and even, on one occasion, for painting the
streetlights of Islamabad in PPP colours. Dr Maleeha Lodhi, a
former professor at LSE and at that time editor of The Muslim
paper in Pakistan, captured the national mood when she wrote: 'If
ministers falling over each other in claiming they had led larger
processions had used half that vigour in coming to terms with the
work of their ministries they would have done the party a bigger
favour.'

The irony was that the battle of rallies which was born out of
PPP frustration at their impotence in fact only added to it. Sharif,
in his sixth year in office, had a well established system and
delegated most of his work, so could afford to go gallivanting

round the country and Punjab would still function. Bhutto, however, with her centralized system which required her go-ahead
even to agree investment projects, and her uneasy relations with
the bureaucracy, found that if ministers were not in their offices
nothing was done.

Eighteen months into democracy, the country seemed in danger
of coming to a halt. Without the Punjab government in her grasp,
Bhutto found herself unable to dispense patronage to her own
MPs in the Punjab, who in turn could not deliver to their constituents and thus feared losing their seats. Frustrated PPP ministers
from Punjab took to holding press conferences to announce totally
fictitious grants, such as one from British Rail to fit air-
conditioning in Pakistan's railways, just to get themselves publicity.
Years of censorship had stifled any idea of investigative journalism
in Pakistan, and many journalists, being poorly paid, receive bribes
from politicians anxious for publicity. Even if they do not, their
paper cannot take an anti-government line for fear of having
advertising stopped, all of which comes from the government.
Javed Jabbar, the Information Minister who took Bhutto's stated
aim of a free press too seriously, was moved elsewhere, leaving the
TV news to deteriorate once more into a round-up of 'what the
Prime Minister did today'. A series on folk music was cancelled
after the first programme when the religious lobby objected. The
promised abolition of the National Press Trust was forgotten —
state-controlled newspapers and wire services were far too useful.
The National Assembly fell to hurling abuse or discussing such
trivia as whether the Prime Minister should be allowed to bring
tissues into the chamber when she was suffering from a cold.

The party's much-publicized development programme had been
prevented from getting off the ground in two provinces. Punjab
was not the only province Bhutto had alienated. Just two weeks
after she had taken office, General Musa, the Governor of Baluchistan, dismissed the Baluchistan government after the Chief
Minister had apparently informed him that he could not keep his
coalition of IDA, PPP and JUI together. There was an immediate
outcry. Bhutto pleaded innocence, but Musa, it was pointed out,
was an extremely old man who had even as a young general never
dared move a tank without orders and now would not so much as
blow his nose without her say-so. Moreover, the previous night

she had had dinner with him – surely he would have mentioned such an immense decision. Bhutto quickly gathered together selected journalists for tea at the Prime Minister's House to plead her case. Few could avoid drawing parallels with her father, who had sacked the Baluchistan government on flimsy pretences to improve his authority in Baluchistan.

Not only had Bhutto alienated another turbulent province, but its new Chief Minister, Nawab Bugti, was angered that he had not been given the job initially, and by what he called 'that woman's attitude'. Baluchistan had always harboured a grudge, feeling that its resources were exploited by the rest of the country. Bugti demanded royalties for the gas from his area, which provided 90 per cent of the country's needs. Bhutto refused and suddenly the incredible had happened – Baluchistan was backing the Punjabis, whom they had always considered their worst enemies. Bugti declared his own war against the centre and refused to let the People's Programme operate, gleefully ordering his bureaucrats to seize federal government Land-Rovers.

For much of the time the President too was not on speaking terms with the young Prime Minister. Bhutto was infuriated by his habit of sending her what she described as 'nasty little notes', registering his disapproval of acts of her government or the behaviour of her ministers. She complained of his frequent meetings with opposition figures and refusal to meet her ministers. An argument which had developed with Ishaq's refusal to sign ordinances, protesting that a democratic government should instead be passing laws through Parliament, came to a head in July 1989, when Bhutto decided that she would retire the Chairman of the Joint Chiefs of Staff, Admiral Sirohey, apparently to show that she was more powerful than the President. However, in her plotting she forgot that the bureaucrats owed first loyalty to Ishaq, so the Defence Secretary immediately told the President of her intention, before informing Sirohey to clear his desk. Ishaq was furious, pointing out that the Constitution clearly gave the President the right to appoint generals and thus the right of dismissal. Bhutto argued that she could dismiss them, and for weeks the battle raged on in the press, the President and the government both using journalists in their pay to push their line.

By then Pakistan's US backers were starting to get edgy. The plot was never meant to be so messy. Benazir was prevailed upon to back down, and made to notice increasing meetings between US diplomats and the opposition. On a trip to Delhi in autumn 1989, the US ambassador warned the then Prime Minister, Rajiv Gandhi, to expect a change of government next door. Mr Oakley reassured leading Indians: 'Take no notice of the anti-Indian statements of the opposition. It's just rhetoric. Whoever is in power in Islamabad, foreign policy will not change.'[8] Benazir was made to think the US were already backing their next horse, just as they had helped her father under Ayub then backed Zia while her father was in power. It was no secret under whose influence Zia had been persuaded to allow her back to Pakistan in 1986, even permitting her to hold large rallies. Zia knew then that the clock was ticking against him – many even believed that they arranged the plane crash, and they certainly made sure there was no real investigation.

But Bhutto still held two cards: whatever grievances people might have against her, they were not convinced the IDA would be better, and there was Sindh, the deciding factor in her appointment originally. The turbulent southern province was a tinderbox on the verge of insurrection, and no one doubted that its people's mandate for the PPP rather than Sindhi nationalist parties was their last chance to keep it within the federation. If their mandate was ignored, Sindh's alienation would be complete and could lead to a further break-up of the country. Pakistan would then truly become the Orphans of Midnight – landlocked and ready prey for the Indian dragon that the majority of the country believes to be breathing fire on its doorstep.

7

SINDH – LAND OF ROBIN HOODS
AND WARRIOR SAINTS

'If you point a gun at a buffalo, he doesn't appreciate that it is
the latest Mauser that can shatter his skull within milliseconds.
But with people you can see this running through their minds,
you can almost hear them worrying about their family. They
get scared . . . and we get rich.' (Hassan Karo, Sindhi bandit)[1]

Hassan Karo, who goes by the title of robber baron, sipped tea
from a china cup as he elucidated: 'The advantage with abducting
people is that they understand the threat.' His luxuriant moustache
seemed to creep like a caterpillar as he spoke. Servants scurried
back and forth with titbits. We could have been making small talk
at an English garden party. But the background music was the
croak of buffalo toads and the other guests were members of
Karo's fifteen-strong gang, gripping menacing weapons misdirected from the war in Afghanistan. We were deep in the forest
of Dadu, Pakistan's most crime-ridden area and the heartland of
banditry for 800 years.

Karo, or 'Black' as he is known, tilted his beaded purple Sindhi
cap decorated with tiny mirrors, and adjusted his ammunition
belt. Pistols in both pockets, a dagger by his side, he looked like a
cartoon villain, narrowing his eyes as he explained why the
dacoits – bandits who infest the forests of rural Sindh in southern
Pakistan – had given up their centuries-old practice of cattle-
rustling and gone in for people-snatching. With its traditions of
vendetta and feuds over land and women, violence is as much a
part of the scenery in Dadu as the dying brown scrubland which

increasingly refuses to yield crops. When the highways were
built in the seventies, enabling feudal playboys to whizz between
their estates and the cosmopolitan cities of Karachi and Lahore,
menacing lorries to transport goods up-country from the port
and bring back drugs, businessmen in jeeps to visit their factories
in rural areas, the *dacoits* saw the roads as literally lined with
gold. Highway robbery was the natural progression. From that
it was only a step to abduction. It was a profitable business.
According to one well-known *dacoit*, Hoth Chandio, members
of the forty gangs terrorizing the roads of Sindh could reckon
on earning a minimum of 200,000 rupees (about £6,000) a year
compared to a national average of about £250 (far less in rural
Sindh).[2]

It has its risks though. Recently three of Black's men had been
killed – or 'neutralized', as the authorities prefer to describe it –
although they took three police with them. They had gone into
a village of mud shacks to buy food and visit women. The
dacoits pay high prices for supplies to help the local economy
and distribute medicines for the needy. Quickly the locals had
brought *charpoys* (string beds) for Black and his gang to rest on.
A fire was lit and freshly killed goat barbecued, and the small
community gathered around in the fading day to hear the men's
tales of exotic brigandry, a welcome diversion from the struggle
to simply stay poor. Later, duly fêted, Black would resolve
minor disputes and give money for dowries. The village was
the home to one of the gang, so they felt safe – they are considered heroes or freedom fighters by most of the rural Sindhi
community, and people bend to touch their feet as they arrive.
Conscious of their Robin Hood image, Black forbids his men
to drink or molest women, and encourages them to pray at
mosques and Sufi shrines.

Black's men only stay at villages of their own tribes, and never
for more than one night because of the network of informers with
scores to settle or eager to make a few rupees. There used to be no
problem. The police are for the most part in their pay, eager to
supplement the meagre £30 a month they earn, and, with their
old Enfield 303 rifles, are no match for the sophisticated automatic
weaponry of the *dacoits*. Seventy-five per cent of police are
thought to be in league with the bandits, receiving a 20 per cent

cut. One of Black's gang has a brother who is a local police officer, and they claim to be able to drive through police check-points and even have on occasion used police vans. Black recalled with glee the time an eager new inspector took over, apparently uncorruptible. He started sending his men on anti-*dacoit* operations which neither they nor the *dacoits* much approved of, so one of the police informed on the inspector and Black's men ambushed his jeep. He soon changed his tune. Being in the centre of *dacoit*-land, Dadu is the most coveted police post, with applicants willing to pay large bribes to get jobs there, knowing how profitable it can be.

For a few years in the mid eighties things had got more diffi-cult – Zia had sent in the 'Punjabi army' and specially trained paramilitary forces, some of whom had recruited sons of land-owners to act as decoys and informers. They had set up army checkpoints on the highways and sent in helicopters to sweep the forests. The invaders were mostly Punjabis, on whom the *waderas* had no influence, and fought hard, cutting down trees and burning villages to track down the *dacoits*. The police had been given sophisticated weapons too – the Dadu police station was even supplied with armed Tiger cars. But with politicians back in control in Islamabad, *dacoits* gained more leverage, knowing that if caught they could rely on the local *wadera* (feudal lord), who was almost certainly the area's MP, to pressurize police and get them off. With the army busy sorting out ethnic violence in Karachi and Hyderabad, Black's men could once more roam free between mountains and jungle on the banks of the Indus, never in one place for more than two days.

Or so they had thought. Every so often the police would have to capture a few *dacoits* just to show they were active. Black's men had been leading them a cat and mouse game, but that particular summer night they were unlucky. While they were recounting their exploits, a group of police had killed their look-out and encircled the village. Suddenly shots rang out and Black knew they had been betrayed. He swore then and there to kill the informant in the most gruesome way he could think of. He directed some of his men to take the women and children to cover and then positioned himself to enjoy the fight. Instead of fleeing, many of the villagers joined in – they were of his tribe.

The shooting went on until the sky whitened. As he and his gang fled, Black realized just how many police there had been – 200, he estimated, to his twenty men. He was satisfied then – a good *dacoit* should be equal to ten police, so three casualties apiece was not too bad. Unfortunately they had not managed to seize any police uniforms – always useful for disguise.

Zia's anti-*dacoit* offensive of the 1980s achieved surprisingly little. But then this is more than cops and robbers – social, tribal, political and economic forces are all at play. *Dacoits* see their fight as a revolt against the stranglehold of the feudal system and a struggle for the rights of Sindhis. Most of Black's men say they were forced into dacoity by a combination of the feudal system, unemployment and the difficulty of eking a living from the unforgiving land through which salinity is creeping like a white plague, rendering thousands more acres uncultivable each year. An Environmental Management Society report in 1989 said that 40,000 hectares of the 20 million cropped go out of production annually while another 4 million people are added to the population, 70 per cent of whom will be dependent on agriculture. Around three-quarters of Sindhis are *haris* or sharecroppers, and when crops fail they die. Deserted villages mark where famine has struck. There are no jobs; one in four children dies before reaching five; the average family has ten members; few have ever seen a doctor and education hardly exists. They rely totally on the *wadera* for making a living, lending money for dowries and sorting out their land disputes.

Naik's story is typical. Speaking softly, his gentle almond eyes like those of an eager puppy rather than a criminal with a high price on his head, he explained: 'I was a peasant, a tenant farmer. We worked on a strip of land for which we got a third of the crop. It was barely enough to live on – there were eight children and my mother needed medicine. For us death is preferable to illness – where would we find money to pay a doctor? One day, another family tried to encroach on our land. They were from the same tribe as the *wadera* so he got involved and had me implicated in a murder case. We could do nothing – the police might as well be working for the landlord. No one can go against the *wadera* and survive – it's like being a fish in a pond with a crocodile. When I was released I could get no work. I had no choice but to become a *dacoit*.'

Land-ownership is at the root of most disputes. Landlords have private armies of *dacoits* to keep troublesome tenants in line. I never heard of a quarrel over land being taken to court – the legal process is too long, expensive and complicated for peasants to understand and they believe it to be corrupt, even though in recent years the national courts have stood up well to political pressure. Often disputes are resolved by the bullet – the murderer then fleeing to join the bandits in the forest.

'An eye for an eye' is how life is run in this area, according to the subdivisional magistrate of Mehar, a dusty two-bit village in Dadu: 'Tribal conflicts often end in murder. Probably only one or two will be involved but the injured party will give the names of fifteen enemies. The innocents will have to pay the police to escape and then will want revenge for being named, while the tribe of the murdered man will want to avenge his killing. Life here is about revenge and counter-revenge. To avoid arrest people end up selling all they have to pay the police – their house and bullocks, and then they are desperate and there is nothing left but to flee to the jungle and become *dacoits*.'

Wringing his spiny hands, the sub-magistrate said he thought the only hope was for a Khomeini figure to emerge bringing 'true Islam'. He was recovering from 'flu, brought on by the endless dust, and sniffed as he complained: 'Having a democracy is no answer – in this area we have two provincial ministers and one federal minister but they can do nothing, they are in cahoots with the miscreants.' The Dadu police superintendent had begun constructing two lines of defence to stop the *dacoits* reaching the highway, in what he described as 'a situation of war'. Over warm syrupy Pakistani Coke substitute, he admitted: 'Dadu is a classic example of where politics and crime are interlinked. Many politicians are involved.'

Landlords have for many years encouraged *dacoits* to be part of their private army to commit crimes against political enemies. Bakar, the youngest and most articulate of Black's band, whom I had been surprised to see squinting at a book of Sindhi legends, had been forced to flee after refusing to join his family's *zamindar*'s army. 'I was in my first year at college but my family was totally dependent on the *zamindar*, who doesn't want anyone to be educated. He dictated us illegal things to do – he wanted us to kill some goats of another *zamindar*, skin them and place their heads on the man's doorstep as a threat. I refused, so he got me arrested to force me. I still refused, but then he took our goat so there was no milk for my mother and then I had no choice. I did some small crimes for him, with police consent, but then thought I might as well steal for myself as for him. So, I became a *dacoit*. I can never go back now – there are eighteen charges against me.'

Further north, at another centre of dacoity, the superintendent of the district jail told me that this is a common scenario. Sitting like a plump cat in front of an enormous and intriguing green-painted safe in a Banana Republic office, he explained: 'The land-lord is king of the village. If he wants to kidnap a girl, he can. People will thieve for him. The police chief is his personal friend. In return the *zamindar* provides him Red Label, women and money, and sends him mangoes to suggest they are on the same social footing.'[3]

The punishment for being a *dacoit* is death, and the superintendent said that 300 had been hanged – and many more arrested – in the past ten years. He called a peon, who brought in some sorry-looking specimens who were not at all reminiscent of Hoth or Black, with their proud bearings like Mughal warriors. Realizing I too had developed a sneaking admiration for the men in the jungle, I questioned whether these convicts were in fact *dacoits*. 'Probably not,' admitted the superintendent to my surprise, 'but they will be when they are eventually released, and we need to make the books look good.'

Arrest or killing is not the answer, argued Mushtaq Ahmed Shah, the police chief in Larkana, the home town of Benazir, who has herself had two servants abducted: 'If we capture five, another five will come up. It's getting so that every family has one *dacoit* son. We need reforms, not bullets.' The scoreboard behind him showed that the *dacoits* were winning – eleven dacoities and forty-four abductions reported in his area in the first six months of 1989. As he spoke he gestured towards the crumbling earth. Along the road a white-bearded old man was sitting crosslegged, sucking a *hookah* pipe and staring plaintively into the distance, where a child was urging on a bullock cart with a stick, churning up clouds of yellow dust. Beneath the old man's flowing robes his limbs were like sticks, gnarled old twigs. 'He sits there every day, watching villages turn to earth and dust, remembering when it was green and lush and full of birds,' the police chief told me. For as far as I could see it was desert and scrub – the harsh brown almost painful to behold. The land looked so unloved that even the few skeletal trees seemed to be reaching desperately for the heavens.

I began to understand better what was happening to Sindh when I visited Sukkur barrage, an impressive sandstone structure with sixty-three arches, built by the British over the river which bisects the entire country and which gave its name to India. The Indus here is hardly recognizable as the rushing torrent I had seen emerging from the Himalayas, where it had seemed a threatening entity waiting to eat up buses and lashing against mountainsides. In Sukkur it has been tamed, sad and green, home to buffalos with shiny skins and blind freshwater dolphins and people living on strange wooden barges.

The Indus is the lifeblood of Sindh, and the Sukkur barrage is the hub of the world's largest single irrigation system. The province has almost no rainfall but most of its population are reliant on agriculture, and until the barrage was built to regulate the water supply, for four months of the year the land would be flooded, often destroying the crops, while for the other eight months the land would be barren. In 1846 one Lt.-Col. Walter Scott conceived the idea of providing a water supply all year round and taking kismet out of agriculture. It was an ambitious project; it took until 1923 to pass through the combined bureaucracy of numerous committees, and the mile-long barrage was finally opened in 1932. The increase in arable land did little to help the peasants. Sindhi *waderas* simply swallowed up more, and Punjabis moved in to claim the rest, beginning a long resentment. By the 1980s there were an estimated 4 million Punjabis in Sindh, most of them in the bureaucratic jobs Sindhis cannot obtain because of their lack of education.

Seven channels take the water from Sukkur to supply 7.93 million acres. It is an impressive system now controlled by numerous computers, and the literature describes it as 'the pride of Pakistan'. But the eighty-five-year-old man who had worked on the barrage since it opened, and as supervisor had power to flood the province or deprive it of water, tugged down his brown Jinnah cap and shook his head sadly. 'There is no pride left in this any more. There has been too much pressure on the canals. We are supplying three times what it was designed for. People are growing rice, which needs far more water, and the canals cannot cope.' He showed me where one of the canals was covered with pangrass and its banks cracked as it silted up. The very small fall of the Indus means there is little natural drainage. 'No one thinks of the future in this country. There is no drainage system and the canals are silting up. Soon the system will collapse and the whole of Sindh will become a desert.' To the naked eye it has already reached that stage. I was seeing in reality what experts in international agencies were scratching their heads over. While the population was set to double in the next twenty years, they were predicting that 800,000 hectares would become uncultivable.

There was a further problem. Taking tea in a village *chaikana*, where a group of ardent young men were explaining Sindhi nationalism to me watched by a circle of staring eyes, a large jeep sped by, horns blaring, scattering children and chickens. In the back I could make out two black-faced men with Kalashnikovs. 'Who was that?' I asked. 'The canal supervisor doing his rounds,' replied Sabu. 'You asked me why there is no middle class in Sindh, that is why. Only the *waderas* get the water.' First I laughed, but then the system was explained to me by Amber, the young son of a *zamindar* collector of photos of *dacoits*. 'You have to pay for water. The more money and influence you have the quicker and better water you get. Those with no money get the dregs at the end or sometimes nothing at all. The supervisor can make life misery. He is a hated man – plenty of people would like to kill him and he is rich so the *dacoits* would like to kidnap him.'

The system of water distribution explained the discrepancies in Pakistan's yield of major crops. I had never understood why landholdings next to each other could have such different rates – one far above the national average, the other far below. There seemed no concept of national interest or efficiency involved in Sindh's farming. 'The *waderas*,' explained Amber, 'want to keep the *haris* down even though it means they too will get less produce. The *waderas* are rich enough – even middle-sized farms here are 30–40,000 acres – to make it unnecessary to worry about efficiency. They are more concerned to make sure the *haris* continue to depend on them for everything so the *waderas* are assured of their votes.'

It is a vicious circle which they would not break out of without education, and the *waderas* will not risk losing votes by opening schools. The World Bank office in Islamabad was sitting on hundreds of millions of dollars of undisbursed aid for education in Sindh because Pakistan would not put up projects. Land reform, it seems, is out of the question – too many *waderas* in Parliament. Attempts to help through cheap agricultural credit have failed – a recent Finance Minister, Dr Mehbubul Haq, found that at least 88 per cent of the money set aside was actually going to the *zamindars*, who were getting tenants to put their thumbprint on applications then collecting the money. One *zamindar* was found to have got 400 loans this way. *Haris* have no hope of raising the money for interest, even if they had understood how to apply – theirs is a cashless economy. Even *bidis*, the scrawny paper cigarettes with a pinch of tobacco, are paid for by barter. Bank managers asked to explain themselves protested that had the cheap credit gone to the peasants they would have used it to buy consumer goods rather than to improve their farming efficiency. This may be the case, but again it comes down to lack of education.

In a corrupt society where so many have to struggle just to stay alive, dacoity with its rich pickings becomes understandable. When dacoits first progressed from stealing animals to abducting people, they restricted themselves to highway robberies. The first reported kidnapping was in 1979. The victim was the son of Rafi Kachelo, a supporter of Bhutto. As arms flooded in from the war in Afghanistan, kidnappings became more common. The arsenal held by Black's group included mortars, rocket launchers, 12-bore shotguns and Kalashnikovs, some of which he claimed come from army depots bought from a middleman they meet in the hills separating Sindh from Baluchistan.

But there were political reasons too. By 1990 official estimates said that Dadu had 160 *dacoits* per square kilometre, the number shooting up in 1983 when the brutal army oppression of the

MRD uprising against martial law sent young men flooding into the forests. Hoth Chandio was one of these. 'The army started raiding villages, burning down houses, stealing cattle and raping women. In my village, Nari, they killed eight people. My brother was wrongly accused of a murder and put in jail. I knew I'd be next. There was no one to help us; our only recourse was to flee into the jungle, where we were branded criminals.'

The army seems to derive pleasure from crushing Sindh. When Bhutto called on the military to restore peace to the riot-torn cities of Karachi and Hyderabad in May 1990, they asked as *quid pro quo* that they be allowed into interior Sindh to carry out operations, as well as power to set up military courts under Article 245 of the Constitution. Benazir refused, at the cost of the final destruction of civil–military relations, knowing that Sindh was her support base and main card and that the Sindhis would never forgive her if she let the army in. Many Sindhis consider the Pakistani army to be as alien as the British troops which were stationed in the province in the last century, when it was ruled by Amirs, as part of the grand imperial strategy against the threat from Russia, whose forces the colonials feared might come through Afghanistan into British India. For no other reason than personal ambition and desire for retaliation after the humiliating British defeat in Kabul the previous year, in 1843 Sir Charles Napier, commanding the British troops in the province, brutally annexed Sindh, sending back the famous cable 'Peccavi' ('I have sinned'). Mountstuart Elphinstone, another famous imperialist, said it had been done 'in the spirit of a bully who has been kicked in the street and goes home to beat his wife in revenge'.

The Pakistani army's behaviour in 1983 was no less unreasonable. It was followed by the setting up of an army cantonment in upper Sindh, and the creation of army checkpoints on all the roads completed the alienation against the centre that had been bubbling under the surface ever since Pakistan was created, occasionally erupting in the form of riots such as those against the imposition of Urdu as a national language. Throughout Pakistan's long spells of martial law Sindh had no representation, there being no senior army officers from Sindh nor any top bureaucrats. Sindhis had little chance of reaching these heights with their lack of education and knowledge of the national language, which only 5 per cent of Sindhis speak.

Secession has been at the back of every Sindhi's mind since the creation of Bangladesh in 1971, according to Dr Hamida Khuro, Professor of History at Sindh University and daughter of Sindh's first Chief Minister: 'Up until then there had been hope that as the Bengalis who were the majority province were also deprived, numbers would prevail and we could all gang up on the Punjabis.'[4]

For a while Zulfikar Ali Bhutto, a Sindhi, seemed to offer hope. But although he was immensely popular among Sindhis, who felt pride because he was one of them, he gave no institutional shape to Sindh's rights, wanting them to rely on him personally. His much-heralded land reform was never really carried out, local *waderas* putting pressure on the administration to falsify figures. Dr Khuro complained: 'His answer was always I'll be here, I'll safeguard your rights. He bamboozled the pro-autonomy politicians with charm and promises to make them sign his Constitution, which institutionalized centralization and had no provincial list of subjects. We [Sindhi nationalists] were well aware of what it meant. When Hafiz Pirzada [Bhutto's Law Minister] came to Sindh University shortly afterwards he was publicly ridiculed and slapped.'

Dr Khuro, a leading figure of the Sindhi nationalist movement, was one of many people who blamed Ali Bhutto for causing much of today's breakdown in law and order by ending the ancient system under which *sardars* (tribal chiefs) would resolve disputes and decide on compensation, and putting nothing in its place: 'Bhutto's slogans "Down with *zamindars*" and "Equal rights for peasants" made great rhetoric, but the reality was that he destroyed the local system and put police in who, being notoriously corrupt, would lock up both accused and victim and demand money from both.'

But Bhutto's removal was a blow – he was one of them, after all. Fearing reprisals in Sindh, army units were stationed as a warning in every district during Zia's regime, unlike previous military rules. Dr Khuro said that this was the final indignity: 'Sindh is not like Punjab, where everyone has a friend or relation in the army. For us it was really men from Mars ruling. The alienation was extreme.'[5]

Hostility erupted in 1983 with the MRD movement, which began in August, was officially called off by its organizer, Ghulam

Mustafa Jatoi, in December, but, according to most Sindhis, continued on a low-key level until 1985. I had many atrocities recounted to me – the most common one was the ambushing of a bus carrying students from the Sindh Students' Federation to Larkana. Nine students died in the shooting and 120 were jailed. That year many villages were razed to the ground, adding to the ghost-town appearance of much of the province. Even after the 1985 non-party elections the army did not withdraw. Dr Khuro says, 'it was a regular process of colonization.'

Adil Rashdie, son of Sindh's only female *wadera*, and opposition leader of Dadu District Council, said the same: 'They tried to crush us with economic sanctions but we were too proud. No Sindhi will ever run to the centre with a begging bowl. So then they tried to break us with force.'[6] As he spoke, with fire in his eyes, we were sitting on the veranda of a politician's house in Sehwan Sharif, the spiritual capital of Sindh. Against the backdrop of wailing pilgrims and the relentless beat of a drum, it was an appropriate place to appreciate Sindhi pride.

A capital of Sindh during one of its many invasions, Sehwan has become its main centre of pilgrimage. The very air seemed to prickle with expectancy and emotion as we walked down the narrow unpaved streets towards the shrine of Lal Shahbaz Qalandar, 'the Beggars' Saint'. The excitement was like that of children at a funfair. On either side were stalls piled high with glass bangles and hung with garlands of green, red and white. Breathing rose and jasmine, I wondered if my eyes too shared the strange unfocused look of those passing us by. The shrine came into view – a white fairyland strung with coloured lights. The drum beat was incessant, inexorably drawing people in.

There was a crush at the entrance as pilgrims touched the doorpost in wonder, praying for children, for food, for strength, begging the Sufi saint to intercede with God and grant them their prayer. Finally we were inside and it was dazzling. We were buffeted by dream-like people whirling, chanting, reaching ecstasy. It took a moment to adjust to the kaleidoscope of colour. On one side were a small group – the drum-beaters, a leading chanter, and all around them a swirling morass of men dressed in bright colours and with kohl-rimmed eyes. Some seemed to be wearing dresses and all were spinning and chanting, chanting, chanting, chanting, whizzing into a trance that would, they hoped, bring them union with God. 'Dama dam mast Qalandar,' they sang, as fireflies gathered round the lights.

On the other side, straining behind a rope barrier, were the women and children. They were stiller, their faces more troubled, though a few were tearing at their clothes and galloping through the others from one end of the barrier to the other. A piper started up, and the music was unbearably haunting as the singer began to weave his tale of love, longing and the struggle for survival. The music conjured up images of a buffalo cart piled high with Sindhis in their coloured printed ajraks, of a tiny child splashing in an unexpected pool of stagnant water, of a scarlet parrot flashing among the trees, but then I jerked back to reality — the scarlet plumage reminding me of the chilling nationalist poster, too familiar in Sindhi villages, of the province, bleeding, with a Kalashnikov across it.

The Sufis' strength, as they wandered across the subcontinent from Arabia, Persia and Afghanistan, was that they spoke in local dialects of hopes and fears all were familiar with. The 'rebels of Islam', they made poverty respectable, and their teaching was addressed to the common man, who did not understand Arabic or complex theological concepts. Their message of love was carried in poems, music and romantic tales of great heroism. Many settled in Sindh, opening kitchens to feed the hungry, and today most shrines still provide free food and shelter.

The intensity of devotion in a Sufi shrine during 'urs', the Thursday night festival, is impossible to resist. The experience is indescribably evocative, easily blotting out the tribulations of the outside world. It is easy to understand why the saints have an immense following in a land of such sorrow. But it is not just the peasants who worship. Waderas all contribute to the local shrine, and Benazir consults a pir, or holy man. Her father was a frequent visitor to the shrine in Sehwan, and, during his rule, the devotional hymn about Qalandar was converted into an informal national anthem which crowds would sing at his public meetings. The scholar Akbar Ahmed holds that Bhutto, shedding tears on hearing Sufi verses, saw himself as a latterday Qalandar in his challenge to the establishment.[7] Ironically, the Persian line on the tomb of his favourite saint, Shaz Baz, says the Sufi prepares to meet death 'dancing on the gallows'.

There could not be more difference between Sindh's whirling Dervishes and the discipline of prayers in the mosque. No wonder Sindhis resented Zia's attempts to impose on the country Punjab identity and what they saw as a straitjacketed form of Islam, far from their mysticism, which Ahmed describes as 'the opposition party of Islam'.

Sindhis are furious at being told how to pray, claiming that it was they who gave Islam to the subcontinent through the invasion of Mohammad Bin Qasim, who landed in Sindh in AD 711. They argue that they were the first province to vote for a Muslim homeland in the 1937 elections (Punjab did not). They are fiercely proud of their heritage and culture, with justification. Moenjendaro (literally Mound of the Dead) near Larkana is 4,000 years old, the site of the oldest civilization in the subcontinent; amid what looks initially like a pile of bricks one can pick out roads, heating systems and covered drains. Unfortunately the rising water table, because of the lack of drainage, is eating up Moenjendaro, and the local violence means that one needs a police escort to visit it, a bitter symbol in a land full of symbolism.

Dacoits are frequent visitors to shrines, where they can slip in with the local people, and some even see themselves as today's warrior saints in a fight to defend Sindh's traditions. Most *dacoits* have become highly political and took an active, if unsavoury, part in the 1988 elections, threatening opponents of their chosen candidates and disrupting their rallies. They gained support in high places from politicians, who relied on them to deliver blocs of votes. Black declared as he buried his latest booty, 'We are not *dacoits*. We are crying for our rights, for the problems of Sindh.'

Like many, he thought that the PPP would be sympathetic and give a general amnesty, and claimed that the MPs they helped secure victory promised them that. However, Qaim Ali Shah, the Sindh Chief Minister and already under fire for being weak, refused on the ground that 'this would be like giving them a licence to commit more crimes'.[8]

Hoth, who had twenty-three charges of kidnapping and highway robbery against him and a £24,000 reward on his head, still had hope, and surrendered in autumn 1989 because he was 'fed up with living like an animal, always on the run'. 'Being *dacoits* was our way of rebelling against martial law. Now I've a good reputation, lots of money and I don't want to end up full of police bullets. We helped the PPP in the elections and they gave us assurances we'd only be tried for police cases and treated leniently. Now everyone's watching what happens to me.'

Waiting in Mehar village jail, Hoth was being treated like a lord. Dressed in freshly starched white *shalwar kamiz* and sporting a gold medallion, he had the awed prison staff dancing attendance on him. While we chatted he was brought tea and biscuits and a small boy ran in with cigarettes. They were the wrong brand and the boy scurried off in shame, his eyes wide at being spoken to by such a local celebrity. Hoth was a powerful presence with his glittering, unblinking eyes and, confident he could walk out of the jail any time, he had, just as an insurance policy, left the rest of his gang in the hills. He was quite conscious of the dilemma he was posing the government.

Qaim Ali Shah summed it up: 'Dacoity is a crime against the person, not the state. Of course we want to end this terror to our highways, but we cannot catch them and if we give them amnesty how do we explain to those who have been widowed, robbed, orphaned or terrorized by *dacoits*? And how do we explain to those suffering prison sentences for one murder or one robbery that you are criminals but those who have committed five or ten or fifty crimes are not?'[9]

Consequently the *dacoits* were losing faith in the PPP, as were the peasants, who had begun turning their support towards the Sindhi nationalist parties they had rejected in the elections, unsure then how talk of independence would solve the immediate problem of where the next meal was coming from. The PPP, having been unable to conjure resources out of nothing in government, were left to watch helplessly as the equally feudal leaders of the many nationalist parties, with their Hitlerian-style propaganda, attracted huge crowds, members burning Pakistani flags. These parties were frighteningly militant, their emblems depicting a bleeding Sindh, tearing away from the rest of the country with Kalashnikovs across it, or the menacing black axe on red flags now fluttering over bazaars in so many villages. Violence and revolution, they said, was the only way to escape repression.

What the nationalist leaders could not agree on was repression by whom, and to what end they should fight it. Were they fighting Punjabi domination or oppression by feudals? To the outsider the latter, exemplified by the practice of *droit de seigneur*, would seem the major injustice, but that presented a problem – almost all the nationalist leaders were feudals themselves. It was much easier in the days when they could just blame Zia. Constantly at loggerheads, they were seriously split over whether they should be fighting for independence – Sindhudesh – or for greater provincial autonomy and fairer treatment within Pakistan.

Zafar Ali Ujan, a Sindhi nationalist who joined the PPP in 1978 and later became a special assistant to Benazir, insisted that Zia's most dangerous legacy was to push nationalist feeling from a small group of intellectuals to every teahouse in Sindh. He said, 'Zia's strategy was classic divide and rule. He deliberately encouraged Sindhi nationalist groups while at the same time promoting Punjabi chauvinism. He wanted to push the PPP into taking up the nationalist cry of their supporters so that they lost the support of Punjab, knowing that if they refused to then they would lose support of Sindh and the other smaller provinces.'[10]

On a bed in a cluttered room inside a white courtyard in the sparse, winding, almost biblical village of Sann, the man recognized as the father of Sindhi nationalism was lying, nursing a broken leg. A grasshopper of a man with the bony head of his hero, Gandhi, G. M. Syed was talking treason: 'The only solution is to break Pakistan and for us to be independent. Punjab is trying to colonize us by bringing non-Sindhis in – every year they settle 600,000 outsiders so now 48 per cent of Sindh's population is non-Sindhi compared to only 5 per cent in 1947. We are being turned into Red Indians in our own province.'[11]

G. M. Syed, head of the Jeay Sindh party, with its no-nonsense slogan 'Sindhudesh' (Independent Sindh), became Benazir's first political prisoner for tearing down the Pakistan flag at Sukkur airport and hoisting that of Sindh in December 1989. Jail was nothing new to him – he has spent twenty-six years in prison or house detention, the first spell in 1936 when he fought for the separation of Sindh from the Bombay Presidency it was then part of. There is no love lost between the two – Syed claimed: 'The present government are stooges of the Punjabis. They won in the elections by using slogans saying to vote PPP is to take revenge against the Punjabis for killing Bhutto.'[12] His release after Benazir was dismissed and his subsequent pronouncement that 'Pakistan

must break' caused outcry among Punjabis, who labelled him a
traitor.

Mumtaz Bhutto, briefly Chief Minister of Sindh under the last
PPP government, and now head of the Sindh Baluch Pushtoon
Front which he formed in 1986, was thought by many to be the
man to unite the nationalists. A well-fed sleek cat of a feudal,
educated at Oxford and Lincoln's Inn, he was hardly a man of the
people, surrounded in his plush Karachi house by ivory figurines,
magnificent carved ebony leopards and a huge Markora goat's
head in a glass case, presumably a hunting trophy. He was not a
man for mincing his words, and told me starkly: 'Sindh is occupied
territory. It is written on every wall, we don't want Pakistan.'[13]
Unlike Syed, Mumtaz believes in Pakistan but he told me that he
saw the only remedy as confederation: 'If Pakistan is to survive
there must be decentralization of power. A multinational government cannot be run like a unitary state. We want a Pakistan as
envisaged by the 1940 resolution – a confederal system with limited
jurisdiction in the centre.'

But Adil Rashdie maintained that so far none of the leaders had
really hit the right theme: 'All the Sindhis really want is self-
respect. We've been under the domination of the Greeks, the
Arabs, the Persians, the British, but we've still remained as Sindh.
Now the Punjabis are trying to take that away from us. We
provide 65 per cent of the country's budget – it's our sweat and
blood which is paying for their F16 fighter jets. The masses know
they are being exploited and cannot understand how talk of separation or confederation can help their needs – that's why the PPP
always beat them.'

Increasingly frustration turned to violence. Like a new plague
tearing across the plains of Sindh, the red flags of Jeay Sindh with
black axes across them seemed to flutter from every rooftop as a
dust-storm whipped across Khairpur Nadam Shah, a village where
they told me that twenty people had been mown down by the
army in 1983. 'This time we have arms too,' they said. But they
were divided over whom to follow, the nationalist leaders all
accusing each other of being creations of Zia or agents of the
army. Rasul Bux Palejo has frequently charged G. M. Syed with
selling out to the army in 1968 and depriving the movement of its
direction: 'There are now two kinds of Sindhi nationalism. One

group comprises agents of Zia or the army who present exaggerated demands which, however desirable, are unrealistic – they even talk of getting the Indian army into Sindh. What we should be fighting against is the economic colonization of Sindh – we should be demanding non-interference from Punjab, law and order so we are safe to use the roads, and complete participation of Sindhis in the services – our message needs to be jobs, lands and civil rights. The *waderas* that talk of nationalism are playing games – their interests lie with sharing the crumbs of the ruling class.'[14] In turn, G. M. Syed often alleged that Palejo was in the pay of the army intelligence, and denied taking support from Zia, though he admitted he found him more sympathetic than other rulers. 'I have worked with all politicians but when I was ill it was only Zia that allowed me to go to hospital and inquired about my health.'

Some even claimed that *dacoits* have been used as tools by the army. One police chief said: 'Their forest warfare is so sophisticated they must have had military training. We need at least ten men to every one of theirs.' But while in many ways they were fighting the same cause, the romance of the men in the forest seemed a world away from the petty squabbling of the nationalist politicians. But, joined by a new wave of students from Jeay Sindh who could not get jobs, the traditional *dacoits* were becoming increasingly politicized.

Among many of the poor villagers of Sindh, natural revulsion against crimes was forgotten in the case of *dacoits*, who were spoken of in hushed admiration, glamorous men who by dastardly plans rob from the rich to give to the poor. Sitting round the fire in a cave in the hills, the sliver of a moon and a million stars standing guard all around, Bakar told me the story of Peroo Chandio, most respected of all *dacoits*, who, like the desperadoes of the American frontier, had even had a film made about him.

Peroo was a barber and the son of a poor peasant – an unremarkable man until the day his family fell into a land dispute with a tenant from another, more influential tribe. The chief of the village had him accused of a cattle theft which he had not committed. Because Peroo was not to be found, the police took his father and mother and beat them. Peroo and his father were then accused of many crimes, and the furious Peroo emerged to kill the police chief before fleeing to the jungle to become a notorious *dacoit*. He was known to have killed more than fifty-three people, and was so feared and respected that he could drive straight through police checkpoints saying 'I'm Peroo.' He wore a police uniform and drove a jeep, and was invited to important weddings at which he would mingle with local administrators. With his help for good causes, setting up clinics and providing dowry money, he became a hero. In 1980 Peroo was arrested and brought before a military court, defended by Abdul Razzak Soomro (now ambassador in Oman), who describes him as a 'noble man'.[15] In February 1982 the court reserved judgement, and in November Peroo organized a daring jailbreak in which thirty-four prisoners escaped. For six more years he led the police a dance, but he was finally tragically betrayed by his best friend, also a *dacoit*, who, in exchange for his own freedom, drugged Peroo at a wedding and drove him into a police ambush in which he was shot dead. Thousands went to Peroo's funeral, including local officials, and respect for him equals that of the warrior saints of the past.

Javed Jabbar, a Sindhi minister in Benazir's cabinet, described the situation in Sindh as 'one of the world's most challenging political problems'.[16] But it was also a social problem and one of economic deprivation. Without an end to the lawlessness no jobs would be brought to the interior, no agro-industries set up, no middle class created. But without an overhaul of the social system *haris* would continue to be driven to become *dacoits*. And while feudals continued to dominate politics, the social set-up would remain.

For Bhutto, Sindh was a major headache and perhaps ultimately her downfall. All too often she was reminded that the deciding factor in the army's hand-over of power was the fear that Sindh would follow in the bloodstained footsteps of Bangladesh, and the belief that she was the last chance if Pakistan was to remain intact. But because she could not afford to lose her support among the Sindhis and because some of her own MPs were intimately connected to the *dacoits*, Bhutto could not implement the necessary crackdown, raising doubts about the worth of an elected government if it cannot maintain law and order and guarantee security for the people.

Just like the starlings singing in the bleak landscape, the election results had suggested there was some hope. In some areas *haris* did not vote like 'animals beaten with a stick' but actually went against the major feudal, though still electing a *wadera* but always from the PPP. By voting for the PPP Sindhis had surely voted to stay in the federation. But later many said it was Sindh's debt for Bhutto's death, and with that cleared it was time to take up arms.

There is no easy solution, and it achieved nothing blaming India, though Pakistan's unfriendly neighbour was certainly well aware of Sindh's vulnerability and had moved divisions from the Punjab border to that with Sindh. Some Sindhis said they were waiting for the Indian army and asked me why it had not yet come. General Beg was right when he told reporters that the army 'could solve the problem in a few hours but that would not be a long-term solution'.[17] By mid 1990 the troops were back. For Bhutto the support of her home province, which should have been her asset, was proving her Achilles heel as, following in the footsteps of previous rulers, she was increasingly falling back on the men in khaki to deal with it, playing right into their gloved hands.

8

DIAL-A-KALASHNIKOV

OF ETHNIC VIOLENCE AND IDENTITY PROBLEMS IN KARACHI AND HYDERABAD

'There is no Bedouinism in Islam.' (saying of Holy Prophet)

The lights went off all at once, and as the sky cracked open, raining bullets, there was absolutely no place to hide. Even the moon had closed its eyes to the urban nightmare unfolding far below in the southern city of Hyderabad. Evening prayers had just ended, and as men poured out of the mosques the massacre began. Within moments masked gunmen on motorbikes or in speeding cars were everywhere, spraying bullets and hurling hand grenades into homes, crowds and shops.

No one escaped. 'They just mowed down anything that came in their way,' an old man told me later. A queue of young men outside the cinema was pumped full of bullets, collapsing into a grisly pile of mangled bodies lying in a pool of blood. Bullets were fired into a bus of fish merchants, killing twelve of the twenty aboard. That Friday was also the last day of Samiya's wedding celebrations. She felt like a queen, dressed in exquisite finery that her father had had to borrow heavily to afford. From under her gold-embroidered veil Samiya glanced shyly at her new husband, seated by her side, as friends and relations sang songs teasing the couple. The first volley of shots did not worry her – 'I thought it was my cousin firing off his gun in traditional celebration. I heard a scream but thought it was the jackals.' But suddenly the air was filled with dust and the choking acrid smell of gunpowder, and rent with screaming. Grenades were thrown into the *shamiana*. 'There was nowhere to run, we were trapped in the wedding tent. I screamed as if my lungs would burst and then the sky came down.' There was not a policeman in sight.

By the time troops arrived the gunmen were long gone, melted into the evil forces of the night from whence they had come. They had killed 186 people and wounded another 250, of which more were to die. Curfew was imposed, leaving many of the victims moaning and dying in the streets, which an eye-witness told me 'were literally scarlet with blood'. Samiya came round to find herself surrounded by corpses, including those of her husband, father, mother and brother. The mosque speakers were broadcasting appeals for blood. Army trucks were everywhere, full of soldiers in hard hats, crouched down or prowling, even in the hospitals where they had been called out to end fighting between people anxious to ensure that their relatives were attended to first. What should have been Samiya's happiest memory had turned into the worst night of her life.[1]

The Hyderabad massacre of 30 September 1988, or Black Friday as it is remembered, was the worst example to date of the ethnic violence in Sindh which has claimed more than 1,200 lives since 1987. Most of those killed were *mohajirs*, migrants from India, whose political organization, the Mohajir Qaumi Movement (MQM), ran the Karachi and Hyderabad municipalities. When the news of Black Friday started reaching Karachi, passed from bus-driver to teahouse, angry mobs took to the congested streets, burning cars and houses in ethnic riots in which a further sixty-five people died.

It was nothing new for Karachi. Pakistan's biggest city, a sleepy fishing village when the British arrived in 1843 and swollen from a population of 400,000 in 1947 to more than 9 million, Karachi is literally bursting at the seams. Life is cheap, and corruption and insanitation, twin evils, stalk the streets. Less than a quarter of the 1,300 tonnes of garbage produced each day is disposed of. Vast areas are controlled by drug barons, and the city is riven by an underground war between rival student factions. Shadowy figures chase death in its alleyways. Residents may not have water or sewerage but most have guns, and if they do not, there is a Dial-a-Kalashnikov service.

In the early 1970s Zulfikar Ali Bhutto dreamed of turning Karachi into another Beirut: a playground for rich businessmen where large deals would be struck by day and large money spent by night. He even built an imposing seafront casino. Today that casino is inhabited only by ghosts, the baize tables rotting, victim of an Islamicization campaign which forbade alcohol and most other forms of entertainment. Karachi is, ironically, another Beirut, but not the jetset playground Bhutto envisaged. Rather it is a city torn apart by ethnic tension in a province alienated from the rest of Pakistan.

Anyone looking to create trouble could scarcely find a riper place. All Pakistan's worst social problems are intensified here; unemployment stands at 25 per cent, population growth at 6 per cent and the city has more than a million heroin addicts. It is home to immigrants from all over the subcontinent, attracted in the vain belief that the streets are paved with gold or because in the lowest depths of the cycle of poverty there was no place else left. As well as 1.5 million refugees from Bangladesh, Sri Lanka and Burma, there are students from Iran, descendants of African slaves, and the poorest remnants from all over Pakistan, mostly crowded together in illegal squatter camps patrolled by drug mafias and at the mercy of corrupt government land officials. Aside from poverty and despair they have one common link – a shared religion – but while this is enough to kill it is not enough to love. Sindhis killing *mohajirs* killing Sindhis killing Punjabis killing *mohajirs* killing Pathans killing Biharis.

The fuse was lit in 1985. Nadeem had arrived from a small village in interior Sindh. A *hari* family in a village destined for the dust by famine, they had been forced to sell the last chicken, and with almost no stocks of wheat or rice left for the year ahead, Nadeem's mother had pressed a bundle of rupees into his hand and told him, 'Go, my son, to the city and find work. You are young and strong and can learn skills and send us back the money.'

He was terrified. With his prayer-mat and Sindhi cap rolled up in a small bundle, Nadeem set out, clutching a scrap of paper on which the village *mullah* had scrawled an address he was unable to read. When he reached the road he sat in the scorching sun staring at the desert and the blue hills in the distance beyond which was Baluchistan, full of wild warriors and tribesmen. A crane perched on a nearby tree seemed to be looking at him quizzically, almost accusingly, as if to say why are you people giving up on this land? We birds who have journeyed from far-off places have not.

When the bus came, Nadeem had to force himself to get on, remembering the skin pulled tight like paper over his mother's bones, and his sister's cough which sounded like a knife being scraped over stones and wracked her entire body. The bus was like an enormous tin monster spiriting him to an alien life. Painted in garish colours depicting evil planes and grinning army generals, it had a skirt of chains hanging from the front and a shoe from the back for luck. The driver was a Pathan – darker-skinned, with black eyes and smoking a papery cigarette which filled the bus with pungent sweet-smelling smoke. Nadeem had never before seen a Pathan and was scared by the man's sullen glare and the strange guttural language in which he barked.

He had hardly set foot on the first step and the bus lurched away, leaving him scrambling to get inside. The bus was packed – there must have been 200 people trying to fit in places for fifty. Nadeem fought his way past the veiled women in the front, through chickens and bundles, big people and small people, some with the hook noses and blue eyes of descendants of Alexander the Great, others with the squat flat noses of Mongolians, fat men with large moustaches and immense stomachs that seemed to have a life of their own, small wiry Baluchis with embroidered shirts and gold-heeled sandals, in all manner of clothes such as he had never seen.

Eventually a round-faced man with a pink Sindhi *ajrak* across his shoulders called Nadeem over, making room between a small man with glittering eyes beneath a wide turban like a sheet piled on his head. Gratefully Nadeem sat, slipping between the damp bodies of his neighbours. After a life on the open fields it was the first time he had been in such a confined space, closed in with people, heat, flies, the smell of rotting meat and stale sweat.

It took several hours to reach the outskirts of Karachi. Nadeem was shocked to see that the other passengers showed no respect for the shrines of Sufi saints passed *en route*. They talked in different tongues, of places and people of which he had never heard. For twenty-three years Nadeem's entire world had been the village of Khairpur Nadam Shah and rare trips to Dadu to the wheat-grinder.

The fat Sindhi's name was Subhan and he 'dealt in land'. Nadeem did not know what that meant, but the man shared samosas with him and when Nadeem stiffened at lorries which seemed to be hurtling straight at them then swerved at the last minute in a battle of nerves, laughed and, gesturing to the Pathan driver, said, 'We call them yellow devils. They use *charas* for fuel. They have to drive fast and pack on many passengers to pay the moneylenders for what they borrowed to buy licences from the police.'

Just outside Hyderabad they joined the Super Highway, speeding into Karachi. The scenery became less desolate: on the left Nooriabad industrial estate was being built, on the right Sorabgoth arms and drugs bazaar, and as they neared the city large blocks of flats and factories sprawled across the desert. Nadeem had never imagined such big buildings all made of cement, bigger even than the Deputy Commissioner's house in Dadu. 'There must be work here,' he thought.

But he became less sure as eventually they reached the city. Never in his wildest nightmares had he imagined that there could be so many people and so much traffic. Everyone else on the bus seemed to have a purpose, and when they piled out they all headed off in different directions, leaving Nadeem for a moment unable to move, transfixed by the new colours, the noise and the people. Besieged by hawkers offering him hairgrips, plastic combs and greasy pasties, Nadeem was caught up in this great wave of humanity. Everywhere there seemed to be hands and people pressing against him, and Nadeem gripped tightly the small bundle that was his little piece of Sindh.

A hand grabbed his arm and dragged him along the street. For a moment Nadeem panicked, then he recognized the fat Sindhi from the bus who had taken pity on him. 'You have nowhere to go?' asked the man. Nadeem showed him the scrap of paper. Subhan looked surprised: 'Nazimabad? Are you sure?' 'Yes, this man will get me a job,' said Nadeem, knowing no such thing. 'He has relations in my village,' he added by way of explanation.

'I can put you in one of these,' offered Subhan, gesturing at the rickshaws which buzzed round like hornets. 'Oh no, I shall walk,' said Nadeem. He had little money and somehow felt more in control while he was walking – he had never seen one of these machines before. Shaking his bulbous head, Subhan said that it was a long way but gave Nadeem directions anyway. 'This is my office address,' he added, scribbling on the other side of Nadeem's precious paper. 'Come and see me if you need somewhere to live.' With that he clambered into a rickshaw, squeezing his huge backside on to the small seat and went pop-popping into the dusty distance.

Nadeem set off walking, his heart pounding every time a rickshaw or bicycle came too close. His feet hurt, he was not used to wearing shoes, and his lungs burned with the fume-laden air, but he forgot this in his fascination with the riches laid before him – piles of gold bangles sparkling in the narrow alleys, entire shops selling tin trunks or cases, whole bazaars devoted to metal pails (Nadeem had only ever seen one before), stalls creaking under the weight of books, young boys bearing tempting sweetmeats or griddlecakes on trays on their heads. 'What wealth!' thought Nadeem. He tried to remember everything so he could tell the rest of the village.

Every so often he would stop and ask directions. Few people understood – according to the 1981 census only 6.3 per cent of Karachi's population are Sindhi speaking. But his paper was like a magic key – there was always someone who could read, and then a crowd would gather, eager to show him the way, usually arguing among themselves. The city was bigger than he had imagined – in fact he had seen only a fraction of it. Because of his newness the young Sindhi peasant was a walking target for beggars, who grabbed at his sleeve. As he pulled away from one shuffling old woman, her veil lifted and he saw a face of exquisite beauty. But as she turned he saw with horror that the other half of her face had been eaten away. Nadeem was shocked – she must be a leper. One of the *hari* families in the village had had a leper daughter and sent her away to live in a colony. He had heard that sometimes they took them out to the desert and dumped them there to die in the hot sun. How could a leper be wandering round the bazaar?

Eventually he came out into the apricot light from the dark streets. The air pollution cast a milky film across the sun but to

Nadeem it was beautiful. There were bigger shops with large signs, and a roundabout jammed with buses, their axles cracking under the heavy load of people hanging from every available space, and impatiently honking taxis. On the way to Karachi, Subhan had told him that the 'yellow devils' get paid a percentage of the fares they take by the rich Pathans who own the buses, which is why they try and force on so many people.

Suddenly Nadeem heard a ghastly commotion. He could not make out what it was – an inhuman mixture of wailing and growling. All around him the shopkeepers began drawing in their wares and shutting up their shops. A deluge of stones and missiles began raining down, and as he leapt backwards an enraged mob appeared in pursuit of a wild-eyed Pathan with a dagger. The Pathan, he learnt later, was the driver of a van which had run over a young *mohajir* college girl, Bushra Zaidi, and the *mohajirs* were out for the man's blood.[2]

Word spreads quickly on Karachi's underground network and soon people were appearing from every nook and cranny, armed with knives, bottles or guns. Nadeem pressed himself against the wall in terror – he could not believe what he was seeing. The Pathans, mobilized by the transport operators, were better armed and organized and exchanges of fire began. Nadeem had never seen such hate – the whole neighbourhood seemed to be aflame. Soon the road was littered with blood-spattered bodies, and taut-skinned men with bulging eyes came thundering at the shops, smashing ahead with iron bars like machetes hacking through the jungle. For a heart-stopping moment Nadeem thought they were charging at him, then he realized it was the cry of Pillage! He tried to run, but each way he turned there seemed to be mobs coming, while in the roads cars were being tossed over like beetles and set on fire.

The atmosphere changed, becoming more venomous, almost as if a chill wind was blowing. Screeching sirens split the air and soon tears were streaming down Nadeem's face. Police had arrived with *lathis* and tear-gas and were charging the *mohajirs*, lashing out in all directions. Nadeem put his sleeve to his mouth, as he saw others doing, to protect himself against the poison gas that the police were spraying. From a nearby shop he saw a group emerge howling, bearing aloft a drum of petrol. He thought they were setting alight more buses but then caught the whiff of burning flesh, a smell he recognized from the frequent funerals in the village. They were burning policemen alive!

Nadeem was to say afterwards that he heard the crack before the iron bar struck him, but as his eyes filled with blood and fire his legs gave way underneath him and he felt his bundle yanked away. Desperately he resisted the waves of blackness and the warm waters of unconsciousness, then dimly he heard calling from up the alley between the grocer's and the cigarette kiosk where he had fallen. Unsure whether this was life or death, a mirage or truth, he dragged himself towards a building from the window of which a woman seemed to be beckoning to him. With the drum of the mob still ringing in his ears, he was pulled into a rotting doorway and up some steps into a cluttered room, where he passed out.

He came round later to find a young girl with frightened doe eyes proffering him lime juice. Nadeem sipped it gratefully, hoping to ease his cracked, parched lips. Gradually he could focus on his surroundings, and found he was lying on a *charpoy* in a small but neat room with plastic-framed Arabic slogans on the walls – he recognized those from the mosque in the village. On a table was a vase of plastic flowers, and by the door some shelves of books. That impressed Nadeem greatly; he had never been in a house with books before. In his hand was a small ball of paper – through the fighting he had held on to it so tightly that his fingernails had cut into his palms, leaving crescent-shaped marks.

Nadeem was lucky. He had been rescued from his unpleasant initiation ceremony into downtown Karachi by a kindly family who had seen his panic and realized he was an outsider. 'This is a very close-knit community,' explained Iqbal, who was a teacher in a local school and fortunately for Nadeem could speak Sindhi, though the rest of the family had to communicate with him through smiles and gestures. Nadeem tried to lean forward to kiss the hem of Iqbal's shirt in thanks, but Iqbal pushed him away. 'We are all brothers – forget your feudal habits here.'

'Is the fighting still going on?' asked the frightened Nadeem. 'No,' said Iqbal, 'the army are out on the streets now – it's shoot on sight curfew so it's moved elsewhere, away from here. This is a *mohajir* community. The Pathans are fighting the Biharis now, further west. That's always messy – these Pathans are well armed and the Biharis make a kind of Molotov cocktail. It looks as if it could go on some days – this is the angriest I remember. They say already sixty people have died. I think the *mohajirs* might take the chance to get at the Punjabis – they're really spitting blood since the police came out with tear-gas.'

Nadeem was confused already, and not just because of Iqbal's stumbling Sindhi. Why were *mohajirs* killing Pathans and why were Pathans fighting Biharis? And where did Punjabis come into it? Weren't they all Muslim brothers?

Iqbal's answer was a revelation to the simple Sindhi. With a passion eloquent in its controlled calm, Iqbal spoke of *mohajir* grievances against the Pathans who had moved into Karachi in search of work. 'Initially they were no problem – mostly they took the worst jobs we *mohajirs* were not interested in. Many of them became drivers, and then about eight years ago they formed a cartel of transport owners who either hire out the buses or sell them at exorbitant interest. The drivers buy licences for about 500 rupees from the police and to pay back all this money the drivers must drive fast with too many people for too many hours. There are accidents every week. They bought influence in the police and got lucrative route permits and immunity from the law. Now they control the city's entire transport system, perhaps the whole country's. As for the police, they are mostly Punjabi and all in league because they rely on money from Pathans to supplement their income. So we can do nothing when these illiterate Pathans run over our children. We can take so much, but every so often the area explodes over perhaps the twentieth accident in a month and they want to lynch the driver. That's what you saw yesterday.'

But Nadeem was lost. People were not killing each other over bad driving. 'Well, it's a question of who controls Karachi,' admitted Iqbal. 'For all this time we've felt it was our city but now we're being outnumbered by Pathans and Punjabis. Vast areas are under Pushtoon control, patrolled by drug and gun mafias supplied by the Afghan war and the army. You must have passed the *bara* market coming into Karachi. That's the headquarters of the guns and heroin trade. The stuff comes down from the north and is sent abroad from here in ships. There are thousands of Afghan refugees living here now and there are just not enough resources. The Pathan leaders are in with the government and get better treatment. If that was not enough, they try and corrupt our children with drugs, they cause violent crime – and with all their arms and money they have respect for no one. The police make lots of money by allowing them to continue their illegal trade, so they won't stop them. But our shopkeepers who are trading legally, just selling groceries, have to pay them protection money which puts up the prices. Our people fighting yesterday were venting frustration at our powerlessness.'

'So why are the Pathans now fighting the Biharis?' asked a still confused Nadeem. 'Well, there are several hundred thousand Biharis who came here after the war and they compete for the factory jobs and places in squatter settlements that the poorer Pathans want,' explained Iqbal. 'Our main battle is really with the Punjabis, because they came in and took our jobs in the civil service or white-collar jobs in banks and places for our children in college.'

It was all too much for Nadeem to take in with his splitting headache. Many of the terms Iqbal used were unfamiliar – he only knew what a *mohajir* was because there was a *mohajir* family in his village. They seemed the same as everyone else but he knew the father had come from India when Pakistan was created, leaving behind his family and business. He was very devout and always looked a little sad. Nadeem had to ask Iqbal one last question: 'Why did you take me in?' Iqbal smiled. 'We're on the same side.'

Nadeem lay back and thought about what he had heard. He had never thought of being on any side – weren't they all Pakistanis, after all? He could not understand why these people should feel a grievance – they lived in a proper cement building, they had books on the wall, and Iqbal was even teaching the daughter to read. No one in his village would believe that; only the *mullah* could read, and the idea of educating girls – well, what was the point?

What Nadeem failed to understand, and would only come to appreciate after some time in Pakistan's nightmare city, was the paranoia of life as a minority community. The paranoid strain of the *mohajirs* was a natural consequence of living as Muslims in India during British rule. Most *mohajirs* came from provinces where Hindus formed the majority, and had lived in constant fear of being economically, politically and culturally overwhelmed by the Hindus.

When after Partition more than a million *mohajirs* flooded into Sindh, they concentrated in the towns of Karachi and Hyderabad, replacing the predominantly Hindu population which had fled to India. Being better educated than Sindhis, they filled the gap left in the professional and administrative sectors and were soon running the cities and dominating the bureaucracy, the country's most powerful institution, and the press, enabling their cultural domination. Special townships were constructed for those who had 'chosen Pakistan', and Pakistan's first Prime Minister, Liaquat Ali Khan, was a *mohajir*. Urdu, the language of the migrants, was made the national language, giving them a further advantage in getting jobs. Within two years the population of Karachi had doubled, despite the exodus of Hindus, and by 1951 refugees comprised 55 per cent of the population. For the first time they were in a majority.

The *mohajirs* rarely mixed with their Sindhi hosts – there was little in common between the hardworking refugees, who mostly tended to be skilled or clerical workers, and the Sindhis, who tended to be peasants or *waderas*. The *mohajirs* were a mainly middle-class community, who believed in meritocracy and saw education as the ladder to success and had no equivalent of the feudal or tribal structure which dominated the lives of the Sindhis and the political processes of the country.

While *mohajirs* were the majority community in the capital, Karachi, and dominant in the bureaucracy, they represented only 4 per cent of West Pakistan's population compared to the Punjabis, who comprised 64 per cent. When Liaquat was assassinated in 1951, many *mohajirs* suspected that it was a Punjabi plot to wrest control of government. As Pakistan drifted into martial law under General Ayub, the Punjabis who dominated the army also became predominant in the civil service, the *mohajirs* being relegated to junior partners. The expansion of manufacturing and service sectors saw an influx of Punjabi and Pathan migrants into Karachi for factory work, whittling away the *mohajirs*' majority, while Punjabi army officers were given lucrative plots of land and jobs.

But the *mohajirs*' biggest grievance was the implementation of

regional quotas on a population basis in government jobs and
college places, and the reservation of seats for students from backward areas. This meant trimming drastically the over-
representation of the *mohajirs*, who saw this, along with the transfer
of the capital to Islamabad, as part of a conspiracy to deny them
power. Complaining that as the better qualified candidates they
should get a larger share of government jobs and college places,
the *mohajirs* switched their support from the Muslim League to the
right-wing religious parties, Jamaat Islami (JI) and Jamaat ul-
Pakistan, and in 1968, when the whole country rose up against
Ayub, Karachi was the epicentre of the movement.

But the JI lost heavily in Pakistan's first elections in 1970 to the
PPP, which began advocating provincial autonomy. This was a
problem for the *mohajirs* who did not have their own province.
Traumatized by the emergence of Bangladesh, which put into the
question the whole validity of the two-nation theory which was
why they had come to Pakistan, the *mohajirs* suspected Bhutto's
populist style, flamboyant habits and imperfect Urdu, which did
not fit with the Pakistan of their dreams. Although overall they
probably benefited more than any other community from Bhutto's
nationalization, which brought them more public sector jobs, they
resented that the top jobs always seemed to go to Punjabis, particularly in the head office of PIA, the national airline and one of
the largest employers, in Karachi. After Bhutto had failed to secure
concrete autonomy for Sindh, the polarization between Sindh and
the centre and Punjab and Karachi was crystallized during Zia's
martial law. National politics was driven underground, and a new
politics emerged of student violence focusing on local or ethnic problems.

Nadeem was soon to find himself in the midst of this. Conscious
of the cost of an extra mouth to feed, he left Iqbal's small apartment
immediately the curfew was lifted and followed directions to the
address on the paper he was clutching. The street was nearby, but
as they approached the house he could hear wailing and sobbing.
Inside, a group of young men were raising their voices angrily,
and a body was laid out on a table. Iqbal spoke in low tones to an
elderly gentleman and found that Nadeem's contact had been a
victim of the riots. Nadeem was crestfallen — now he really was
alone in the big city. He wanted to stay and express his condolence,

but a worried-looking Iqbal pulled him away. 'Didn't you notice the men looking at you?' he asked. 'They are members of APMSO, that's All Pakistan Mohajirs Students Organization. They are angry at Sindhis because they think they are taking their college places.'

Nadeem had never heard of a Sindhi going to college, but after the events he had seen on his arrival he appreciated that Iqbal knew better. He was angry when Iqbal told him it might be better not to wear his Sindhi cap – he was proud to be a Sindhi.

His view changed a little the following day. Iqbal had told him of a factory where they were recruiting labour. It was a textile mill, and the air inside was stinging with pieces of white fluff which choked his lungs. The hours were long and the work looked hard but it meant earning money for the first time in his life. In the village they had simply taken a share of the produce and bartered crops for milk or medicine. There was a long queue of applicants and the Punjabi foreman looked each man up and down, feeling arm muscles and tapping a stick across their spines. The young and fit gave their names, the old or weak were cast aside. Nadeem was lithe and strong from his work in the fields and had no doubt he could do the work. But to his surprise the foreman, on taking his name, pushed him away and said, 'We don't want any lazy Sindhis here.' Nadeem, feeling as though he had been hit, realized then that all those taken on had been small wiry Biharis or tall proud Pathans.

It was the same story at every factory he went to, whether it was for pharmaceuticals, food processing or cotton. Already the bazaars seemed hot and overcrowded rather than the Aladdin's cave he had experienced on his first day, and this made Nadeem angry. He slunk back to Iqbal's with almost no self-respect left, and told him he now understood about Pathans and Punjabis. It was a shocking revelation.

Nadeem was luckier some days later. Iqbal had suggested he try the fishing harbour, as the fishermen mostly being Sindhi he would have no language problem. The stench was overpowering as he trudged through the oozing black mud around the port, watching with envy the men bringing in their catch on colourful wooden boats. Inside the market, where the servants of Karachi's élite were selecting the choice specimens and the poor were bargaining for the rotting remains of the previous day, and in another room Biharis were deheading shrimps, Nadeem found a job as a sweeper. It was hardly learning a skill as he had promised his mother, but it was a job – soon he'd find something better. In fact he was fortunate to get the job. As he was beginning to discover, most things in Karachi are run by a cartel and contracted out, whether they be jobs, transport, land or services. Jobs are passed on from father to son, brother to cousin, neighbour to neighbour. Usually both the employee and the employer pay the contractor. The previous sweeper had died of tuberculosis and left no family. The contractor was out of town and the market supervisor was desperate for a sweeper. The father of one of Iqbal's pupils was a buyer from the market; he had put a word in for Nadeem and the job was his.

His chest swelling with pride, Nadeem decided it was time he found a place to live, and went to the office of Subhan, his friend from the bus. Outside the dilapidated hotel from which Subhan operated, a group of Pathans sat on their haunches in that peculiarly subcontinental way, staring ahead. Nadeem stiffened, remembering the fury of the Pathans in the riot. But these men had no rage in their empty eyes. They had given up on Pakistan and were queuing up to buy applications to work as construction workers in the Gulf. Trading in people was one of the many activities Subhan was involved in, as Nadeem was later to discover. On the stairs, across which green fungi was creeping, was a line of Biharis come to plead for a delay in paying the instalments of their debts for the purchase of land. The high interest rates meant that they would never finish paying.

Emboldened by his success in obtaining a job, Nadeem waved his crumpled paper at the peons sitting in front of piles of dog-eared files and was shown into the office in which Subhan sat at a huge desk, with three lilac plastic telephones in pride of place. It was surprisingly plush, and he welcomed Nadeem like an old friend.

Subhan was a *dalal* or landgrabber. Like many of Karachi's entrepreneurs his business was in illegal squatter settlements, in which 4 million of Karachi's inhabitants lived, constantly under threat of the bulldozer. Through contacts in the authorities Subhan would take over a piece of government land, having paid them to look the other way. He would then stake it out in plots and sell

those, lending the money at exorbitant rates. A builder's yard
would be set up of cheap cement and bricks and timber for the
residents to buy for building their houses, and water lorries com-
missioned to deliver water. The resulting shanty towns are far
superior to the slums of Indian towns, and because the initial
outlay is relatively low it is rare to see Karachi dwellers sleeping
on pavements or under plastic sheets like their neighbours in Delhi.
But the *katchi abadis*, as these illegal townships are known, have
two snags – the payment is constant, the *dalal* demanding more
and more money for services or interest on their purchase, and if
they won't pay, the threat is demolition, which an ardent government servant might decide to do anyway. Residents find themselves paying out to the local authorities and police to prevent the
bulldozers coming in.

And so it was that two years later Nadeem was like the Biharis
on the steps, back in Subhan's office begging for an extra month
to make his payment for the plot he had bought. Karachi had
taken its toll – Nadeem had the sallow complexion and sunken
cheeks of the city-dweller. The biggest change was in his eyes,
with their betrayed expression. His meagre earnings had saved his
family in the village but now he was chained to Karachi, constantly
harassed by the land mafia for a debt which seemed to get ever
bigger, like a monster devouring his life. Ever since Nadeem had
moved into the *katchi abadi* people had been trying to fleece him.
Whenever he refused to pay 'residential taxes' or 'protection
money', one of their representatives would appear with a bona
fide demolition order issued by the authorities. Anyone who dared
refuse would find their house suddenly up in flames, or their body
would be found riddled with bullet-holes as a warning. The mafia
controlled everything – water supply, garbage removal, resolution
of disputes, even burials in Karachi's crowded cemeteries. It was a
feudal system without any niceties.

Nadeem understood all about discrimination and oppression
now. Unable to keep up his payments, Subhan had arranged for
him to act as watch on a fishing boat smuggling contraband in
from a cruiser further out. He had made more money that night
than from a month's sweeping, and his heart had stopped thudding
when the customs boat actually waved to them – was everyone in
Subhan's pay? Later he discovered that Subhan was only an agent

– somewhere there was a Big Boss, whom no one he knew had met but who as far as Nadeem could see seemed to control everything in Karachi.

The Big Boss was a Pathan, and the Pathans had been very angry that a Sindhi had been given this lucrative mission. One night a group of them had burst into his shack, smashing the roof that had taken so long to build from scraps he had collected here and there. They beat him unconscious but, worse, the next day he heard a choking throttled sort of noise outside. He dragged himself out and saw the old monkey man with the white beard rocking something in his arms. The old whitebeard was a Sindhi from a village near Nadeem's, and they often talked long into the night about the sun and the stars in the village and the special gold of corn. Even poorer than Nadeem, he made his money from a monkey which he walked along the bazaar and, when he could afford the bus fare, to the beach. He would blow a pipe and beat a drum and the monkey would dance or stand to attention. The old whitebeard loved that monkey and would always share his few crumbs with the poor bedraggled creature. Nadeem felt a sinking in his stomach like the days when he could afford nothing but grey gruel as he saw the old man's shoulders shaking. In his arms lay the small furry body, completely still and matted with blood, and wordlessly he showed Nadeem that the Pathans had put out the monkey's eyes with a hot iron, then carved 'Sindhi bastards go home' across its chest with a knife before slitting its throat.

Nadeem turned and retched. But within a year students from Sindhi and *mohajir* organizations would be committing worse atrocities – this time on people. It was not just Nadeem's stomach that was protesting – his mind was reeling with the hate that could exist between Muslim brothers and the depths that could be sunk to. Images flashed through his mind of the riots on his first evening in the city and again at the end of the following year, when 200 people were killed in Orangi. Nadeem had nearly starved then, because the curfew clamped over a third of the city meant that he could not get to his new job in a Sindhi-owned factory. Curfew was so frequent that many factories, including Nadeem's, had been forced to close. With no work and no money Nadeem could not keep up the payments for the *katchi abadi*. A group of heavies had threatened to throw him off the land. That was when he had thrown himself on the mercy of Subhan, who had arranged the smuggling job which had tided him over but engaged the wrath of the Pathans.

Now as he comforted the old whitebeard, Nadeem vowed to avenge the death of the monkey that was all his friend had. He determined then and there that no longer was he going to let himself be trampled by Pathans or their Punjabi sidekicks – he would join a Sindhi nationalist group and fight for his rights. The whitebeard was disapproving. 'Not in our stars, my boy,' he said enigmatically.

But Nadeem was decided, and for the last year he too had become one of the shadowy silhouettes which stalked the city's streets gun in hand whenever trouble was brewing. When riots broke out he would fight and pillage, making more money in one night than in a month's work in a factory. He convinced himself that he was not really robbing – like the *dacoits* in the forest, he was struggling in the name of Sindh. He attended meetings where speakers recounted with fire the injustices to their community, and he too burnt with resentment. Nadeem's feeling of falling into an abyss came to a head one night when he found himself back in the neighbourhood where he had first experienced mob violence. As he leapt back from the flames of a van he had set light to, he found himself face to face with Iqbal. Nadeem's new friends had persuaded him that the *mohajirs* were just as much to blame as the Pathans and Punjabis and must all be destroyed to reclaim Sindh for the Sindhis. But Nadeem had never really thought of fighting individuals.

The two communities had been at each other since 1987, when the government claimed to have discovered a pamphlet distributed by Sindhi nationalists which advocated co-operation with *mohajirs* to oust Punjabis and Pathans from the province then turning on the *mohajirs*. This revelation set *mohajirs* and Sindhis on each other. Almost overnight a new party had emerged, demanding the recognition of *mohajirs* as a fifth nationality. Suddenly everyone was talking about Altaf Hussain and the Mohajir Qaumi Movement. Every wall seemed to be covered with graffiti depicting men with Kalashnikovs and proclaiming 'Mohajir power Super power'. Red, green and white flags of the MQM fluttered in the streets of *mohajir* townships.

In response to this *mohajir* militancy, new ethnic groups sprang up to represent Sindhis, Pathans and Punjabis, and those already in existence became more militant. The easily obtainable flow of sophisticated arms from Afghanistan meant that streetfights turned into bloodbaths. The tension was exacerbated in December 1987, when the MQM swept local body elections to take control of Karachi and Hyderabad Municipal Councils. Since then battles between Sindhis and *mohajirs* had frequently engulfed much of Sindh, particularly in Hyderabad, where there were three assassination attempts on the *mohajir* Mayor.

No one knew where the MQM had come from – many people claimed that it was a creation of Zia's, as part of his divide and rule strategy to keep tensions high and justify continued army rule. Kamal Azfar, a lawyer who had been a young minister under Ali Bhutto, said that Zia had approached him in 1985 suggesting an attempt to harness *mohajir* support, a proposal he rejected. Within two years of emerging out of the All Pakistan Mohajirs Students Organization (APMSO) at a mass rally in Karachi in August 1986, the MQM had become the most significant force in southern Pakistani politics and a personality cult had grown up around its leader Altaf Hussain, the uncrowned king of Karachi. Known as 'Altaf bhai', he played up the godfather aura, running his organization in cells and sitting in his office in a small white-painted house surrounded by pictures of himself. Everywhere he went his followers, sporting Altaf rosettes, leapt to attention.

Behind the sinister image portrayed by the dark glasses, the protection rackets and the mystery of the MQM's origins, Altaf was Pakistan's most charismatic politician. The country's only political leader to rise from the masses, he would ride through the streets on a Honda 50, preaching revolution and collecting funds door to door. It was not just talk. The MQM, funded by public subscription, runs schools and clinics, and the first time I met Altaf he was setting up stalls to sell fruit and vegetables cheaply to force the shop prices down. All sorts of people were giving a hand: the stalls were manned by doctors, engineers, clerks and medical students.

Altaf complained that *mohajirs* had been forced to assert their own identity aggressively because of the treatment given to them by the rest of the country. 'We've been treated as third grade citizens for the last forty-one years. We would like the people of

Pakistan to be one nationality, but how can that be when primary
education books show four pictures of the nationalities of Pakistan
– Punjabis, Pathans, Baluch and Sindhis? We are the ones who
sacrificed our wealth and assets to come here, yet it seems we are
not considered full Pakistanis. If we had been treated as equal
citizens there would have been no need to raise slogans of *mohajirs*.'[3]

But one could not help thinking that the *mohajirs* feel their
sacrifices made them more equal than the rest of the country.
Constantly they would talk of how much they gave up, yet the
entire MQM leadership consisted of young men born after Partition in Pakistan. Altaf, at thirty-six, was one of the oldest, while
the MQM Mayor of Karachi was only thirty. Less than a quarter
of the *mohajirs* had even been born in India. Yet they considered
themselves the religious superiors of the rest of Pakistan and despised
the romanticism of the Sindhis. Feroz Ahmed, writing in the
Journal of Asian and African Affairs, explained that 'their intellectually
oriented view of Islam leaned heavily towards fundamentalism or
other conservative interpretations which contrasted sharply with
the more tolerant Sufi-influenced syncretic Islam of the Sindhis'.[4]
They thought Urdu a superior language and the only Islamic
language, and, continued Feroz, 'considered the indigenous peoples
of Pakistan to be not only lesser Muslims but also less civilized'.

For the *mohajirs* Pakistan really was the Promised Land, and if it
did not live up to their expectations then that was because it was
not following orthodox Islam, which they associated with speaking
Urdu in proper idiom and wearing *sherwani*, dark coats buttoned
up to the neck. When the Muslim League seemed to have deviated
from this path they put their support behind the Jamaat Islami
(JI). But with the first countrywide general elections in 1970 and
the restoration of four provinces to replace the One Unit, suddenly
they had to face the reality of Sindh. Not only were the Sindhis
clamouring for the acceptance of Sindhi as the official language of
Sindh but one of them, Zulfikar Ali Bhutto, was bidding for and
attained national leadership. Feroz Ahmed explained: 'For twenty-
three years the *mohajirs* of Karachi had never even thought of
being in Sindh; a vast majority had never seen a Sindhi or heard
the language being spoken. Their youth had grown up thinking
that Karachi was a *mohajir* enclave or world unto itself.'

Initially when Zia took over he seemed to offer hope. He purged thousands of Sindhis from public corporations and proclaimed on television that the *mohajirs* deserved special favours because of the sacrifices they had made. With his lower-middle-class background, the identity he was putting forward for Pakistan seemed to coincide with what the *mohajirs* strove for. But they were soon disillusioned. The identity Zia promulgated was too associated with Punjabis, who took over the leadership of the JI and flooded Sindh's colleges and government institutions. The disproportionate third of top civil service jobs that the *mohajirs* had in 1973 had been pushed down to 20 per cent by 1983. Moreover, the increasingly frequent and vicious attacks on *mohajirs* by Pathans showed, they felt, that the government was not interested in protecting them.

With the formation of their own party, the MQM, *mohajirs* were for the first time portraying their interests as a particular ethnic group or 'fifth nationality' rather than what they thought should be the national interests of Pakistan. The MQM's creation undermined the *raison d'être* of Pakistan, and meant following the age-old Pakistan syndrome of voting for people because of who they are rather than what they say – with the exception of Ali Bhutto in 1970. But the *mohajirs* believe they had no choice. Altaf explained their frustration to me in April 1989: 'If a Sindhi, Pathan or Punjabi is killed, Islamabad shakes, but no one raises slogans against the killings of 200 *mohajirs* because they don't consider us human. We feel pain just as anyone else – we're not animals. In the last two and a half years more than 1,000 *mohajirs* have been killed and nothing has been done.'

As young women rushed in and out with plates piled high with tea and cake, Altaf's impassioned rhetoric pulled me away from my fascination with the office, where even the plants and fish-tank were decorated in the red, white and green of the MQM, and from the problem of deciding whether he would think it rude if I did not eat or rude if I did. He was insistent but it was Ramazan, the fasting month, and there is nothing more off-putting than wolfing food in front of people who have not eaten since 4 a.m. and cannot eat again until 8 p.m. I nibbled a samosa half-heartedly while the former pharmacist spoke, with all the fire that he had given to his addresses to mass rallies, of the *mohajirs*' grievances against the quota system which limits the number of jobs and college places for 'urban Sindh'.

'We're discriminated against in all walks of life – professional institutions, national games and even in the 1981 Census, where they deliberately reduced our population. We are at least 45–50 per cent of Sindh, concentrated in the cities, but they put us at 22.6 per cent. Karachi's population is 10 per cent of the country's total and produces 63 per cent of federal revenue, yet it gets only a 2 per cent quota of jobs and facilities. To make things worse, anyone coming to Karachi can for a small bribe get proof of domicile and compete for these jobs, whereas we *mohajirs* have no place else.'

The MQM was hated by the establishment. Altaf said he saw his mission as not just rights for *mohajirs* but for 'all oppressed and suppressed people of Pakistan. We want to show people they will never get their rights until they join together to struggle against the exploiters, who have been creating disturbances amongst us and hatred between *mohajirs* and Sindhis, *mohajirs* and Punjabis. The problems of the common man can only be solved by the leadership of the common people.'

However, it was hard to see how the MQM could capture more votes than in the 1988 elections, when it swept urban Sindh, capturing the third largest block in the National Assembly with all but one seat in Karachi and Hyderabad, and a third of all seats in the Sindh Assembly.[5] For a while there seemed a hope of peace in the streets of Karachi when an alliance was signed between the PPP and MQM in the form of a fifty-two-point Karachi Accord, the main aim of which was to work together for law and order. But by April 1989 it was obvious the alliance would not last – the Sindhis and *mohajirs* were locked in a battle for jobs and power, and with Karachi's already overstretched resources Bhutto could not give to one community without taking away from the other. The Accord was failing dismally. Gunfights in the street had begun again, the army were back in the racecourse and sports centre. Pitched battles closed the universities, and when they dared to open they resembled prison camps, armed guards patrolling. Tariq Rahim, the Parliamentary Affairs Minister, was making weekly visits to the MQM to persuade them to stay in the alliance.

Altaf complained: 'We supported the PPP to show we are not against Sindhis – if we had stopped Bhutto being Prime Minister every Sindhi would have turned against us. But everyone knows the PPP are cheating us — if we started behaving like them the Accord would be finished within two days.' There is no doubt that many in the PPP who had campaigned on Sindhi nationalist slogans were anxious to end the Accord which their constituents saw as selling out. The *mohajirs* were loathed by Sindh's feudals, who considered them 'urban upstarts'. Both sides blamed the other for the killings. Some fighting broke out among rival MQM groups, as the Hyderabad branch put increasing pressure on Karachi HQ to break off the agreement and began displaying Zia posters to signal their disapproval. An aide to Sindh's PPP Chief Minister told me: 'The Accord can never work because our aims are poles apart. Peace is the death of the MQM.' But the MQM are so paranoid, one wonders if they could ever be satisfied. As, conforming to Islam, we did not shake hands at the end of my interview, Altaf stated dramatically, 'When a Sindhi comes to power, the Sindhis are against us; when a Pathan is in power, the Pathans fight us. Will whoever come to power always victimize us?'

By October 1989 the Accord had collapsed and Karachi was once more a free-for-all, its 3,000 available police either too corrupt, ill-equipped or demoralized to cope. The army was being increasingly dragged in to clear up the mess, as the student wings of the MQM and the PPP turned the city into killing fields where violence had sunk to new depths. The latest wave started in January 1990, just after the MQM, along with other opposition parties, had staged what was reportedly the largest and best organized political rally in Pakistan's history. The demonstration in Karachi was within earshot of Benazir Bhutto, recovering from the birth of her second child in a nearby hospital. There were killings in rural Sindh soon after, apparently carried out by members of the APMSO and the PSF, the student wing of the PPP.

In retaliation the PSF, believing that they now had the Sindh government behind them, launched a kidnap and torture campaign against the more numerous APMSO. The APMSO struck back with twice as many victims. Soon hospitals were filling with young men maimed by burns with hot irons, cigarettes and electric drills. Obscene slogans were carved across the chests and stomachs of captives. In the first month of fighting, eighty-one people were killed and hundreds wounded.

Demonstrating their strength and damage potential for the country's heavily Karachi-dependent economy, the MQM brought Karachi to a standstill with a general strike bringing the army into the streets. It was the men in khaki, too, who had to oversee the messy business of exchanges of twenty-seven political workers captured by both sides in tit-for-tat abductions. An army officer who helped work out the trade at 5th division said: 'It was a very distasteful thing, but if we had not become involved there would have been twenty-seven additional bodies.'[6]

Bhutto changed her Chief Minister, but again to someone considered weak. Iqbal Haider, an adviser to the former Chief Minister, said in their defence, 'The seeds of ethnic violence are easier to sow than uproot.'[7] But many felt that the Bhutto government was not even trying. The MQM claimed that the PPP wanted trouble as a pretext for arresting the MQM leadership. 'They will then kill us and say we resisted arrest,'[8] alleged Altaf Hussain. For their part the PPP contended that the MQM wanted to make Sindh ungovernable, to create a crisis to bring down the Bhutto government.

In the city of hooded figures and evil silhouettes the situation had become so bad that people were suggesting dividing the province (the MQM's demand) as the only answer. With no money to ease the social problems, the government began turning increasingly to the army to sort out ethnic riots, leading many of their own supporters to ask the question, 'If the army is controlling, what is different to martial law?' But a week of violence at the end of May 1990, which left more than 250 people dead, persuaded Bhutto that there might be no alternative to the military option her father had always warned against, though ultimately he had not heeded his own advice. As General Beg had said, bringing the army in would provide no long-term solution to a deep-rooted socio-economic problem, of which breakdown of law and order is only the manifestation.

It was over control of the worsening law and order situation in Sindh more than any other issue that uneasy relations between Benazir and the military finally came to a head. The army maintained that the PPP's inaction reflected a lack of will to come down on members of its own party who were believed to be providing protection to *dacoits* as well as its student wing, which

had long been involved in bloody clashes with the MQM. Under
pressure to take action before the army finally took things into
their own hands, a 'clean-up operation' was planned, with joint
lists of suspected terrorists prepared by both military and police.
Arguments raged, with the Sindh government wanting to restrict
the operation to the cities while the army insisted that if it was not
to be one-sided it must take in rural areas too.

However, on 27 May 1990, while General Beg was out of the
country the Sindh government decided to launch a crackdown
based only on police lists and centred on Hyderabad, the bastion
of MQM power. Shoot-on-sight curfew was imposed, and a
police house-to-house search begun. There are conflicting reports
over what happened next but, in what became known as the
Pucca Qila massacre, crowds of *mohajirs* emerged from Hyderabad
fort, fronted by women and children holding Korans over their
heads. The PPP claim that behind them were snipers who began
shooting at the police, while the MQM claim that the police,
unprovoked, brutally began firing at the women. Thirty-one
women and children were killed, sparking off as usual a chain
reaction in Karachi. According to some reports, the final death toll
was seventy in Hyderabad and more than 250 elsewhere.

Finally the army intervened, quickly restoring peace and
welcomed by banners calling for martial law. Iqbal Haider said
that the army's intervention caused confusion because neither the
federal nor the provincial government had called on their support.
Senior PPP officials alleged that the whole incident had been
orchestrated by the army in order to boost their 'saviour' image,
underlining the total breakdown in trust between civil and military. Tariq Rahim claimed, 'We have tapes of Azim Tariq and
Imran Farooq from the MQM meeting an army commander in
Hyderabad before the incident, showing there was total connivance. We know too that curfew was broken with the aid of
local commanders and army trucks were used to transport snipers.'

Tension increased as Sindh police carried out a wave of arrests,
taking in more than 3,300 people in two weeks. Most of these
were *mohajirs*, and Azim Tariq, chairman of the MQM, described
it as 'the greatest crackdown on Benazir Bhutto's political opponents in Pakistan's history'. Referring to the Pucca Qila incident,
he added, 'The killing we faced during PPP government was

even worse than when we fought for Pakistan against British colonialism. It seems as if we're not living in the twentieth century but back in tribal days.'⁹ Alarmed by the growing clamour for martial law in Sindh, the PPP returned to negotiations with the military, but the generals had a high price. If they were to help they did not just want to be policemen clearing up what they saw as the government's mess. They wanted powers to set up military courts and would only agree to be deployed under Article 245, which suspends the administration and high court's jurisdiction, so that they could initiate an 'impartial' clean up.

The army list of suspected terrorists supposedly included the names of five provincial ministers, and the government was aware that if Article 245 was granted the army would start arresting their own people. After four weeks of often stand-up rows during which 30,000 troops continued to keep peace but without constitutional cover, the army was given as a compromise the right to detain, arrest and interrogate suspects. The army command was not satisfied, but many believed that to give them further powers would be tantamount to inviting in Pakistan's fourth martial law.

Bhutto's refusal to surrender Sindh to the army on this basis kept her the support of the Sindhis, but at great cost. Pressure mounted as industrialists and traders staged a one-day shut-down to pressurize the President to dissolve the assemblies. Her government, moreover, had failed to start the political reconciliation crucial to restore peace. The hawks in the armed forces increased their demands for Bhutto's removal, pointing out that if they were having to control Sindh then the whole *raison d'être* for allowing her to take power had vanished.

When the balance tipped and the government was finally dismissed, the army moved quickly to bring Sindhi nationalists and the MQM to the same table, General Gul once more using his influence on the latter. After a two-week respite, however, kidnappings and outbreaks of violence resumed, and it was clear that this would continue until a truce could be worked out between the PPP and the MQM as the two major political forces in the province. Mr Jatoi, the caretaker Prime Minister, said, 'Law and order is my main priority. I am not scared of coming down with a heavy hand.'¹⁰ He later confided, however, 'With feelings so high and missiles freely available on the open market I think only a dictator can solve this problem.'

If there was any hope left in Karachi it was in Orangi, probably the world's largest squatter camp and mostly due to the work of one elderly man, Akhtar Hameed Khan. 'You are now entering the Middle Ages,'[11] said Doctor Sahib, as he is known, by way of welcome. Curfew is the government's only contribution to life beyond the green line that marks off Orangi from the neat villas of the civil servants and the marble palaces of politicians and businessmen.

Home to more than a million people, Orangi began in 1965 to accommodate the first floods of migrants from India and then Biharis from the newly created Bangladesh. Today it is a microcosm of Pakistan, with every kind of problem – poverty, disease, ethnic tension, drugs mafia and guns. It has *mohajirs*, Baluch, Pathans, Punjabis, Biharis and local Sindhis all competing for scarce jobs. Inside Orangi's 8,000 acres there is no government – residents are provided with no water, no power, no sewerage, no health care, no transport and no education.

Once the poorest part of Pakistan, with typhoid and malaria cases in every one of its 90,000 houses, Orangi has become a hive of industry, even exporting textiles abroad and bricks to affluent Karachi suburbs. The transformation is mostly due to Mr Khan, who persuaded the people that 'the government was never going to give them anything but promises – if they wanted to live like humans they would have to do it themselves'. They did. With the help of Mr Khan and BCCI, which set up the Orangi Pilot Project, providing just over a penny per head, they constructed houses and drains, reducing waterborne diseases drastically. Within ten years there were schools, a mobile health clinic, women's work centres, a bus service and even a bank lending money for enterprise projects. Residents had laid their own water pipe to a nearby dam. Electricity was bought from entrepreneurs who had invested in a generator, or pirated from overhead cables, often with the palm-greased connivance of the local authorities.

Nadeem arrived in Orangi when he was in the depths of hopelessness. The Pathan Big Boss had discovered his clandestine activities with the Sindhi nationalists, and some heavies had beaten him and set his house on fire. In Pakistan it is often cheaper to hire hitmen than bullocks. He had hidden at the foot of the Jinnah tomb on the hill, somehow hoping that this memorial to the father of Pakistan, who had left it an orphan within thirteen months, would watch over him. Having more significance historically to the Pakistanis than Lenin's mausoleum to the Soviets, in contrast the last resting place of the 'Great Leader' always seemed empty apart from a few beggars seeking shade in the trees. As Nadeem marvelled at the smoothness of the marble and looked over the city, which was eerily quiet because so much of it was under curfew, Nadeem thought there had to be an answer besides the barrel of the gun. 'This is not why Pakistan was created,' he decided. He would go back to his village with many unanswered questions, but first he must earn some money.

He walked and walked through the pre-dawn streets, kicking the dust, oblivious to the jumble of Gothic architecture and intricate designs of the buildings and balconies. Eventually he came to Orangi, where the motor bazaar was just starting up. A four-mile stretch of hammering, piles of tyres and vehicle parts run by Pathans, this is the hub of Pakistan's motor industry. They can fix, copy, renovate anything and no scrap of metal goes wasted. The hubbub generated by blackened figures soldering and hammering that morning was particularly frenzied because the curfew break was only four hours. Small children covered in oil scurried in and out of more inaccessible parts of engines, chattering like birds.

Nadeem had never fulfilled his mother's wish of learning a skill. He had come now to Orangi with only his strength to offer. But this, he discovered, was in demand. Manpower at cheap rates was needed for residents who had, with Mr Khan's encouragement, got together in the lanes into which the township is divided to elect Lane Presidents, who would collect money and organize labour to build septic tanks and lay drains. OPP's band of fervent young helpers had developed a manhole cover and latrine costing a fraction of those previously available. Since the project began in 1980, more than half of the lanes had built drains, and the concept had been so successful that 180 self-help organizations had sprung up covering everything from sport to religion.

What the World Bank in a recent report called 'Orangi's uneasy mix of co-operation and discord' had at times exploded. The worst occasion was in 1986 when Pathans, angered at the bulldozing of their drugs market at Sorabgoth, marched on Aligarh Colony, turning Orangi into a battlefield. Subsequently, at the first hint of trouble in Karachi, Orangi was always one of the first places to be put under curfew.

This was not really fair. Gradually the inhabitants of Orangi had been getting richer through their own efforts and saw that they had something to live for. The different ethnic communities were starting to intermingle. It was one of Pakistan's few success stories. But the local authorities were uneasy at the growth of this rival economy, which the World Bank described as a parallel state parasitic on the legal one. The administration called Mr Khan an Indian or Israeli agent.

Mr Khan was unknowingly Nadeem's saviour. In return for lodgings and a bowl of food, he was soon working day and night building latrines. To Nadeem every spadeful of dirt he dug was more useful than all the blows he had struck against his fellow men, and he toiled like a man possessed. In his rare breaks he fashioned kites for children out of scraps of paper and wire. Soon they were bringing him bits of material and ribbon from the machine rooms. His kites created a magical new world for the adults too, soaring and diving like free spirits. With no electricity or telephone lines, the kites could fly freely, only occasionally snagging on the TV aerials of the *mohajir* colonies. Here was something all could enjoy regardless of ethnic background, and Nadeem's designs were always flowers or birds, symbols of peace.

One day one of the OPP helpers suggested he apply for a loan to buy materials so that he could sell the kites. Since 1987 OPP had lent 2.5 million rupees to residents of Orangi. Nadeem was terrified, remembering the moneylenders' extortion and forcible methods. But OPP were used to reluctance, and a deal was suggested whereby Nadeem would borrow a small amount to buy wire and material, then when those were sold he could use the profit to buy more. Soon he was in business selling his kites to shops in the city and later even to Hyderabad. As he watched a wide-eyed child stare transfixed at a red kite dancing in the wind, Nadeem remembered with a dull pang the parrots flitting through the trees back in his village and realized he would soon go back. Things would never be quite the same – he had tasted freedom, resentment, anger and fear and now knew of life outside the *waderas'* oppression. He had seen both how Pakistan could and could not

work, and discovered that his kite pirouetting across the rooftops
was a far more effective weapon than the cold steel of the Kalashnikov.

9

PROPHETS AND LOSSES

THE IMMORAL ECONOMY

'At what stage does man prefer a bag of grain to the vote?'
(Bertrand Russell)

At first encounter Pakistan does not look like a particularly poor country. In the main cities few sleep on the streets, and the shops are well stocked with everything from non-alcoholic Barbican beer to Heinz baked beans. The roads are jammed with Japanese cars. Neon signs advertise foreign computers and locally made air-conditioners. Large houses are strung with coloured lights for wedding ceremonies which last for weeks, the peacock-like guests arriving dripping with gold and diamonds in chauffeur-driven Mercedes. Inside, tables groan with mountains of saffron rice decorated with silver-foil and pistachios, trays of plump chicken breasts and huge skewers of succulent lamb. In one room men discuss politics while in another, like a South Asian version of Dallas, women with heavy make-up and bouffant hair gossip slyly and compare shopping trips to New York and London above the twang of a sitar and the clink of 7-Up bottles.

There are some impressive statistics too. The world's second largest exporter of cotton and the third of rice, in the 1980s Pakistan averaged 6 per cent growth a year. Its $390 per capita income is one of the highest in the developing world,[1] and certainly higher than neighbouring India, as Pakistanis love to remind people.

But there was something strange going on. Karachi's Sindh Club, a sandstone vestige of the Raj, overlooking perfectly manicured lawns dotted with bent-kneed gardeners trimming the occasional errant leaf, is a favourite haunt of the old business community. On the colonnaded terrace, under labouring ceiling fans, businessmen sipping pomegranate juice and nursing their paunches were muttering in anxious tones about the economy, their every move monitored by servile bearers in crimson jackets and too-tight trousers. In the run-up to Benazir Bhutto's first budget, the government had taken out advertisements in the newspapers to explain that there was no money and was so poor that it was having to print money to pay government wages while civil servants had to get permission even to refill pens.

But then lots of things about Pakistan did not make sense. Pakistan is supposed to be the Muslim Homeland, yet here was this senior economist telling me that the country's biggest export is people. The government even has a minister to arrange it. The remittances they send back amounted to $3.2 billion a year at the peak in 1984 – almost as much as Pakistan's total exports.[2] Consequently the Iraqi invasion of Kuwait in August 1990 was a serious blow to the Pakistan economy, meaning a loss in remittances for 1990 of $300 million according to government estimates.[3]

I had met some Gulf workers on the plane to Karachi. They had piled on at Dubai like part of a circus parade, barefooted, heads swathed in bedlinen, illiterate and unable to decipher even the seat numbers. The centuries had clashed on that flight – these wild tribesmen sitting cross-legged in the vinyl seats, who could not read numbers yet were wearing digital watches, who were returning to villages with no electricity yet proudly clutching ghetto-blasters and multifunctional food processors.

Even these impressive tribesmen, whose carved features and crude dress seemed so much more alive than the pale Westerners I had left behind, had been affected by the consumerism which permeates Pakistan society. Some of the goods they were carrying would be sold in the underground market of Rawalpindi or the original *bara* (smugglers') market in Peshawar to rich Pakistanis, who see foreign items, particularly gadgets (the more buttons the better) as marks of status. But many would be taken back to remote hilltop villages to which power lines would never travel and placed ceremoniously in clay huts almost as objects of worship. Freezers would be lugged across mountain tops to be used as wardrobes.

Ostentation is an important way of showing one's place on the social ladder. Somewhere there is an unwritten code of Pakistan etiquette which often seems to have more influence on the lives of the élite than the Koran. It dictates that a person's house should be far too big, the air-conditioning so powerful that one moves from near-oven to freezer temperatures, that there should always be too much food on the table, too many phones in the office and too many cars parked outside. Foreign items have particular kudos, and it is not unusual to find Harrods soap in a feudal house in the middle of the most backward village in deepest rural Sindh, where most of the inhabitants have never heard of London.

Despite the country's superficial affluence, it does not take much travel to see how little it extends nor too much digging to understand why the government has no money. Without the remittances from Gulf workers, most economists say Pakistan's economy would crash. Rather than addressing fundamental structural problems, governments always looked outside for help. When the Gulf crisis doubled Pakistan's oil import bill, the government, rather than considering rationing, sent round an *aide-mémoire* requesting additional assistance from donors to help meet an estimated $1.5 billion extra burden on the budget. For years the economy had been on the edge – saved one year by a good harvest, another by borrowing, and sustained for the last decade by generous handouts from the West in return for Pakistan's support for the Afghan resistance, and then for its transition to democracy.

But by the end of 1989 there were many other fledgling democracies competing for Western aid, closer to home, in eastern Europe or central America. With the withdrawal of Soviet troops from Afghanistan, Pakistan had lost its importance in the superpower battle and was receiving severely declining funds for the 4 million refugees it plays host to. Remittances from the Gulf standing at $1.88 billion were on the decline. Servicing of the foreign debt of $14.4 billion and the internal debt of $15.5 billion, along with defence and non-development expenditure, were eating up 80 per cent of current expenditure, leaving the government with little room for manoeuvre.[4] Benazir inherited a government living on borrowed time. On the day of presenting her first budget, she complained, 'We took over an economy in shambles. It seems no bills were paid.'[5] People were clamouring for promised jobs and houses from the new government. Suddenly all Pakistan's chickens were coming home to roost.

So why does Pakistan appear wealthier than India, which has a far more solid industrial base? Where do people get the money to buy those tins of Heinz baked beans at the cost of three days' average earnings? Much of it is made illicitly from drugs and smuggling – Pakistan's thriving black economy is estimated to be anywhere between half to twice the size of the white. It is not difficult to work out why a survey of students at Karachi University found the most sought-after (and thus lucrative) career to be working as a customs official. The US Drug Enforcement Agency believes the country's earnings from the sale of heroin to be more than the total export earnings.

Little of these ill-gotten gains actually benefits the official economy. Pakistan has one of the world's lowest domestic savings rate – 4.5 per cent of GDP compared to India's 22 per cent.[6] According to the system of Islamic economics under which Pakistan theoretically operates, banks cannot give interest, but they get round this by calling interest-bearing accounts 'profit and loss' accounts and the government seems to ignore it altogether, offering 15 per cent return on its bonds or Khas certificates. The stock exchange is more remarkable for the blood on its walls than for the volume of trading. An American banker told me, 'The only country I can think of with as little stockmarket activity is Colombia.' No one saves, and few invest in industry, because of the unstable political situation following three periods of military rule and two dismissals of governments. But in a catch-22 situation the uncertainty gravely restricts any government's ability to raise resources and thus stay in power. What confidence there was in the country has not recovered from the shock of Zulfikar Ali Bhutto's ruthless overnight nationalization campaign in the 1970s.

Most of the money is kept overseas or spent on land, grotesquely large wedding-cake houses and unnecessary consumer items. The government has no intention of stamping out the black economy, which employs many people – an important factor in a country with 25 per cent unemployment – because of the fear of people voting with their stomachs, or, worse still, preferring economic well-being under martial law to hunger in a democratic system. In fact, so desperate was the government to take advantage of the parallel economy that it offered its own laundering operation, selling bonds to legalize unlawful gains. The last ten years had seen the creation of a *nouveau riche*, mainly consisting of smugglers who act as patrons to members of both government and opposition to ensure that the butter remains on their bread whoever is in power. Zia's years saw a general improvement in purchasing power, though as usual it was the rich who benefited most. According to the 1988 government economic survey, both rural and urban income distribution had worsened even compared to the 1960s, when it was revealed that twenty-two families controlled more than two-thirds of the country's wealth, owning 66 per cent of industry, 97 per cent of insurance and 80 per cent of banking.[7]

Sometimes it seemed as though Pakistan was run by an exclusive club – a clique of people one meets at airports and hotels, giving the impression of a much smaller country. Only in Punjab had a middle class developed, mainly through its domination of the military and civil service. In the rest of the country inequalities widened, first under General Ayub, when they were deliberately promoted as a necessary precondition for economic growth. Wages of industrial workers in West Pakistan fell during his rule by nearly 12 per cent, despite a countrywide boom and a 72 per cent increase in industrial production.[8] Ali Bhutto's often incoherent economic policy, as he tried to be a socialist while looking after the interests of the feudal classes, hampered growth, his devaluation and nation-alization deterring investors. Under Zia the lot of the working people improved, not through government policy, but by a combination of luck, Gulf remittances and turning a blind eye to the doings of smugglers who joined the élite club, their profits trickling down to a range of people from poppy farmers to truck-drivers.

It would be harder to justify the continued freedom to smuggle if the official system was more efficient. But it is beset by bureaucratic procedures and corruption. In 1988, for example, the government estimated that 122 billion rupees (£4 billion) were embezzled compared to a total development budget of 56 billion rupees (£1.8 billion). Dr Mehbub-ul Haq, a former Finance Minister, put leakage at 50 per cent.[9] Investors call Pakistan a 'skimocracy', complaining that in setting up projects, palm-greasing is necessary all the way down the line, from the minister to the man in the local telephone exchange, and never stops.

The lack of trust in the official system was exemplified by a visit to Peshawar's money market. Edging into the main square in the old city, opposite the impressive glass frontages of the country's leading commercial banks, was a higgledy-piggledy row of seedy shacks. The banks were empty, employees in their grand halls outnumbering customers. The shacks were crowded with craggy-faced Pathans swathed in woollen shawls. One of them was the servant of a smuggler with a weakness for the South of France. After each successful shipment, the servant would take a large brown paper package to the owner of one of the shacks. The Egyptian who runs it would take him into the dark interior, extract the latest model in digital phones from a crate and call Karachi for spot prices. He would then press a few buttons on his calculator and give the servant a chit. His master's money would be waiting in a Swiss bank ready for his next trip to Europe.

In the next shack was an Afghan commander collecting funds for the *jihad* (holy war) from a Swiss bank account. The money came from the sale of a Soviet armoured personnel carrier to a German arms dealer. The vehicle had been dismantled and transported in pieces by Baluchi tribesmen across the Iranian desert to the Persian Gulf, from where it was freighted out. Behind the Afghan was Kalim, a small boy whose father was a construction worker in Dubai. On the first Tuesday of every month he paid half his salary to a local money dealer, and two days later Kalim could collect the money, less a small commission, in Peshawar.

These were all customers of the Peshawar part of the world's most extensive underground banking system. *Hundi*, as it is known, is faster and more reliable than commercial banks in this part of the world. From the humblest stall equipped only with an ancient wooden abacus, to the Egyptian with his huge safe and direct line to the country's stock exchange, they were dealing in millions.

Salim had been President of the moneychangers' bazaar for the past nine years. He explained that not only was their exchange rate much better, but Pakistani citizens were officially only allowed $1,000 in foreign currency for two years. 'Here, one can change any amount, and,' he whispered conspiratorially, 'there's no paper-work involved.' Even the most law-abiding citizen, who has tried official routes to transfer money in or out of Pakistan and become inextricably enmeshed in a network of lost telexes and leering stenographers whose masters are never at their desks, could not fail to appreciate this point. Pakistani businessmen will do anything to keep off the books, including paying more, and whole sections of the economy do not officially exist, though those that do tend to overstate their business to obtain government incentives, so perhaps in the end there was some measure of balance on the books.

Business in the Peshawar money bazaar was so good that the crumbling shacks would fetch at least $50,000. Mansur Ahmed had worked in the bazaar for the past five years and averaged more than $1,000 a week. Most of his foreign currency came from India, and he dealt mainly in pounds, marks, dollars and Saudi riyad, though he said he could arrange anything for 1 per cent commission.

The only legal currency dealing in this totally open trading was that in afghanis. The Peshawar market is interlinked with the Chicken Street moneychangers in Kabul, and as such, had become a barometer on the state of the Afghan war. Floods of refugees pushed down the price of afghanis, which had become worth less than half what they were before the war relative to the rupee. The biggest buyers of afghanis were agents from Pakistan's Inter Services Intelligence, for bribing officials in the Kabul regime.

Inspector Asis from the Federal Investigation Agency (FIA) told me he had, quite remarkably, patrolled the bazaar for two months without catching sight nor sound of any foreign currency. Standing in front of a large pile of sterling, he expressed confidence that his fifteen informers (also in the pay of the traders) might be on to something, and said severely that if he was to catch anyone selling foreign money other than afghanis, they would be sent to prison 'forthwith'.

Everyone, it seems, was out to make money in that grey area between legal and illegal, and officials were in on it too. In the modern state banks in the square of Peshawar City, clerks would tell customers they had no foreign money to encourage them to use the *hundi*, for which they too will receive a cut. People often question why Pakistanis abroad tend to be more hardworking and entrepreneurial than at home, but the fact is that most Pakistanis are entrepreneurs, only not in a conventional way and usually parasitic on the official economy. The telex operator who claims

'lines are down' until slipped a few rupees, or the post office
assistants who say smugly, 'Stamps not available here' and direct
people to the pavement sellers outside, where stamps are most
certainly available, if a few *paisa* above the official price – all of
these can be called entrepreneurs.

'Pakistan's main economic problem is moral,' explained Mr
V. A. Jaffarey, the Government Economic Adviser and architect
of the 1989 budget.[10] A classic example, and the main reason the
government has no money, is tax collection. The taxman works
on a bizarre system of commission. Offer him more than the
commission and the tax is forgotten. Hence, out of a population of
110 million, only 1.1 million are registered and even fewer pay.
Mr Jaffarey, peering over his large glasses, elaborated: 'They have
numerous ways to get round it. A company can be making a
profit for fifteen years but never pay a penny in tax, because the
owner says he is bringing in new machinery and thus claims
exemption for modernization. That alone costs us 0.5 billion rupees
a year.' A British team, visiting Pakistan to suggest how to tighten
up tax collection, concluded, 'There is nothing wrong with the
system – it's the people. No one believes that they should pay
tax.'

But it is not just the public who have no concept of national
interest. The government is guilty too. Economic policy is determined by short-term or political considerations for the benefit of
the few, with disastrous consequences for the many. Ali Bhutto's
later nationalizations of cotton ginning and rice husking mills were
specifically designed to hit political opponents, and it was during his
rule that economic activity was really replaced by political activity.
Introducing lateral entry to the civil service enabled him to use the
organization for political patronage. From the political workers
given jobs in state corporations to the businessman awarded a
lucrative licence for contributions to party funds, suddenly holding
the right party card or knowing the right politician became an
essential prerequisite for amassing wealth. It was the resulting pre-
eminence of politicians for the first time in Pakistan's history that
eventually earned Bhutto the hostility of the army and bureaucracy.

An all too common story in Pakistan is of changes in duty
structure to favour the industry of a political supporter, far more
subtle than outright corruption. It can be starkly demonstrated by

a visit to the shipbreaking yard in Gadani, an hour's drive along the coast from Karachi. By 1982, a decade after it was set up, the narrow strip of golden sand at the edge of the Baluchistan desert had become the world's third largest shipbreaking site, drawing in busloads of tourists fascinated by the spectacle of thousands of men tearing apart huge ships with their bare hands.

On any given day in the mid 1980s some 35,000 men would be dismantling 100 ships under a 100° sun, crawling like ants across the huge metal hulks equipped with nothing more sophisticated than hammers and winches, earning just over a pound for a twelve-hour day. By 1989, because of changes in the tariff structure making shipbreaking uncompetitive, the 'Graveyard of the Ships' had become a ghost-town with only a handful of workers to be seen.

Like an eerie metal memorial, the edge of the beach is lined with ramshackle huts constructed from unsaleable scrap in a hotch-potch of metal piping, corrugated iron sheets, rusted barnacle-encrusted doors and the occasional funnel for a chimney. They stand empty. The army of fearless Pathans who travelled the 1,000 miles from the Frontier province in search of work no one else would do has dwindled to a few hundred. Thirty shipbreakers have gone out of business, and only one of the remaining sixty is working. Standing, arms crossed, amid the sea of rusted leftovers, Hasan Jaffri, the secretary of Pakistan's Shipbreakers' Association, made a sorry picture. 'This is the end of Gadani,' he mourned in April 1989.

From an annual import of 1 million tonnes in 1982–3, it had dwindled to seven small ships or 26,000 tonnes in 1988–9 because of what Mr Jaffri called 'discriminatory duty' on shipbreaking. Between 1982 and 1984, duty on ships was raised from 30 per cent to 85 per cent, apparently because of the fall in the prices of ships from $190 to $65 per tonne. Since then, however, the price had shot up to $230 per tonne while the rupee had depreciated significantly.[11] The final straw came with one of President Zia's last acts, which was an Ordinance in July 1988 exempting re-rolling mills from central excise duty but imposing it on shipbreaking for the first time, making the overall duties on ship scrap three times those on the shredded scrap used in the melting industry.

Inside the former ship's captain's quarters which forms the office of Abdul Majeed, chairman of the Shipbreakers' Association and the largest shipbreaker, controlling 30 per cent of total business, the atmosphere was gloomy. Mr Majeed said dolefully: 'Breaking ships is no longer profitable. I used to break a minimum of 100,000 tonnes per year – this year I've only bought two small ships.'

The highly labour-intensive shipbreaking had been effectively priced out of the market, while the melting industry experienced an astronomic boom. In 1988-9 private sector furnaces produced 1.1 million tonnes of ingots, compared to only 200,000 tonnes in 1982-3.[12] It was, it seemed, no coincidence that Pakistan's largest steel foundry was owned by the family of Nawaz Sharif, Zia's protégé, who was made Chief Minister of Punjab in 1985. Since Sharif was first picked up by Zia in 1983 to be Punjab Finance Minister, the family company, Ittefaq, had progressed from running a fairly unremarkable textile mill and foundry to being one of the wealthiest private companies in the country, if not the most wealthy.

Shebaz Sharif, the likeable younger brother who runs the company, put its success down to 'hard work and the grace of Allah'[13] and, despite great efforts, the Bhutto government failed to substantiate its allegations of corruption against the family. Even claims that Ittefaq was cheating on electricity bills, something almost every industrialist does, by having a sub-station within the foundry and the meter inside the factory, backfired when Sharif incredibly managed to prove that WAPDA owed them money. Allah, it seems, looks very kindly on the Sharif brothers, who now own four textile mills, a street of houses, a private hospital, a sugar mill, and have almost completed the biggest sugar mill in Asia.

But it certainly did no harm having a family member as Chief Minister, declaring land they had bought a tax-free zone, enabling it to be sold at immense profit, having banks at his beck and call eager to lend money at preferential rates, and obtaining duty benefits for their industries. After Sharif took office, two major incentives were introduced for the sugar industry including a 50 per cent excise duty rebate for the first two years of production, with retrospective effect, which made the industry one of the country's most profitable. By 1988 three-quarters of Pakistan's private mills were owned by politicians from Sharif's party and sanctioned during the Zia regime.

Benazir Bhutto's government tried to play the same game. Much of its economic policy seemed directed at getting back at opponents. Opposition politicians believed the withdrawal of exemptions on sugar duties imposed retrospectively in June 1989, landing Sharif, for example, with a bill for £2.7 million, to be deliberately aimed at them. Sales taxes introduced in the 1989 budget were on items such as cement, which Ittefaq produces. Sharif complained that Bhutto's moves had cost his company an extra £50 million for 1989–90: 'She's deliberately taxing everything we make.'[14]

But Bhutto was less adept at uncovering scams than Sharif and Co. apparently were at making them. Not only had they covered their tracks carefully and made figures open to the foreign press in a show of apparent openness, but some of the projects were partnered by generals or senior military figures whom Bhutto could not afford to upset. Sharif, for example, had a fleet of different-coloured Mercedes cars which he was most unlikely to have paid the 250 per cent import duty on, but then so do many top army officers.

Unable to prove anything, the PPP was left looking amateurish and vindictive. The Public Accounts Committee, under the chairmanship of Hakim Ali Zardari, Bhutto's father-in-law and one of her MPs, a job traditionally held by an opposition member for scrutinizing government accounts, instead concentrated on those of the opposition, producing lists of unpaid bank loans. Journalists walked out of his press conference in disgust when he asked them to print lists of names of allegedly corrupt IDA members but was unable to produce evidence.

Unfortunately, it is often the common man who suffers in these wranglings. Ittefaq laid off 3,500 workers in summer 1989, alleging that the government was trying to force the company out of business by instructing Pakistan Railways to refuse to cart scrap, imported from the US from Karachi dock to the company's works in Lahore. Shebaz Sharif called it 'a deep-rooted and sinister conspiracy motivated by political vendetta'.[15]

The US ship MB *Jonathan*, which arrived in Karachi on 14 June 1989, was carrying 28,000 tonnes of steel scrap to be molten in Lahore. Ittefaq claimed to have had a contract since 1980 with Pakistan Railways, to be provided 1,200 wagons every forty days, and was their biggest private customer. This time the railways said the carriages were needed for 'items of national priority'; Shebaz Sharif, however, argued that more than 1,200 carriages were lying idle in Karachi, and some of his workers blocked passenger lines in protest, causing chaos.

Despite a Supreme Court ruling that the carriages must be provided, eleven months later the ship still had not docked, amassing demurrage charges of more than $2.5 million. Not only did it cost Ittefaq in lost production but, Sharif pointed out, also meant a considerable loss in revenue to the country and was not looked on kindly by the US. The US ambassador in Islamabad wrote to the President and Prime Minister expressing his concern at the behest of the US supplier concerned, who was ultimately responsible for the charges. 'This is an unfortunate incident which muddies the water for other potential investors,' commented one US diplomat.

Benazir Bhutto's own government was soon heavily tainted with corruption charges. Her husband, Asif Zardari, became known as Mr Ten Percent, for his alleged rake-offs in deals. The view was so widespread in Pakistan that it no longer mattered whether it was true – perception was all. Certainly some Western businessmen I spoke to in Karachi claimed to have been offered invites to attend one of Benazir's dinners for a fee. A lucrative contract to supply mobile phones to Karachi went to a company whose Pakistani partners apparently included one A. Zardari, instead of to the big British telecommunication set-ups which were expected to win it. Land around the Bhutto residence in Karachi was said to have been forcibly seized so that the First Couple could build a compound. There were any number of such tales about the polo-playing Mr Zardari to be heard around dinner tables from Karachi to Peshawar, and a favourite diplomatic game became guessing 'does she know?'.

Corruption may have been no greater under the Bhutto government, but it was undoubtedly more blatant. One American banker said, 'Certainly there's always been corruption but it took on grotesque proportions with respect to Asif Zardari.' In an investigative report titled 'Take the Money and Run', just before Bhutto's ousting, Newsline, Pakistan's award-winning news magazine, detailed instances of use of the state-owned development finance institutions (DFIs) and nationalized commercial banks (NCBs) in which it said political patronage was being played for 'mind-boggling stakes'.[16]

According to the report's findings, 'Since the Benazir Bhutto government came into power twenty months ago the DFIs and NCBs have approved loans totalling billions of rupees for projects whose chief merit seems to be the political connections of their sponsors. 294 million rupees for a textile mill to a federal minister who probably wouldn't recognize a bobbin if he tripped over it, 900 million for a papermaking plant based on twelve-year-old second-hand machinery from Britain, 2,300 million for a cement plant to a federal minister's son barely out of his teens ... so wholesale has become the plunder that in the words of a former DFI chief executive, "the whole financial sector appears to be in danger of collapsing".'

In 1989, loans sanctioned by the National Development Finance Corporation (NDFC) went up 242 per cent while those by Pakistan Industrial Credit and Investment Corporation (PICIC) increased 310 per cent. Bhutto maintained that this was a reflection of her push for industrialization, necessary for progress, but Karachi bankers pointed out that the heads of these institutions were changed and people connected to the PPP or Zardari installed, while by mid-1990 the institutions were all on the verge of bankruptcy. The recovery rate in the first quarter of 1990, for example, was only 7.83 per cent according to State Bank figures. Several stiffly worded letters were sent to the Finance Secretary from World Bank officials, and according to Mr Jatoi, 'loans were given so freely the World Bank has stopped disbursements to credit institutions'.[17]

The more stories circulated about Benazir's husband and ministers 'looting the country', the more widespread became corruption at all levels. The Collector of Customs in Karachi explained, 'When ordinary people read in the papers of ministers making millions they think why shouldn't I? They know if their children are to have a better chance they must have education, but there is no state system and they earn less than school fees so in many ways they have no choice. In fact if they do not take bribes people think they are stupid.' He added that over the last two years things had got so out of control that in the customs service he could barely name two or three honest people.[18]

After her dismissal, accused of four charges of corruption, Bhutto of course denied everything. Seated inside her house after her first court appearance in Karachi, face blotchy and voice one note from hysteria, an emotional Bhutto obviously could not believe what was happening to her. 'I'm outraged that I'm the only Prime Minister who did not take an industrial unit, whose relatives did not have bank loans written off, yet those who looted the country go scot-free and dare to point their fingers at me.'[19]

The main target seemed to be the husband with whom she appeared so much in love. He was on bail facing serious allegations, and even Bhutto's closest supporters said his arrest might be useful, considering him a liability. Bhutto maintained that the whole accountability process was a political vendetta aimed at hindering her election campaign. 'People said there was a lot of hanky panky. What hanky panky? Tell me about it. Are we living in the civilized world or are we back in medieval times where people were burnt at the stake as witches? If there was corruption why did no one bring me facts?'

In fact her opposition had got themselves in a fix. As the Bofors case, which brought down Rajiv Gandhi in India, showed, corruption can take a long time to prove, and as those making the allegations were themselves hardly angels, the whole thing smacked of vendetta. In a speech to the Asia Society in Washington on 11 September the US ambassador said: 'In my view, if there is to be accountability for those holding political office it should not start from the 16 November 1988 elections which brought in the PPP but should also include the 1985–8 period, when the IDA parties and politicians ran the government.' Bhutto's main rival, Nawaz Sharif, argued: 'I've been undergoing an accountability process for the last twenty months. Now it's their turn.'[20]

Moreover, ordinary people expected corruption of politicians, and attending a few of Mr Jatoi's *jalsas* or corner meetings in rural Sindh in late September 1990 it was obvious there was little response to his allegations. Instead the PPP was once more riding high on a sympathy vote, and the Bhutto government's incompetence was being forgotten in what she was successfully portraying as victimization. Bhutto always excelled at the martyr role, and somehow, as if she were a screen goddess, no one, even the press or diplomats, could find it in them to blame the lady herself, though they were happy to castigate the ministers and advisers she chose.

Shortly after taking power, one of Bhutto's ministers told me he intended to make as much money as possible in the first year in office because they might not last much longer. But this attitude is accepted in Pakistan. People would be more shocked if those in positions of power did not take monetary advantage of the fact. A journalist friend of mine, who was one of the very few I knew who was not in the pay of any politicians or intelligence agencies, once confessed that his mother refused to speak to him because he would not accept cars or other pay-offs, and accused him of being selfish. 'Don't you ever consider how your "principles" affect others?' she had asked, adding, 'How can they be principles when everyone else is at it? What does it achieve from you going without?' In Pakistan that becomes a very difficult question to answer. A former Mayor of Peshawar told me that when he had first taken the job he had been determined to be clean and stamp out corruption. 'But then I discovered that 99 per cent of my staff were totally corrupt, from the sweepers and streetcleaners to the bureaucrats in charge of finances.'

The most common way for politicians to supplement incomes or do favours for friends was through bank loans from the nationalized banks, which guaranteed an instant profit. Most of the projects 'sanctioned' only ever appear on paper, enabling investment figures to look better than they are. There are several popular scams. Up to 70 per cent of the value of the 'investment' can be borrowed at cheap rates. This can then be lent to someone else at a higher interest. Or if the project in question is for a 'priority' industry, or the borrower's friend in high places declares it priority, he can then get a further 20 per cent in equity and, by over-invoicing imported machinery, get the government to pay more than the total cost. So without putting up a single rupee of his own money, a businessman can find himself in possession of a sugar mill. Moreover, there is a good chance he will not have to pay it back. In 1988, £1 billion of loans from nationalized banks were declared 'non-performing'.

The longest-running absurdity of political considerations determining economic policy was the non-imposition of tax on agricultural income. For years the World Bank and numerous economists had been saying that the only answer to Pakistan's balance of payments deficit was to bring in a tax on agricultural produce, the country's biggest sector, comprising 70 per cent of export earning and employing 55 per cent of the workforce. While feudal landlords dominated Parliament this would never be

introduced, because it would shrink their own earnings. Nawaz
Sharif, one of the few non-landlords in politics, had no such
qualms and claimed that were he Prime Minister, he would seek a
constitutional amendment allowing the chief executive to impose
taxes, then bring in land tax as a way round having to get it
through the Parliament. Few believed he had the gumption even
to suggest such a move.

While there is no land tax businessmen cannot see why they
should pay tax. One complained to me, with some justification I
thought, 'Across the road from me is a house belonging to a
landlord. There are always three Pajeros (Japanese jeeps) in his
drive and often a Mercedes. He has similar set-ups in Karachi and
Islamabad as well as his feudal seat and a flat in London. When I
earn just about enough to feed and clothe my family, why should
I pay tax when he does not?' Many industrialists would get round
this either by not registering or by getting together with a landlord
and declaring their earnings as agricultural income.

It was not just political factors which deviated from balancing
the budget. Regional tension not only caused outbreaks of violence
but also prevailed against better economic judgement. For nearly
forty years the provinces have been at loggerheads over the issue
of the Kalabagh dam, which is desperately needed to help ease Pakistan's massive power shortfall. Kalabagh, on the border between
Punjab and NWFP, was earmarked by engineers in 1953, after
expensive surveys, as the most suitable site for a dam. But while
the Punjab assembly keep voting in favour of building it, the
Frontier argues that it will cause the flooding of villages around
Nowshera and Attock, and Sindh and Baluchistan maintain that the
dam will lower the water level causing droughts further down the
Indus. Dr Khuro, a Sindhi nationalist leader, believes, like many
Sindhis, 'Punjab just wants the key to the control of the Indus.'21
The arguments continue, more money is wasted on surveys of
other even less suitable sites, and the power deficiency gets worse.

With Pakistan's current economic woes, the time for *ad hoc*
measures would seem past. But under Benazir Bhutto, shortsighted
policies continued. Villages were still being electrified for political
effect when there was no power to supply them, and he with the
most money continued to get the irrigation water. With little
government money at her disposal, Bhutto hoped that private and

foreign investment would provide the jobs her supporters expected. It was a foolish hope. If anything industrialists began moving out of Pakistan to Dubai, frightened off by the unstable political situation, tensions with India and ethnic violence in Karachi, the country's commercial centre, where 47 per cent of industry and all major headquarters are based.

By the end of 1989 the security situation was so bad in the southern port city that provides nearly three-quarters of government revenues that business was down to 50 per cent. Chamber of Commerce officials said Karachi was losing $48 million per day because curfew in the most populated areas prevented workers reaching factories.

While it hurt their pockets, businessmen in their marble whitehouse replicas a few miles south and a world away from the squalor and overcrowding of real Karachi had always been protected from the ethnic violence. But not any more – by 1989 they were running scared from a new wave of violence directed specifically at them.

That year saw no willing entrants from Karachi for the usually hotly contested awards for the twenty-five best-performing businesses. Potential winners knew that their names would top another list – that of a group of kidnappers spreading fear through Pakistan's business community, seizing wealthy industrialists or their relations at gunpoint and demanding ransoms of $50,000 or more. The *dacoits* of rural Sindh had come to town in search of richer pickings. With arms easily available and police incapable of coping, they had been joined by members of drug mafias freelancing on the side, political activists claiming to be 'struggling for the rights of Sindh', and even some of the city's estimated 10,000 unemployed medical graduates. It was of little solace to the businessmen targeted that their abductor may have a PhD or could speak eloquently on Sindhi nationalism.

Leading business organizations brought in kidnap experts from the US and Italy after more than eighty businessmen had had to pay ransoms in six months. By August 1990, according to the chairman of Adamjees Insurance, Mr Chaudry, the number of kidnaps had reached one a day and several hundred businessmen held kidnap insurance with Lloyds of London through the company. Victims had become more political and included the son of the State Bank Governor and the head of the stock exchange. Brian Janjua, chairman of Woodward Pakistan, explained the feelings of the business community: 'When I leave the house in the morning I do not know whether I'll be back. I breathe a sigh of relief after 2 p.m. when I call home to see if my children have returned safely from school. Fear dominates our lives.'[22] Not surprisingly, investment was drying up. A business leader who employs 100 heavily armed guards for his home and family said: 'There is no reason to invest here if your life is at stake.'

Qaim Ali Shah, the Sindh Chief Minister, was under fire for his weak handling of the situation when I met him, and was later removed. Half the city was under curfew that night in August 1989; the previous day there had been a gun battle inside Hyderabad jail, and incredibly he was claiming that the situation was under control. He was a nice man, small and walrus-like, and I wanted to believe him, but he was floundering as if he was trying to climb out of a glass box. 'The feeling of insecurity is artificially created by screaming headlines in the papers,' he protested. 'These incidents were happening more before but not reported because the press was not free. I blame the press 50 per cent.'[23] Not only was this an unconvincing line to take with a journalist, I thought, but it was totally undermined when during an hour-long dinner he received several emergency calls reporting gunfights and by his own admission that the problems kept him working till 2.30 a.m. every night. I left convinced that the problems were actually worse than I had imagined.

In fact, senior police officers I spoke to said that most kidnappings are not reported, victims being anxious that their assets should not be known either by potential future kidnappers or by the taxman, while police are keen to keep the crime records low in their areas, on paper at least. Businessmen allege that the police are often in league to supplement their meagre incomes. Ghani Talpur, a wealthy landlord who was held in 1989 for nine days, said afterwards, 'I am positive that without their [police officials] help, I could not have been kept so long.'

Bashir Ali Mohammad, chairman of the All Pakistan Textile Mills Association, whose members had paid out more than 39 million rupees in six months, was furious at the government's lack of action. 'Every day we hear of people we know personally being kidnapped or robbed. The highways are so unsafe that for over a year we have not been able to visit our factories. We cannot understand why the government is allowing business and industry to be driven out. Ultimately Sindh will be the loser.'[24]

Eventually, patience wearing out, APTMA joined with other business organizations, pumping money into a hard-hitting advertising campaign. Front-page newspaper advertisements, headed 'SOS to the Prime Minister', depicted industrialists held chained in caves by armed bandits or *dacoits* and declared, 'Dacoities are being committed round the clock. The police is either helpless or in league.' Qaim Ali Shah intervened to stop the adverts, summoning the APTMA chief to his house late one night and keeping him there until he agreed to withdraw them. They had succeeded in making the point, however, and Aitzaz Ahsan, the Interior Minister, set up an Emergency Cell. After six months all this had come up with was the impractical requirement that people must get permission to repaint their cars. So bad was the situation that when businessmen met Benazir Bhutto, instead of their usual pleas for tax concessions, they would ask for arms licences.

By September 1989, night-time Karachi was almost unrecognizable as the lively place I had first visited nearly two years earlier. Flashy Mercedes had disappeared into garages, people preferring to travel in less conspicuous second-hand Suzukis – a great sacrifice for those used to an ostentatious lifestyle. At socialite dinners which were ending a good few hours earlier than I remembered, almost every guest had a tale to tell of a colleague or relation who was kidnapped at gunpoint from his house, car or while out shopping. Instead of the usual gossip, they compared precautions such as taking different routes to the office every day and leaving at different times. A year later people were staying at home.

The Ladies' Bar of the Sindh Club was once where women in cocktail dresses sipped gins and waited for their husbands, who were perhaps playing snooker in the rooms which still bear the signs, 'Ladies and Indians are not allowed'. More recently it has become frequented by lawyers discussing cases and businessmen puffing cigars while making deals, with nothing stronger than an orange juice in sight. Too often the conversation turns to discussing who offers the best 'cover for terrorism' or kidnap insurance, available at high premiums. Some fear that the list of subscribers may fall into the wrong hands. Most businessmen employ armed guards from one of the twenty private security agencies which have sprung up to match the new kidnap boom, some even offering to mediate in negotiations. According to Adamjees, the largest insurance company, at least four clients a day were reporting cars stolen at gunpoint.

The inevitable result of the wave of kidnappings was the flight of capital to Dubai and north to Punjab, where in 1988, for the first time in Pakistan's history, there was more industry sanctioned than in Sindh. Despite Pakistan's obvious advantages of a large domestic market and its position as a springboard to the wealthy Gulf states, foreign investment has always been pathetically low, partly because of political uncertainty. Dr Salim Habib, President of the Overseas Chamber of Commerce, said in summer 1989, 'foreign investment has been negligible for the last three years and with kidnappings going on and families not safe, no company will invest here.'

This sounded suspiciously like the death knell for Bhutto's hopes of foreign investment providing jobs, and some believe it to be even more fatal. Akhtar Hameed Khan, the director of the Orangi Project, said, 'We are looking at the destruction of Karachi and that means the destruction of the Pakistan economy. Pakistan is trying to destroy itself.'[25]

Pakistan certainly seems to be destroying its future. Drug addiction, illiteracy and population growth are on the increase, beyond their already appalling levels. Most countries would be worried if in thirty-five years their population trebled from 33.7 million in 1951 to over 103 million in 1986 and was set to double in the next two decades. But in Pakistan under Zia, the Islamic Ideology Council declared family planning un-Islamic. Maulana Maududi, one of the greatest influences on Islamic public opinion, wrote a book on birth control in which he condemned family planning, denouncing it as a Western plot to erode Islam.[26] According to latest official surveys, average fertility per woman is 6.9, and Benazir made no move to tackle this controversial issue.

'Knowledge is Light' proclaim billboards outside bookshops. But Islam means the rejection of Western scientific methods and English language, and has wrought havoc on education. There are only a few hundred PhDs and thirteen physics professors, and while government figures put literacy at 26 per cent – lower than at Partition – these are inflated and the reality is thought to be worse. Leading scholars such as Dr M. Afzal have put only 8 per cent of the population as educated to primary standard and 2 per cent to secondary. Shahnaz Wazir Ali, the junior education minister, told me she was shocked when she took office: 'Incredibly for a country with 110 million population we are talking in terms of thousands at college.'

There was plenty of foreign money around to tackle these social problems. But neither the feudal politicians nor the religious fundamentalists wanted the spread of education, the former preferring this to remain the preserve of the élite. Much of the money disappears into the pockets of officials, and for many projects the Pakistan government cannot afford to put up the matching rupees. A World Bank official told me they have between $2-4 billion in undisbursed aid. So schools remain a few children grouped under a tree, and in some areas, such as rural Baluchistan, female literacy is less than 1.8 per cent (government figures). This is frightening, particularly given Pakistan's demographic pattern in which in 1981 45 per cent of the population was under fifteen.[27]

Islam in its present form in Pakistan does not seem equipped to run a twentieth-century state. Having a modern secular Western-educated woman at the helm seemed to make little difference – she too was a prisoner of attitudes so entrenched that only a revolutionary could change them. Thus while Bhutto herself took on the sanctioning of investment projects to speed them up, the delay was never really at government level – her nod did not make the man in the local telephone exchange or the customs officials at the dock any more efficient. Simply to stay afloat at its present miserable level, Pakistan had to continue to run cap in hand to Uncle Sam, until in 1990, suddenly rediscovering Pakistan's nuclear programme, he turned the other cheek, leaving as Pakistan's only hope its friends in the Islamic world, to whose aid in the Gulf War it was quick to send troops despite widespread criticism at home.

IO

THE GREAT GAME REVISITED

OF BLOOD FEUDS AND TRIBAL WARS

'The Game itself is a Hobbesian war of all upon all which may
start as a battle of wits but must end in violence for its laws are
take or have taken from you, strike before you are struck, kill or
be killed.' (Mark Kincead-Weekes, introduction to *Kim* by
Rudyard Kipling)

In a land with no laws I had dinner with a smuggler. The directions,
which sounded bizarre, were precise: the sixth fort on the left past
the sign for the English grammar school for young ladies, half-way
up the Khyber Pass, travelling in the opposite direction and far less
style to past conquerors such as Genghis Khan, Alexander the Great
and Tamberlaine. No cavalcades of elephants or camel loads of
courtiers for me – just two sultry Pathans squashed in the back of
my small Suzuki, clutching Kalashnikovs and discussing how much
a healthy young Englishwoman would fetch on the open market.

As I waited for the huge door of the smuggler's fort to swing
open and swallow me up, I felt rather as I had one Easter vacation
when I was fifteen and trying to sell unlikely household gadgets to
women with clipped accents and matching Pekinese in heartland
suburbia. 'This multi-action pump dispenser soap brush is just
the thing for your Venetian blinds, Madam.' Now I was on the
other side of the world, with gunshots echoing across the cloud-
mountains of the valley in a place which has been a continuous
battlefield since man first set foot on it. I could not help noticing
the anti-aircraft guns mounted on one of the eight watchtowers.
They don't have those in Carshalton Beeches.

Over syrupy tea in the best Coalport china cups, and nasty pale yellow sawdust cake topped with silver balls, my host explained that his family had had a long-standing blood feud with another tribe since his cousin had abducted one of their women. The score on revenge killings was four-three, so the other side was eager to even things out and a constant watch had to be kept.

A bit more violent perhaps than the neighbourly arguments over who should trim the laburnum tree growing over the fence, but it seemed reasonable. Only the night before, the manager of an agricultural credit bank had told me of the difficulties of ensuring that field officers in the Frontier were not posted to areas where their families had feuds and might be shot.

Feuds and smuggling are a centuries-old way of life in the tribal areas of the Frontier, to which the laws of Islamabad are quite irrelevant. In the days of the Raj the tribesmen were allowed to build gun factories inside their mud forts, to stop them stealing British arms and because it was assumed that they would build inferior guns in those far-off days when British was best. In the last decade the large spillover of sophisticated weaponry from Afghanistan had made tribal clashes far more grisly. My smuggler friend complained wistfully as he showed me round his marble-floored fort: 'It was far more fun in the old days when enemies often had to be stalked for years with a Lee Enfield .303 bore. Now with Kalashnikovs and rocket launchers whole families can be wiped out in minutes.'

Often they are. Not always over family feuds. The craggy hills of the Khyber Pass provided the dramatic backdrop for the Great Game, in whose rocky nooks and crannies until Indian independence British officers played the tribes off against each other, occasionally reminding them who was master with mini-wars, the British taking hostages and razing entire villages. This is the land where government has no authority, and 'stalky men' such as those portrayed in Kipling's *Kim* from the Indian secret service were used to maintain the supremacy of the British Raj.

The most powerful tribe in these Leviathan antics which Pakistani political agents continue today are the Afridis. It is said that if you find a snake and an Afridi in your bedroom you should kill the Afridi first. Spread across both sides of the Pakistan-Afghan

border, in the days of the Raj the 600,000 Afridis guarded the
Khyber Pass in return for money and the freedom to collect
protection fees and raid caravans on what was once the main route
between Kabul and the riches of Delhi. In reality the British never
controlled the pass, and from when their troops first marched up it
in 1839 towards the First Afghan War, losing hundreds of casualties
to the Afridis, right up to Partition, pickets had to be mounted
along the road to ensure safe passage of their convoys.

Malik Nadyer Khan is an Afridi chief. A small dapper man in
his late fifties, somewhat shrunken in his oversized black coat and
clutching a large black furled umbrella, he would not be out of
place on a central London underground line, were it not for the
gang of seven Kalashnikov-toting heavies who trail him everywhere.

Inside his crumbling mud fort the *malik* (tribal king) serves
freshly slaughtered sheep on three-foot skewers and sweet Russian
champagne (courtesy of the Afghan government cellars) in a
darkwood-panelled living-room with heavy brocade curtains. Despite his harmless favourite-grandfather appearance, Nadyer Khan
is more likely to be found burning down friends' forts than settling
down in slippers with a cocoa in front of the television. One gets a
hint of his real nature with the glint in his pistol-grey eyes when
he bites into the skewered lamb and meat juices run down his
fleshy chin.

Since the age of twenty-two, he has controlled the Zakakhel
tribe. The Zakakhels and Kukikhels are traditionally the most
important of the eight Afridi tribes, because they control the road
and the border at the main smuggling route between the two
countries. The fort-lined road along the Khyber Pass was built by
the British in 1842 after the first of three Afghan Wars as part of
their 'forward policy' to stop the threat of Russian invasion. At
the narrowest point, where the cliffwalls almost seem to touch but
were actually widened to build the road, it is easy to imagine
Surgeon Major William Brydon emerging on a half-dead horse,
the sole survivor of the battle of Gandamak, in the final humiliation
of that first war in which 16,500 British soldiers were slaughtered,
giving them a lesson it took both them and the Soviets, more than
a century later, a long time to learn. From the road one gets
tantalizing glimpses of the thirty-four tunnels of the Khyber Rail-

way, along which the Khyber Mail has clung perilously to the knotty cliffside since the railroad was built in the 1920s for the then exorbitant sum of £2 million.

The traditional struggle between the Zakakhels and Kukikhels brings in the governments of both Pakistan and Afghanistan, each putting their weight behind one of the two tribes which change sides regularly according to who is currently offering the best deal. It's their equivalent of switching supermarkets. After the Soviet troops entered Afghanistan in 1979, the stakes increased enormously, the Great Game played as vigorously as during the British-Afghan Wars. The tribes assumed new importance, with Pakistan eager to use Afridi territory for *mujaheddin* bases while the Kabul regime was anxious to cut off the main supply route of the resistance. Stalky men again ply back and forth, gathering intelligence for the master strategists of both sides.

Nadyer Khan was in Pakistan's pocket when we met in April 1989, and getting things all his way since his main rival, the top Kukikhel *malik*, Wali Khan Kukikhel, had recently died. Wali Khan had been the first to fall out with Pakistan, shortly after Partition, of which most Afridis did not approve. Following the British example, the Pakistani government bulldozed the obstinate *malik*'s village and he crossed into Afghanistan, where he stayed until 1962 when he was lured back by President Ayub who gave him a seat in Parliament.

Nadyer Khan then automatically sided with Afghanistan, joining Ghaffar Khan in the struggle for Pushtunistan, an independent land for the Pushtun tribes of which the Afridis are one of the most powerful. Apparently supported by the Soviet Union from 1972–4, they took up arms against the government of Zulfikar Ali Bhutto, who in retaliation used as terrorists some of the very men now leading the Afghan resistance movement. After the Soviets entered Afghanistan, the Pushtunistan issue was shelved and Nadyer Khan returned to Pakistan, leaving the sister-in-law of the now President Najibullah living in his house in Kabul. Nadyer Khan spoke condescendingly of Najib, whom he knew well in his twenty-five-year stay: 'Najib was nothing in those days, he used to clean my shoes,'[1] he said in a voice that carried the gravity of some ultimate Zakakhel slight.

While Nadyer Khan did a deal with the Pakistanis, Wali Khan Kukikhel took the Afghan side, receiving vast amounts of money and arms to hinder the resistance from operating in the tribal areas. Nadyer Khan admitted that he also took money and weapons from Kabul agents but used them to help the *mujaheddin*, who these days frequently stop for tea and boiled sweets at his fort before or after sorties. For months the road was unsafe with reciprocal kidnappings, but in classic colonial carrot and stick treatment in 1985, President Zia sent in troops to bulldoze Wali Khan's fort and paid him handsomely to stop causing problems.

The latest clash between the two tribes was over plans to build a road to Tirah, the most inaccessible part of Afridi land. The only Westerners that have ever seen it were those abducted. There is a lot of road-building going on in the tribal territories — according to an official from a US agency, the money is coming from US funds meant for cross-border operations but given to Pakistan in return for its assistance, to enable them to develop the tribal areas and thus bring them under control.

By spring 1989 the *mujaheddin* and their Pakistan backers were in serious danger of losing the Afridis' support. The *mujaheddin* had closed the road between the border post at Torkham, which they had won control of the previous November, and the Afghan city of Jalalabad, and were demanding large tolls from users of this, the main smuggling route, seriously affecting the Afridis' main source of income. To many tribesmen, already fed up with bombing attacks suffered as a result of allowing the *mujaheddin* to use their territory as bases, this was the last straw. The bloody March offensive on Jalalabad had not only failed but had caused a spillover of 28,000 more refugees into their already overburdened land, and the regime's reply of Soviet Scud missiles had blown up the passport office at Torkham, where long-haired hippies once smoked dope, and caused considerable damage in the tribal areas.

Smuggling is of course illegal anyway. But the government has no authority on either side of the road from Peshawar to the border, and customs officers watch helpless as heavily laden smugglers leading donkeys with fridges strapped on their backs pass by a few feet from the road. It is not just for security reasons that

tribal smugglers dwell in forts. Inside the high mud-walls can
be found piles of Soviet refrigerators and microwaves, smuggled
from Kabul. The Russians may have lost in Afghanistan but across
the border they had won another major battle.

Prices of smuggled Soviet goods undercut the once-popular
Japanese items by so much that these are now seen only rarely
in Pakistan's bazaars. Few homes are without a Soviet air-
conditioner. Until the Soviets left Afghanistan a roaring trade was
done in Russian vodka, known locally as 'Gorbachev'. In the
smugglers' bazaar just outside Peshawar one can buy anything
from Chinese toilet-paper to Bulgarian beer, Scotch whisky to
Soviet caviar. Smuggling has become a complex business. No
longer can a self-respecting operator rely on a few mules laden
with Afghan cigarettes. These days loudly painted government
trucks fight it out on the highway between Kabul and Peshawar,
packed with all manner of luxury goods, paying 'taxes' to resistance commanders who control the road inside Afghanistan and
'commission' to customs officers in Pakistan. Some of the heaviest in-fighting between *mujaheddin* groups has been on the main
route between Kabul and the Soviet Union, which each group
wants to control so that it can hijack Russian goods destined for
the capital, though the vodka and caviar have stopped since the
Red Army went home.

Not all the contraband entering Pakistan originates in the Soviet
Union. Goods entering from Karachi are marked for Afghanistan,
which being landlocked uses that as its nearest port. From there
they are taken in bonded trucks through Pakistan and just past the
border town of Torkham, where they are dumped in a warehouse,
stamped, and smuggled back into Pakistan, thus avoiding Pakistan's
prohibitive import duties.

Many of the weapons destined for the *mujaheddin* from US and
Saudi funds are sold off in frontier arms markets. On my first
night in Peshawar, a roomboy at Greens' Hotel tried to sell me a
Chinese rocket launcher at what I later discovered to be an extremely low price. A tribesman is not considered dressed without
a gun, and Nadyer Khan had his first pistol at the age of six. A
half-hour's drive (and a week long's fight with bureaucracy for a
permit) from Peshawar is a one-street village called Darra Adam
Khel. I thought I had arrived on the set for a cowboy movie from

the Wild West, bullets ricocheting across the low roofs. But the men wore turbans, not stetsons, and in this scenario Trigger was a moth-eaten mule. Darra is the gun-factory of the Pathan areas – a town where every kitchen doubles up as a gun-forge. Inside young boys and old crane-like men using the most primitive tools fashion perfect reproductions of everything from pen-pistols and mortars to multi-barrel rocket launchers and anti-aircraft guns complete with serial numbers, a far cry from the simple rifles made when Darra's unusual industry was set up in 1897. One of the craftsmen even offered to supply the Pakistan airforce with copies of US F-16 fighter aircraft. The workmanship is outstanding but the materials are poor, and with the real thing so readily available, Darra is doing more trade in smuggled weapons; though visiting journalists usually fall for pen-pistols engraved with 'Souvenir from Darra', if only to have them confiscated at the airport.

Aid organizations such as the United Nations High Commission for Refugees take the smuggling factor very seriously and are, for example, hesitant about sending mules to Afghanistan to replace the estimated half-million oxen killed there in the war. They fear the mules would end up pulling Pakistani ploughs instead. In 1989 a consignment of Texas mules intended to be used by the Afghan resistance fighters were switched for Pakistani specimens long before reaching their destination.

Governments would make occasional threats to burn the *bara bazaars*, showing footage of leering customs officers standing over bonfires on the television news. The officials were almost certainly burning packaging while the contraband found its way into their homes, and the government will do nothing to stop the centuries-old trade which is an easy way of keeping the unruly tribals happy. Bare subsistence is the most tribesmen can hope for from harsh surroundings which yield barely a blade of grass but where everything has a price. To obtain a wife or a gun they must loot or smuggle – to the short-term-minded government a much cheaper alternative than providing industry, schools and dispensaries. According to Malik Mir Aslam Khan Afridi, President of the All Tribal Unity organization, 80 per cent of Pakistan's 7 million tribals survive on smuggling.[2]

Not surprisingly, then, angry voices were raised in the smart Peshawar offices of the 'Businessmen's Association' after *mujaheddin* had stopped the traffic on the main Jalalabad–Torkham road, arguing that the trade bolsters the regime and forcing smugglers to find much longer and harder routes over mountain passes. Smugglers all, seated cross-legged on the floor, weapons across their knees and munching sultanas, the officers of the Businessmen's Association said business had never been so bad in the Peshawar smugglers' bazaar. Turnover had dropped from an average 2 million rupees per day ($100,000) in August 1988 to a few hundred thousand in spring 1989. Shelves once bursting with Japanese televisions, Russian refrigerators and Thai silks were standing empty save for a few boxes of French perfume and a battered video. To the accompaniment of Pathan back molars grinding sultana cloves and the sucking of saliva, occasionally collected into an old brass spittoon, Haji Mohammed Yusuf, the bazaar chairman, presented the figures. It was worse than they thought: 'Business is down to 15 per cent and fifty of the 210 shops in the bazaar have gone bankrupt. It is time for the Pakistan government to get these *mujaheddin* in line.'

But not all the tribesmen were unhappy with recent events. Beneath the romance of the Frontier is the sordid reality that aside from their gun factories many tribesmen have built extensions – heroin laboratories, processing poppy mostly grown in Afghanistan and growing rich on the proceeds. The Afghan war had made Pakistan the world's largest supplier of heroin, and by 1989 drugs were bringing in at least $4 billion a year – more foreign exchange than all Pakistan's legal exports combined.[3]

Inside a typical crude fort one producer even had a jacuzzi and Lear jet. He was considering putting up a picture of Benazir, for to his surprise he had been very pleased with the new government. Hedging his bets, he once funded politicians on all sides of the political spectrum. Now he was more powerful than they.

Chuckling in a way that contorted his rubbery face, he explained: 'When Benazir became Prime Minister she launched a big campaign against the drug barons. We had an emergency meeting and sent out warnings – a business associate of the Prime Minister's husband was abducted and several narcotics officers killed – the usual things. One of our number gave himself up and, for a while, we were worried that he might name names, but the appropriate threats went out and he was released through lack of evidence.

Laughable really – he'd even been named on BBC Panorama, everyone knew he was in on it.'[4]

The release of Haji Mirza Iqbal Baig was an embarrassing setback for Bhutto's government. On taking office Bhutto had promised the US she would take firm action against drug barons, whose wares supply the streets of London and New York as well as the more than 1 million addicts at home. She had, she said, 'declared war on the drug barons' and insisted 'no one will be spared' – a tall promise considering that no drug lord had ever been jailed in Pakistan. Haji Iqbal's surrender in July 1989 was heralded as the first of many, and the Narcotics Minister called a press conference to name him 'the kingpin of the international heroin trade'. Brave narcotics officials appeared, to tell how they had heroically resisted threats and bribes and were continuing their fight despite the fact that the drug underworld had put a $250,000 reward on each of their heads. But Bhutto, it seemed, had expected Baig to be taken off her hands through extradition orders, none of which came, and rumours began spreading of Baig's funding of both sides in the elections. Within a month he was a free man.

One of the problems for the government was that a symbiotic relationship had grown up between Western intelligence and the tribal chiefs, whose co-operation was vital for the CIA to continue their cross-border operations. Trucks from the National Logistic Cell, a transport unit created by the Pakistan military intelligence (ISI) for the Afghan operation, had been bringing arms from Karachi to the border and apparently taking back heroin to be sold overseas. Several times when these trucks had been involved in accidents witnesses reported seeing white powder pouring out. The irony is that the CIA were using for their Afghan policy, through ISI, the very people the State Department, through the DEA, were trying to stop. No wonder DEA officials said Pakistan's tribal areas, thought to hide several hundred heroin laboratories and supply forty gangs, are now the world's safest haven for drug processing – their compatriots are providing the protection.

There is a further irony. The producer explained: 'All these Western aid projects have helped opium production in Afghanistan through irrigation, and the Americans have produced a new incentive – offering bribes to those who destroy their crops. They don't learn – they tried that in Pakistan and production went up.'

Not surprisingly Bhutto, despite the political will, was able to make little dent in the narcotics business, though Iqbal Baig was finally re-arrested. After her dismissal she claimed, 'We arrested seventeen top drug barons and would have eradicated poppy in Pakistan by 1992. That's why the drug barons wanted us out.' However, the former Collector of Customs in Karachi said, 'It depends how you define drug barons. In fact those arrested were just couriers.' He added that the government had once more refused to act on the names that the Customs Intelligence had provided. Moreover, more than three-quarters of the poppy processed was grown in Afghanistan, and poppy-smuggling had been little affected by the road closure as it is usually brought by donkey or just carried over mountain paths. More badly hit were the Pakistani political agents, the sole government representatives in tribal areas, who use their cut from the smugglers for slush funds to buy off tribals in order to solve disputes.

The Peshawar political agent, seated under a wooden board engraved with the famous names of heavyweight predecessors, complained that because of the road closure he had so little money that he could no longer afford biscuits. But bribery was not the only time-tested method to maintain authority. We met on one of those subcontinental spring days when the roads shimmer with the threat of damp heat and the electricity flickers on and off with the falling levels of the dams. Outside an angry buzz was audible over the usual jumble of street noises. The wooden verandah around his offices was crowded with ancient hawk-nosed Pathans sporting a range of beards, from wirewool to soft flowing, waiting for the agent to convene a *jirga* or tribal assembly to solve a dispute over the abduction of a Pakistani child, probably taken to be a bride. The old men were muttering moodily because the agent had seized some of their people as security until the matter was settled.

Despite the wild atmosphere the tribal areas are run very democratically, on the lines of Athenian democracy. As part of the strictly followed tribal code of Pushtunwali, *jirgas* are held to solve disputes with both concerned parties and other tribes participating. Usually they are convened by tribal chiefs – only if the matter is very serious or affects Pakistan's sovereignty would the political agent get invo... ..!. There can be as many as 5,000 people attending and they can go on for months until consensus is reached. While the *jirga* is in process, a peace accord is made, called 'putting a stone' or *tiga*. If this or the decision of the *jirga* is broken, the tribe burn down the offender's fort and kill his animals, dividing the loot between them, and the offender is ostracized by the tribe until he apologizes. Nadyer Khan frequently has to supervise repercussions for such breaches of tribal law. Unlike the Pakistani legal system, in the tribal jungle there are no special favours for friends or relatives. Over lunch Nadyer Khan told me: 'Last week I burned my best friend's fort down because the *jirga* had ruled that his son had stolen a car but his son had run away. Now he's apologized and I'm helping him rebuild it.'

The system seems to work, with the threat of feuds acting as a powerful deterrent. Despite the proliferation of arms and the violent appearance of the tribals, there are in fact fewer killings than on the streets of New York. Nadyer Khan explained, 'It is an eye for an eye and Afridis always take revenge. I won't dare kill because then for the rest of my life I will be in danger and my family will always be under threat. If your brother kills mine it is my duty to kill someone in your family. If I can't kill your brother then I kill you, then your brother must kill me.'

In the past the political agents could rely on *maliks* such as Nadyer Khan to keep law and order. Since British times they have been given power and financial assistance. Nadyer Khan receives regular payments from the political agent and his area gets free electricity as part of government policy to bring the areas under central control. Nadyer Khan said, '*Maliks* were like small kings. It was a self-propagating system because only *maliks* could afford to study, and the system was so strong that it was still continuing just the same when I returned from Kabul in 1979.'

But the influence of the *maliks* is waning because of the influx of drugs and arms. The *malik* is no longer the richest man – Nadyer Khan's wood-panelled fort was quite modest compared to the marble extravaganzas of some of his neighbours. With the spread of new wealth and ever more powerful arms, *maliks* fear that tribesmen will increasingly resist the old ways. Many *maliks* are against developments like the proposed road to Tirah, because they fear with exposure to the outside world they will lose their power over their tribes.

In neighbouring Baluchistan, Pakistan's most backward province, an inhospitable land of arid desert and rugged mountains coloured in the kind of ochres and blacks that are painful to look at from the air, the tribes are so strong still that three-quarters of the elected MPs are from the families of *sardars* (tribal chiefs). The provincial assembly in Quetta is a meeting place for a bizarre selection of tribal headgear. A strange domed building, it seems as out of place as an abandoned spaceship between the neat avenues of the military cantonment and the chaos of the city, where men with black-rimmed eyes and high-heeled sandals decorated with gold studs walk hand in hand among shacks piled high with mounds of the ladylike footwear. As the surrounding hills turn pink in the evening sun, providing light relief from the otherwise overwhelming brownness, shadows fall on serrated clefts in the rockface, reminders of one of the biggest ever earth tremors, which wiped out the city on 31 May 1935, killing 23,000 people in Quetta alone. Inside the assembly building tinny music begins heralding the start of a session. The beards and turbans take their places, passing legislation as though it is going out of fashion – in marked contrast to the national Parliament. One of the younger tribal MPs later told me bills were passed so easily because 'no one understands them'.

Presiding over the session, looking like a caged crane eager to spread its wings, was the biggest *sardar* of them all, resplendent with white handlebar moustache and flowing robes. The Chief Minister was Nawab Bugti, who talks of cutting off ears and noses in blood feuds in a clipped Etonian accent. Feuds and homosexuality seem to be the main way Baluchis can get their kicks in a province so conservative and dull that for many the annual highlight is a visit to Hanna lake, where they sit for hours staring at the brown water surrounded by brown hills. The women, kept in strict *purdah*, cannot even do that.

Sixty-four per cent of this unruly province is still under tribal laws with no police or government, where the only rule is survival of the fittest. Each of Baluchistan's tribes is ruled by a *sardar*, whose authority until recently had been rarely questioned. But at a coronation ceremony for the new *sardar* of the Tareen tribe in summer 1989, many of those attending felt it might be the last such occasion. 'We are becoming figureheads like the Queen of England,' said one.

The fourteen-year-old boy whom they had all come both to assess and congratulate looked a bit confused by it all. A week earlier he had been sitting in uniform in his public school reciting English verbs. Now, wearing a flowing white and gold headdress and swathed in embroidered shawls solemnly presented by other *sardars* whose daring exploits had made them his childhood heroes, Mohammad Qaddafi Khan Tareen was being crowned the most powerful man in the Tareen tribe. After his grandfather's death the previous week, the title had passed to him, his father being in delicate health. With the crown came the control of the destinies of the 20,000 Tareens. On the say of Mohammad Qaddafi Khan they would live or die, prosper or starve.

The celebratory lunch, for a mere 5,000, resembled a scene from the court of Henry VIII, with row upon row of chieftains sitting cross-legged and munching great haunches of meat, tossing the bones carelessly over their shoulders, exuding power and masculinity. A total of 172 sheep and eighteen cows had been killed for the occasion, and an entire room was filled with 10,000 pieces of flat unleavened bread.

There was much mumbling in the ranks of the eaters at seeing a white female in their presence. Five thousand pairs of eyes seemed trained on me, and I could think of no better question for the new *sardar* than 'How do you feel?' Immediately I remembered how that had made me grimace when, training to be a television reporter, the colleague I had gone with to the scene of a fatal motorway accident had asked the mother of the victim the same question. Conscious of the total silence aside from the munching of bones, I tried to improve it, but the boy seemed terrified, more the type I would expect to see hiding behind his mother's *chador* than the proud Goliath-like figure one expects as a leader of a tribe.

The heyday of the *sardars* was like their frontier counterparts, the *maliks*, during the Raj. When the British took over the unruly region in 1846, they followed a policy known as 'masterly inactivity'. This meant dividing it into British-governed settled areas; an independent state called Kalat ruled by a Khan; and tribal zones into which British administrators were forbidden to cross. But the tribes relied on looting and raided the settled areas continually, knowing that the British were powerless to follow them.

Matters came to a head in 1867, when 1,500 armed raiders struck at the frontier district of Dera Ghazi Khan in Punjab. The British Deputy Commissioner there, Robert Sandeman, raised a force of local tribesmen and drove off the invaders, killing 120 and taking 200 prisoners. Later he concluded a treaty under which the *sardars* promised not to raid his district. To discourage tribesmen from looting, he provided employment in tribal forces and, arguing that continued warfare with the unruly Baluchis was not worth the effort, set up a treaty in 1876 covering the whole area, which left them to their own devices in return for the security of the Bolan Pass, the main corridor through the vast range of mountains which extends from Baluchistan along the Frontier province and was probably the first passage between India and the Persian Empire.

After Indian Independence the Baluchis, along with the Khan of Kalat, were reluctant to become part of the newly created Pakistan, preferring to remain a feudal state. A year later the army moved in to persuade them, hanging Baluchi leaders and creating a hostility against the centre which continues today. At first they were allowed to keep their old tribal ways but, in 1958, President Ayub amalgamated West Pakistan into one province. He imposed Pakistani laws on the tribal areas and ordered the surrender of unlicensed firearms. The furious Baluchis, feeling that part of their identity was being denied, refused to give up their weapons and revolted. Many *sardars* were imprisoned. Eventually a compromise was reached, and when the provinces were reinstated in 1970, 85 per cent of Baluchistan went back under tribal law. But the Baluchis had maintained a simmering insurgency, and this exploded in 1973 after Zulfikar Ali Bhutto sacked the leftist Baluchistan government. Once again a Pakistani was trying to interfere with Baluch rights and a second rebellion began – this time, instead of romantic Robin Hood acts, outright rebellion, from which many feel even today there can be no going back. Some 80,000 soldiers were sent in, razing villages in a massive ground and aerial operation, while the Baluch People's Liberation Front, partly funded by Moscow and trained in Afghanistan, attacked army convoys. There are almost no Baluchis in the army, and officers despised these underfed men who were arrogantly demanding autonomy. The uprising was ruthlessly suppressed, using methods repeated in

Bhutto's own province, Sindh, in 1983. Leaders of the rebels were arrested and thousands killed. After President Zia imposed martial law in 1977, the leaders were released and went into exile in places as diverse as Kabul and Ealing.

Apart from the rich Saudis who arrive in chartered jets to hunt sandbirds in the desert and contribute to Islamic funds, no one really cared what happened in Baluchistan. Though almost half the territory of Pakistan, it is the only province not watered by the Indus and is home to less than 4 per cent of the population. The world only noticed it when the Soviet Union invaded neighbouring Afghanistan. Huge and hard to defend but strategically located, bordering Afghanistan and Iran down to the Arabian Sea, the West feared that Pakistan's soft underbelly would be used for a Russian push supported by disgruntled tribesmen to reach the 'warm waters'. Panicking, the West began pouring in aid to this strange place in such quantities that by 1988 it amounted to $1,000 per head. According to the Baluchistan Chief Secretary, who runs the province like a no-nonsense headmaster with a school full of naughty boys: 'All usual restrictions were relaxed to give us far more aid than we could possibly absorb. We could not provide enough proposals but the World Bank and other donors were happy to give for irrigation schemes they had never seen.'5

But the Chief Secretary's authority extends little farther than the capital, Quetta, and many sardars refused to allow development in their territory, fearing that the spread of education and communications would weaken their powerbase. Tribal forces were sent to scare off federal officials, and those trying to build roads or power lines risked being shot by tribals convinced that this was the work of the devil or a central government plot to colonize the province. Even today in these areas a radio is a novelty and the people are governed by medieval laws. Suspected criminals are tried by walking across burning coals; if their feet burn they are guilty.

The Soviet failure to establish a hold in Afghanistan was a big blow to Baluch nationalist dreams. But it did not damage support for the cause within the province – in the 1988 elections the Baluch Nationalist Alliance, headed by Nawab Bugti, emerged as the largest party. Ironically the BNA's main organizational strength comes from the Marxist Baluch Students' Organization, which advocated an end to the *sardari* system. Bugti refused to see any hypocrisy in him as the main beneficiary of the system heading such a group, commenting only, 'Everything in life is a contradiction – night and day are contradictions, as are happiness and weeping.'[6] The Baluch *sardars*, it seems, have come to the same realization as the feudal landlords in Sindh and Punjab, that in order for them to retain their family's local standing, they must have political power.

But unlike the feudals and their Frontier counterparts, some *sardars* were increasingly coming to the conclusion that the only way to retain support was to set up development projects themselves. Perhaps the most progressive of the tribal areas is that of the Magsis. As early as the 1930s the Magsi chief made education compulsory and built the area's first school, with jail sentences for fathers who failed to let their sons attend. According to Tariq Magsi, one of the present *sardar*'s family and himself an MP: 'Now there are more educated Magsis than uneducated. Many have gone abroad, there are 25,000 working in the Gulf and many have got government jobs.'[7]

This is a revolutionary exception in a province with only 2 per cent rural literacy, but the Magsi *sardars* have maintained their grip and tribal customs still reign supreme. Tariq Magsi said that one member of the *sardar*'s family must always be present in the area to sort out feuds: 'The biggest problem is killings caused by feuds over women, land, guns and cattle.' Blood must be avenged by blood – if the offender is absent, then his nearest relation is slain; if he is from a different tribe, then a section of that tribe must be killed. The system is called *ghairat* and Tariq Khetran, a *sardar*, explained: 'If someone challenges me I must murder them. For example, when I was seven my father was murdered by my cousin so my family killed my uncle and the *ghairat* was started.'[8] With the influx of sophisticated arms from Afghanistan there can be hundreds of deaths. Despite the violence, like the Pushtun chiefs the Baluch *sardars* argue that their system is efficient. Magsi claimed that he had on occasion decided 520 cases in two nights and 'can decide a murder case in one hour. In the courts it would take years and witnesses could be bribed to give false statements – with me they cannot because I would know. It is the *sardar*'s job to know all that goes on in his area.'

Known as the last of the great *sardars*, Nawab Bugti (who with his striking appearance has been described as looking like Sean Connery playing a tribal chief) loves to shock foreigners with his gory tales of feuds, told matter-of-factly in the polished tones of one educated at Aitchison College, Pakistan's Eton. 'Two years ago,' he told me as I took my first mouthful of an unidentifiable curry, 'I sorted out a feud in which 250 people had died in thirty years and people kept cutting each others' ears off.'9 Such tales did little for my appetite. Tribal law is so strict in Bugti areas that Bugti women still hang themselves if their husband as much as sees them with another man. If she fails to take this 'honourable' way out, the husband must kill them both.

Today even Nawab Bugti has come round to allowing developments that he previously blocked vociferously. The discovery of Asia's largest gas field at Sui in the Bugti area brought money into the district, making the tribesmen less bound to traditional allegiances. Since taking office Bugti had regularized labour at Sui, given considerable funds for Bugtis killed in encounters with law-enforcing agencies, and was building a road.

But the grand Nawab takes the line that if there is any development to be done, he is the one to do it, and in true Baluch tradition waged war with the federal government of Benazir Bhutto, whom he referred to disparagingly as 'the young lady'. Her administration, trying to carry out the ill-fated People's Development Programme through its own party organization in Baluchistan, had its bulldozers seized and was chased out of the province. The fertilizer, sewing machines and bicycles they were due to distribute, the Nawab said he would dump.

Baluchistan's past exclusion from state power and thus patronage is reflected in a literacy rate of only 6 per cent and a share in industrialization of less than 1 per cent, while per capita income is only half that of Punjab, despite the fact that it is the repository of most of Pakistan's mineral resources. The Sui gas fields, for example, provide 80 per cent of the country's gas, saving some $300 million a year in foreign exchange, yet royalties to Baluchistan are minimal, totalling just $1.2 million in 1980.10 Bugti's fight with the centre, particularly over the Sui gas royalties, resulted in the unlikely spectacle of Baluchistan supporting its traditional enemy, the Punjab, which under the leadership of Nawaz Sharif had for the first time joined the fight for provincial autonomy. Bugti insisted, however, 'I support myself,' and at a joint meeting with the IDA in Lahore to discuss 'the federal usurpation of provincial autonomy' he told his new allies:

> 'I am hungry, you've food in your belly
> I am naked, you are clothed
> I am homeless and you have a home
> How can we have the same view of life?'

The Nietzsche-loving Bugti seems to come from another age, far more suited astride a black stallion than in his government Mercedes, even if he had replaced the Pakistan flag with a BNA pennant. But he is a dying breed. Although the 1988 elections showed a return to voting for candidates because of who they are rather than what policies they favour, for the first time someone from Bugti's own tribe dared to stand against him. The life of the *sardars* in the 1990s is one of strange contradictions. While tribesmen still fall at their feet and touch the hems of their shirts, the new generation of *sardars* are more likely to be watching Michael Jackson videos and eating French fries than slaying foes in the mountains. But their power continues, because tribesmen have more faith in the tribal system than the government administration, where cases can take years to come to court and corruption is rife. Just as in the 1960s and 70s leading *sardars* embraced the locally popular Marxism in order to retain their support, now it seems that they will spearhead moves to progress though it will be of a limited nature, ensuring that the *sardar's* family is always one step ahead. Jan Jamali, a young tribal provincial MP, has twenty-four cousins at the country's top school, Aitchison. He explained: 'To keep our power our family must keep members in the army, government service and politics. Our name is no longer enough – we have to be able to deliver the goods.' Sardar Tariq Khetran, then provincial Minister for Food, had a constant flow of tribe members in his house and office whom he could never turn away but must be able to help. He agreed with his contemporary, Jan: 'We are the pragmatic *sardars*.'

'RESISTANCE TOURS LTD'

AFGHANISTAN – THE WAR ON THE BORDERS

'We told [the US] you screwed up in Korea and Vietnam; you better get it right this time.' (General Fazle Haq, on Pakistan's confidence that Washington would back their decision to support the Afghan resistance)[1]

'How many insurgencies have you covered?' drawled the moon-faced American who was, he said, on his fifth. Somewhat taken aback, I explained that this was my first, and immediately the faces which had turned round with interest at this newcomer in their midst swivelled back to the bar, leaving me staring at an array of backs hung with khaki jackets stained with varying degrees of faded blood – cherished marks of battle.

I didn't care. I had come from reporting knitting exhibitions in Birmingham and gas strikes in Coventry to join the ranks of these, the war correspondents of Peshawar's American Club – hangout for mercenaries, missionaries, spies, hacks and general misfits. We had all been drawn there by the war in neighbouring Afghanistan, which had made Pakistan America's most important ally in Asia and, then into its ninth year, taken 1.2 million lives and led to the migration of almost a third of Afghanistan's population, mostly into the frontier regions of Pakistan.

Arriving in Pakistan, I had gone straight to Peshawar, braving the Grand Trunk Road on a local bus service rather aptly named the Flying Coach, driven by a Pathan who was certainly floating on something. My excitement mounted as we weaved between lorries and oxen carts on Pakistan's crude equivalent of the M1 motorway, diverting across fields where bridges had collapsed, past mud settlements with names like 'Hope Village', which house some of the estimated 4 million Afghan refugees the country is host to. It was just weeks before the Soviet forces were due to begin their long awaited withdrawal from one of the world's poorest countries after nine years of occupation – the first time Soviet forces had lost a war since an attempt to conquer Poland in 1921. The bumpy road was packed with tarpaulin-covered trucks bearing weapons from the not-so-covert US arms pipeline to the Afghan resistance for their expected final push.

Of all the descriptions of the 2,000-year-old frontier town, arriving in Peshawar in the fading sun and rising dust, the one coined by the nineteenth-century British Commissioner, Sir Herbert Edwardes, 'Piccadilly of Central Asia', seemed far more appropriate than the literal translation 'valley of flowers'. As the headquarters of the Afghan resistance, its population has swelled from 200,000 to more than a million in the last decade. The Flying Coach terminates at the overspill of the old city under the shadow of the enormous cliff-like fort built by Babur, the first Mughul emperor, to keep out the wild tribesmen who nowadays have turned Peshawar into their capital city. Dumped there with my far too large suitcase, containing everything from a pink felt rabbit to a tape of Mahler's Fifth, it all seemed overwhelmingly foreign. The trees shading the Mughul gardens had been felled long ago by the Sikh emperor Ranjit Singh, and those remaining by the Afghan refugees for firewood 170 years later, and the flowers had long since died. Instead the city pulsated with exotic peoples from Lebanon to Mongolia, all of whom seemed to be selling things to each other.

Like Churchill and Kipling and many fellow-countrymen before me, a love affair had begun in which I would spend days walking through the labyrinth of the old city, forever finding something new. Behind the huge grinning sets of false teeth advertising dentists I discovered a tiny courtyard overlooked by an exquisite carved balcony from which Juliet could have called her Romeo, though she might have been whipped had she done so. Hours could be happily whiled away in the teashops of Qissa Khawani, the picturesquely named 'Storytellers' Bazaar', where passing merchants and tribesmen from the hills have swapped tales for centuries, joined now by Afghan guerrillas. Out of the jungle of brass pots and pans one day a small wide-eyed boy emerged, and took me by the hand to a bird market full of wooden cages. And the greatest find of all – up a narrow alley lined with garlands of paper money for weddings, a surprisingly Hindu custom, across a bridge over something which looked and smelled suspiciously like a sewer, and into a rickety hotel. As I mounted the fragile stairs the most indescribably enchanting music was coming from behind a closed door on the top floor. Inside huge tears were rolling down the pitted cheeks of an old man in a yellow turban. This face, which looked as though it had survived a thousand storms, could not withstand the humbling strains of the voice of the chubby-cheeked boy singing of love and torment:

> 'Do not ask my sky-high mountain peaks
> Their stones are suffering
> Leave the agonized trees alone
> Avoid the flowers, their boughs grief-stricken
> Do not ask the gentle breeze, do not ask.'[2]

The destruction of Afghanistan and the deaths of its sons and lovers provided most evocative material for the songs of the Pushtu music bazaar, where grown men weep over intoxicating melodies conjured from the yellowed keys of a strange box-like instrument by a gipsy musician.

It was not just the sounds of the Pushtu music bazaar that the war over the borders had affected. Signs of war were visible everywhere in Peshawar. Men on crutches and children with stumps of legs and arms hobble through the bazaar, sprayed with mud by Japanese Pajero jeeps containing Afghan commanders and their bodyguards *en route* to negotiate some lucrative arms deal. Suzuki vans packed with *mujaheddin* yelling 'Allah-o-Akbar' (God is Great) race along the Khyber road to the battlefront, ignoring the constant scream of ambulance sirens bringing back the maimed. Huge anti-aircraft guns guard the airport from which in 1961 the hapless Gary Powers set off in a U2 spy plane on his ill-fated State Department Mission, to be shot down over the Soviet Union. Frequent bomb blasts rock the city – apparently the work of agents from KHAD, the Afghan secret police. The Great Game relived, there were eyes and spies everywhere creating a smog of distrust – a casual word here against one of the resistance parties and another Afghan would disappear. Merchants from far-off republics with picturebook names, Tajiks and Uzbeks, hawk carpets and lapis outside the gates of Deans Hotel, in the fading British glory of which Churchill once stayed and where I had made my temporary home.

Peshawar is a city that feeds on rumours, and within my first week I had heard first that the Afghan town of Jalalabad was to be attacked, then that it was not, then that it was; the garrison of Khost was about to fall, then it was not, then it was; the Soviet troops were not really leaving; the Indians were flying Afghan planes, all according to 'very reliable sources' and not a word true. This misinformation was so popular that the US Embassy put together a situation report, 'sitrep', each week mainly consisting of it, and had funded an Afghan Media Resource Centre to make up more.

It felt like a journey into hyper-reality. A British diplomat had to my amazement offered to arrange my trip into Afghanistan with the *mujaheddin*, though warning me to take my own cup – 'One never knows what one might catch'. I thought sharing a dirty cup probably one of the lesser dangers in a war zone and ignored his advice. Driving back from the American Club, where I had gone for tips on 'going inside', bullets whizzed over the top of the rickshaw. Two groups from opposing tribes were firing at each other across the Khyber Road. I tried to ignore that and the well-armed guard who had appeared outside my room, checked to see if there really was a secret microphone behind the picture, and wrote my mother a postcard about the charming view. Well, if you knew it was there you could imagine you could see the hills of the Khyber Pass.

The sense of unreality was heightened when one evening I returned to find a bunch of turban-clad black-bearded *mujaheddin* polishing their Kalashnikovs on the veranda outside my room. They looked like a Hollywood rent-a-crew but were in fact the real thing, come to sort out arrangements for my first trip 'inside'. The previous day I had been to the headquarters of Jamiat Islami, one of the seven Peshawar-based resistance parties, where after initial reluctance because of my sex, and copious quantities of watery green tea, they had agreed to set something up. My evening visitors had come to inform me that we would be leaving for the border at dawn and advise me on what to take. I began to feel as though I was booking a holiday: 'Resistance Tours Ltd' — the ultimate in war-zone trekking trips for journalists, soldiers of fortune and public schoolboys eager for adventure in their year off.

In the city's Banana Republic store I had already bought a standard US army sleeping bag, canvas rucksack, and not yet bloodstained khaki jacket. These were supplied to the *mujaheddin* as part of American support and immediately sold off in the bazaars — inside Afghanistan I only ever saw them on Western journalists. Dressed in my baggy fawn Pathan *shalwar kamiz*, my hair screwed into a floppy wool Chitrali cap, thin wool *petou* or shawl across my shoulders, I thought I looked quite the part but the commander was not happy. My fair hair, pale skin and green eyes would be an instant giveaway to the Pakistani borderguards.

After a long discussion and much rearranging of my shawl and cap and smearing of dirt across my face, it was decided that there was no way I could ever be mistaken for an Afghan guerrilla. I did not think that this discovery would adversely affect the rest of my life but for the moment it meant I would have to cross the border disguised as an Afghan refugee. I was rushed across town to the Afghan bazaar by the canal and a shopkeeper was awoken from his slumbers to open up his small shack and sell me a huge shroud-like garment called a *burqa*. In the flickering light of the candle produced by the eager salesman the shop was like something out of a horror movie, the walls hung with these grotesque pleated tents with sinister embroidered grilles for the eyes.

It was even worse wearing the surprisingly heavy *burqa* — a living hell in which the majority of Pakistani women and many Afghans spend their lives, it is like being trapped inside a sauna, with life reduced to fragments of passing scenery through the small grille. But the commander was still not satisfied. At 5ft 9in I was considerably taller than the average Afghan, and my pink socks and sneakers were clearly visible under the *burqa*. Eventually plastic flipflops were agreed upon, and a small boy was produced to hold my hand and add to the authenticity. Solemnly I was rechristened Lela and presented with my *mujaheddin* survival kit — a packet containing a few boiled sweets, some oral rehydration powders, a small waterproof plaster and two antibiotic pills. We piled into the back of a pick-up and were off towards the hills, which rippled in the morning heat.

I soon gave up trying to piece together the scenery through the grille, which seemed to correspond more with my nose than my eyes. Over the next eight hours we switched from pick-up to bus to ancient jeep, like goons in a spy movie — a bad B version. The route was through Pakistan's tribal areas, which are off limits to foreigners, and each checkpoint successfully negotiated brought a sigh of relief from the group, who lost no pleasure in telling me that they often had journalists arrested. I concentrated on not noticing the bumpy road through the hard wooden seats and the blazing 40° heat turning my *burqa* into a furnace. Trapped inside the *burqa* was like having no identity, and I struggled to make myself heard by the Afghans, who seemed intent on ignoring me. It was like sitting on a London tube with a blanket covering one's head and trying to strike up a conversation with fellow passengers. Eventually Nakib, a weak-looking character with a droopy moustache, who had been assigned my 'husband' and was thus responsible for my protection, took pity on me. Through a laborious combination of my muffled mutterings, waved hand actions and drawings in my notebook, I had my first Pushtu lesson. For some reason I never understood, Nakib insisted on teaching me 'How big is your goat?' — not an expression I ever found particularly useful but perhaps some obscure Afghan joke.

Eventually the air cooled and the protesting van with a broken axle, which was our last and least suitable vehicle, laboured up almost vertical tracks, occasionally overhanging an edge and forcing us to reverse. From the *burqa* the view was alarming — all I could glimpse was patches of sky in the wrong place and steep drops. Finally we went through the last checkpoint — we had reached the border post of Terimangal, its one street crawling with *mujaheddin* loading sophisticated arms on to donkeys and camels. It was rather like looking down into an ants' nest, and once through I could throw off my *burqa* and look around. What bliss! We were surrounded by rugged chocolate-box mountains, capped with snow, though the once lush pine forests had been stripped for firewood. On the other side where the sun was disappearing was Afghanistan. I could not help sharing the excitement of the Afghans and the emotion when Habib, the surly commander, turned to me and said: 'Afghanistan – the most beautiful country in the world.'

I remembered his words that evening while lying in my sleeping bag on the roof of the staging post, staring at millions of stars. There had never seemed so many or so close – the Afghans say there is one for every victim of the war. But if Afghanistan was one of the world's most beautiful countries, it was also one of the poorest. Infant mortality is one in five, literacy less than 10 per cent, and even before the war in 1979 average life expectancy was only forty-one. Four-fifths of the population live at subsistence levels. Yet stacked against the walls of the shack that was our home for the night were some of the world's most sophisticated weapons. The war had brought heat-seeking Stinger missiles, radio-communications and satellite maps to a people most of whom had never even seen a transistor.

There were several other journalists staying at the post, which was the first stop for guerrillas from the Jamiat party *en route* to the battle zone and a re-supply centre for commanders deep inside Afghanistan. I was glad not to be the only one having difficulty eating the greasy goat stew with my hand, and was interested to work out the rationale behind the pecking order for who was served first – as the only woman I was served last. If anyone had brought their own cup they did not produce it. After dinner it was war games. As strategy was discussed, using matchboxes and an ashtray made from the cover of a Stinger, for a planned attack on a Soviet convoy near the town of Jaji, it became clear that no one had a clue quite what they were to do. The commander waved the radio about outside in an apparent effort to contact other groups, but he might as well have sent smoke signals – the set had no batteries. One of his men was firing rockets at a tree in an unsuccessful attempt to gather firewood. I began to understand why in nine years the *mujaheddin* had been unable to capture a major town, particularly when we were warned not to walk away from the hut because there were hostile *mujaheddin* groups nearby.[3] Weren't they all on the same side?

High up on the exposed mountainside we snuggled into our sleeping bags, listening to the whoosh and thud of rockets in the distance, until we were driven in by the icy wind, then out again by the plague of giant fleas into whose territory we were intruding. It was a short night – time has a different meaning in Afghanistan, where the sun and moon are autocratic, there being no electricity outside the main cities. Even the centuries are different – the Afghans are on 1368 (after Prophet rather than after Christ). Our early rising was dictated by the first prayers of the day – a strangely disciplined affair – rows of pyjama-clad warriors of God prostrating themselves on the mud roof, a sight I was to see again and again even in the midst of battle. This was more than a guerrilla insurgency against an occupying force – it was *jihad*, holy war, where the cry of 'Allah-o-Akbar' could invoke as much fighting spirit as that induced by drugs in some armies.

Breakfast arrived in a cloth bundle, unwrapped to contain strips of long stretchy *nan* bread, still warm, to be dipped in goats' cream and washed down with the already ubiquitous green tea, drunk with boiled sweets because there was no sugar. A strangely effeminate fighting force, the *mujaheddin* sat around preening themselves in pocket mirrors or snuffbox lids, which seem an essential part of their uniform, snipping nostril hair, drawing on eyeliner and greasing down moustaches. Some went for walks, often hand-in-hand, picking yellow flowers to wear in their caps or simply to hold. At that time I found this amusing, and not at all the image of the heroic freedom fighters I had had from media reports back in England. It took me several trips before I realized that to the *mujaheddin* flowers growing in their country is a sign of peace and hope. Treasuring beautiful flowers was no sign of weakness – they have values we have forgotten.

But that first morning on the edges of Afghanistan I had little patience with the lethargic guerrillas I seemed to have ended up with. They refused to move until we agreed to hire a taxi – the last thing one expects to find in war-torn Afghanistan, where even before Soviet jets started bombing there were very few roads. This taxi was a pick-up with a broken axle and coated in dried mud for camouflage. It also had something called a 'Computer Laser Disco', which consisted of a string of fairylights around the broken windscreen that flashed at not quite the same speed as the discordant music. Afghans love gadgets, and there was another one too – a device for letting us know when we were going uphill, which seemed just as unnecessary.

We bumped along for a while until the track ran out, then walked for hours, passing destroyed or abandoned villages, occasionally finding blackberries along the wayside to eat. At the top of a mountain we came across a small fly-ridden puddle of water. Next to it was a guerrilla wrapped in his *petou*, shivering, obviously dying of malaria. The commander filled a rusty tin can with some of the water and presented it to me. It was a difficult moment – I was desperately thirsty and my lips were already parched and cracked. It could be hours before we saw any more water. But I had no desire to contract hepatitis or malaria or any of the other nasty things no doubt lurking in the muddy pool. I compromised, taking a sip to moisten my lips then discreetly spitting out the rest, not guessing that on later trips I would be desperate enough to drain such an infested pool.

The next day I was given a donkey, much to my chagrin. Not only did I want to show that I could climb as many mountains as the guerrillas, but I have never got on with donkeys since one bit me at an early age at a circus. This particular mule was laden with Kalashnikovs, rocket launchers and mortars, so was hardly a comfortable ride, nor did I feel particularly secure knowing I was sitting on several pounds of explosives. Somewhat bruised when we reached the next staging mount, I refused to remount the beast, to our mutual relief.

For several days we saw no signs of fighting, though occasionally a shout would ring out and we would fling ourselves on the ground as Soviet jets flew over, shattering the stillness. Was the earth trembling or were we? The throb of fighter engines seemed to be the only sound in this country of silence, with none of the background hum of traffic and lawnmowers and modern living. Occasionally we met other travellers and, if they were not of a hostile group (as surprisingly many seemed to be), swapped news. They would try to outdo each other telling fabulous tales of shooting down helicopters with Lee Enfield rifles or attacking tanks with sticks and stones, reminding me of the TV cameraman who had covered the war from the start and told me, 'For ten years the fighting was always in the next valley or the last town – anywhere but where I was.'

But there were shocking reminders that this was more than a *Boys' Own* adventure. Stopping at a cluster of small huts on a hillside in the hope of some *chai*, we came across a tragic scene –

the body of a young man killed in action stretched out on a slab of wood, black moustache and black eyes on a chalk-white face, hands clasped on his chest. The *shaheed* or war martyr was surrounded by his family, a small boy at his head desperately chewing his lip and trying not to cry in front of his weeping mother. Like many boys his age, the war had prematurely made him the head of the family. Despite all the Western aid money there were few medical facilities inside Afghanistan, and for those wounded in battle it was a long and dangerous way to the hospitals of Peshawar, requiring valuable manpower. Those badly injured were more often left to die, their deaths marked by narrow slate graves under tattered coloured flags, small triangles of cloth fluttering in the wind. And for every death there were five maimed.

The closest we came to danger on that first trip was in the taxi, driving past a camp belonging to one of the other parties, that of Abdur Sayyaf. Bullets whizzed past our ears and we ducked down on the floor. They were after our arms to add to their already vast stocks, which could be seen inside the heavily guarded walls. To my surprise I could see Africans and Arabs wandering around inside the compound – Sayyaf's party is probably the richest, receiving large funds from the Wahabis and the Arab world, and its impressive publicity machine draws in recruits from Palestine to Algeria.

We escaped by handing over some arms, lightening our load somewhat. By the time we reached the mountains overlooking Jaji we were ill-prepared for battle, more rockets having been traded *en route* in a dubious exchange with other guerrillas in which we seemed to come off worse, though once we got eggs for dinner, which made a welcome change from our staple diet of *nan* in the morning and rice in the evening. Now finally nearing our destination, the men seemed strangely reluctant to go on. All sorts of excuses were proffered – that the route was mined, that they were tired and, incredibly, that they might get hurt. It was a fitful night filled with the boom of rockets and the whirr of engines, scouring the sky trying to pick out plane lights among the zillions of stars. Vaguely I was aware of morning prayers, then as the sky lightened I slept deeper, dreaming I was on a ship.

When I awoke I realized that what I had thought was the crash of the sea was in fact tank-fire. Panicking, I stared at my watch and saw that it was 8 a.m. – we were supposed to have set off two hours before. For a moment I thought I had been left behind, but the hut was thick with hashish smoke and sleeping *mujaheddin*. Having overdone the *hookah* pipe they were hard to rouse, but eventually they came to and after what seemed an interminable wait while moustaches were preened, tea made (though there was no bread left to fill the gnawing hole in my stomach), and Kalashnikovs cleaned, we set off, climbing to the top of the mountain. With the aid of high-powered binoculars, we could see far below some smoke and just make out a burning tank. A few rockets shot across the valley somewhat unenthusiastically, and men could be seen running about the streets. It was the tail-end of battle and the Soviet convoy we had come to ambush had passed through – we were too late.

Sensing my annoyance, the commander dug deep in his pocket and produced a dark green foil packet marked US army rations. I pulled it open to reveal cold baked beans – a food that could not be more alien to the *mujaheddin*, and they watched incredulously as I wolfed them down. It seemed an awfully long and hazardous journey to make just to eat one of my least favourite convenience foods, and I half expected a beaming adman to appear proclaiming, 'And all because the lady loved . . .'

Back in Terimangal base some days later, more journalists had arrived. There was even an American TV crew, so the guerrillas felt compelled to lay something on. We were taken to a launch pad, where they fired off several rockets after borrowing my penknife to cut off the detonator. We all took pictures and looked suitably impressed, and the television reporter did a dramatic piece to camera – viewers, it seemed, would never know what side of the border we were on. I returned to Peshawar relieved to have suffered nothing worse than a sunburnt nose, but knowing that I had seen little of the real war where heroes – not media stars – are made.

In the American Club back in Peshawar I asked what had happened to the romantic heroes I had read about, the brave men from the mountains driving back the might of the Red Army with their bare hands. Arguing that the Soviets were leaving as much because of domestic pressure as their inability to shake off the guerrillas, I was pounced upon by journalists from right-wing American papers and branded a communist. No answers there, so I wandered round some of the ninety-five Western aid agencies that had sprung up in Peshawar, creating an almost entirely new suburb called University Town. There was everything from sewing projects for refugees, cross-border road-building projects to facilitate the transfer of aid (read arms), olive-growing schemes, to camouflaged ambulances and sheds full of artificial limbs, manned by earnest young things, debs doing something worthy, and loud Americans. Many were front organizations more interested in intelligence-gathering than in good works. Peshawar during the time of the Soviet withdrawal had one of the world's highest concentrations of spies – from Mossad to the CIA they were all there. The Islamic world was well represented too, the Muslim Brotherhood and other organizations setting up hospitals and schools from where they could spread the word, often upsetting the Afghans, whose faith is far more tradition-laden.

One resistance leader with no time for tribal customs was Gulbuddin Hekmatyar. The then chairman of the seven-party Islamic Unity of Afghan Mujaheddin, known as the Alliance, which had been created under Pakistani pressure to show a semblance of unity and make arms distribution easier, he seemed the obvious person to talk to. According to the US, his party, Hezb-i-Islami, contained the most effective fighters and thus, on the principle 'we give most to those who kill most Russians', was the recipient of the lion's share of arms, at one stage getting as much as 40 per cent. It was hard to be objective about the man. His party had a ruthless secret police organization, gathering intelligence kept on computer, and according to a former refugee commissioner running jails inside some of the camps. The few Afghan intellectuals who had remained in Pakistan said they had received threats from him and believed him to have ordered the assassination of Professor Majrooh, while British intelligence suspected him for the death of Andy Skryopski, a British cameraman who was killed while inside with Hezb.

With such thoughts in mind, the setting for our first meeting was perfect. Near the railway line in University Town, on the corner of a leafy street, is a red-brick fortress topped with evilly barbed wire and with lookout posts on the corners from which Afghans with AK47s scoured the streets. This was the newly built Alliance headquarters, where, after depositing my shoes, having my bag checked and passing through a corridor in which gaggles of Afghans were sitting on their haunches drinking green tea, I was taken into a room with a telex where day after day pages of accounts of wildly exaggerated battlefront activity were sent all over the world. A slimy assistant of the great man introduced himself, corrected me to say Engineer Hekmatyar rather than plain Mister (he read engineering at Kabul University and failed), and gave my clothing the once over. I had been in Peshawar long enough to hear tales of Hekmatyar's threats to women whom he considered not properly dressed (i.e. an inch of flesh showing), and his activities in throwing acid into the faces of unveiled women when he was a student. Afghan women in Peshawar trying to be independent lived in fear of him. Tajwar Kakar, a former headmistress who spent years in Kabul's notorious Pul-i-Charki prison for her work in the resistance before escaping to Pakistan in 1983, where she set up a school for girls, was finally forced to emigrate to Australia after repeated death threats from Hekmatyar, warning her against teaching women that they need not wear burqas.[4]

After having another shawl put round my shoulders I was finally admitted into the presence of the most ruthless of the Peshawar Seven. He seemed surprisingly gentle, but under his black turban his deep-set eyes were impossible to read, and his long fingers played uneasily with a string of black worry beads. This man did not want to speak to me and my questions were answered dispassionately through an interpreter until I asked about foreign interference. Speaking fluent English, he raved about a joint British and Soviet plot to bring back the former king Zahir Shah and 'cheat the resistance of their victory'. This was a familiar theme in interviews to come, and its hysterical note belied Hekmatyar's otherwise controlled calmness.

Hekmatyar, as the only leader with a shred of charisma and the darling of Pakistan's military, was intensely disliked by the other party heads, one of whom, the outwardly mild Professor Mojadiddi, reportedly pulled a gun on him in an Alliance meeting. Since the creation of the Alliance in 1980 its unity had always been paper-thin, most often splitting 4–3 between the fundamentalists such as Hezb, favouring an Islamic Republic, and the moderates such as Mojadiddi's ANLF, which want a traditional royalist state. There is little love lost between them, particularly when it was leaked that Hekmatyar's commanders had been instructed to stay back during battle to let the other parties take the brunt of attack, then move in for the booty and claim credit for victory.[5] The lack of unity was arguably an advantage in fighting the Soviet troops, because it meant that there was no centre of command that could be taken out and no way of predicting what the guerrillas would do next – they themselves did not know. But it was to prove disastrous when it came to trying to wrest back control of towns from the Afghan army once the Soviets had left, as the ill-fated attack on Jalalabad was to show.

An early symptom of the impending problems came with a visit to Alikhel, a garrison not far from the Pakistan border which had been seized by the *mujaheddin* in late May 1988 after the Soviets had drawn back. The streets were littered with arms, and unable to decide how to distribute them, commanders from the seven parties were jealously guarding piles of missiles and Kalashnikovs, using megaphones to warn people to keep away. Fighting would occasionally break out between the groups. Two months later, when the guerrillas captured Kalat, the capital of Zabul, there was so much inter-*mujaheddin* fighting over loot that the Afghan army were able to take it back and have held the town ever since.

The lack of unity among the resistance was an inevitable consequence of Pakistan's divide and rule strategy. Major resistance figures such as Hekmatyar and Burhanuddin Rabbani had been funded by Pakistan since 1973, when Daoud took power in Kabul in a coup which many believed paved the way for the communist takeover in 1978. They and several others from the Kabul University-based Islamic Movement fled to Pakistan and were allowed to set up headquarters in Peshawar. Ali Bhutto used them in retaliation to Daoud's training of Baluchi insurgents, and in an effort to force him to recognize the Durand Line as the border. The line had been drawn up somewhat arbitrarily in 1893 by Sir Mortimer Durand to divide the British and Afghan empires, the border previously having been just somewhere in the peaks. But it also divided Pathan tribes, and the tribesmen, who recognized nobody's sovereignty and to date wander across the border at will, thought of themselves as Pathans first and thus raised the cry for an independent homeland – Pushtunistan.

Daoud had always been a strong advocate of the Pushtunistan issue, believing that cities like Peshawar and Quetta should again be part of Afghanistan as they were before British times. Attempts to stage armed insurrections in Afghan towns in 1975 collapsed, and Hekmatyar fell out with the more moderate Rabbani, leaving to set up his own party. After the summer of 1979, as fighting in southern Afghanistan intensified and refugees began pouring into Pakistan, huge numbers of organizations were set up, mostly on tribal basis, by leading Pushtun families, who had for centuries been Afghanistan's king-makers and were not about to surrender control to people like Hekmatyar, of whom they asked condescendingly, 'Who is his father?'

By mid 1980, according to General Fazle Haq, there were 170 groups operating, most of whom Pakistan had no control over.[6] To 'eliminate the confusion', all but Islamic parties were banned, and it was announced that the large amount of military and financial support which had begun flowing from Saudis and the new Reagan administration would go only to the then six members of the Alliance. To guarantee support for these organizations it was made mandatory for refugees to join an Alliance party in order to be eligible for rations. With 2 million refugees arrived in camps by 1982, and 3.27 million registered by 1988,[7] this provided a massive constituency. Sayyaf was brought in to head the Alliance as a neutral figurehead. But he soon saw his own opportunity for power, and on a trip to Saudi and Kuwait he lined himself up a large amount of private funding and thus the seventh party was born.

These days the resistance leaders live in much greater style than the one room Hekmatyar, Rabbani and Ahmat Shah Massoud shared back in 1973. Some own property abroad, and in Peshawar run huge complexes like Sayyafabad, an Arab-funded well-provided township for about 40,000 people just outside Peshawar. Despite all the trappings, the 'Unmagnificent Seven' are still reliant on the backing of the Pakistani military, who made them leaders and could as easily unmake them. The only party with any ideological basis is Hezb – the others rely on regional following, such as

Rabbani's Jamiat Islami, the only party led by a non-Pushtun, or spiritual, such as the National Islamic Front (NIFA) of 'Pir' Sayed Ahmed Gilani, a former Peugeot salesman who claims to be a direct descendant of the Prophet but looks more like a character from a cigar advert.

Although all the parties claimed immense followings, none of them really wanted elections which could disprove this. Given the distorted nature of their support through their respective access to arms and money, and the atmosphere of paranoia in the refugee camps where people were frightened to speak out against the leaders, it was impossible to judge the extent of support for the parties, but further into Afghanistan fighting tended to be localized tribal warfare with *mujaheddin* in traditional tribal rather than party groupings. 'These parties are just as alien to us as Najib's PDPA' was a frequent refrain in refugee camps, and a survey by Professor Majrooh in 1987 among 2,000 refugees found that less than 1 per cent of those polled would want one of the seven leaders to rule Afghanistan.

The resistance leaders were well aware that much of their support would last only as long as they could provide the next Stinger, commanders regularly changing party when no arms were forthcoming, as they too would lose the support of their men if they could not supply weapons. How US and Saudi arms were distributed was left entirely to Pakistan's Inter Services Intelligence Directorate (ISI), giving the organization complete control over the relative power of the seven parties, none of which had been allowed to grow too strong. When, like the cleric and former MP Nabbi Mohammadi, one leader started controlling large areas, their arms supply would be slashed as his was in 1981. To prevent leaders speaking against each other and preserve mutual suspicion, President Zia always saw two at a time, and to maintain control a senior ISI officer was always present at meetings of the Supreme Council of the Alliance, usually a Brigadier who used various names but was known by Executive members as the Kingmaker. To put the leaders in an even weaker position, ISI built up its own network of 400 commanders, whom it supplied directly in return for carrying out specific operations. After the death of Zia and General Akhtar Rehman, who had set up the ISI Afghan operation, ISI found the Alliance far harder to control, and sometimes

General Hamid Gul, the head of ISI from 1987, could not hide his
frustration. A member of the Supreme Council told me, 'He
would insult us in front of the other leaders and say we don't just
control you we control your commanders.'[8]

The Soviet invasion of Afghanistan on Christmas Eve 1979 to
back up the PDPA government had presented a great opportunity
for Zia, and he used it to the full. Relations between Pakistan and
the US were at a low point – aid which had been suspended
because of Bhutto's refusal to drop the nuclear programme, and
reinstated when Zia took power, was cut off after Bhutto's execution, and matters had been worsened by the burning down of the
US Embassy in Islamabad in November 1979. But Washington
was anxious to check Soviet expansionism, and with the fall of the
Shah of Iran was left with Pakistan as its only ally in the region.
The CIA maintained strong links with the Pakistan military for
intelligence on the Gulf. General Fazle Haq, Zia's strong-man and
then Governor of the Frontier, had no doubts that if Pakistan
declared all-out support for the resistance the US would back
them, despite what he describes as the 'quivering of the Foreign
Office in Islamabad', and claimed that even before the occupation
the CIA was secretly transferring money to fund the rebels. He
said: 'I told Brezinski [Carter's hawkish US National Security
Adviser] you screwed up in Vietnam and Korea you better get it
right this time.' Within a week of the invasion Brezinski had
publicly affirmed that Washington would support Pakistan with
military force if necessary.

But it was under the Reagan administration that the cause was
really taken up in the US, and in the autumn of 1981 a six-year
package of $3.2 billion economic and military aid was agreed,
making Pakistan the third largest recipient of American aid. US
support not only gave Zia international legitimacy but the vast aid
programme helped shore up the country's economy and supply
sophisticated toys such as F-16 advanced fighter jets to the army,
who he admitted were his only political constituency. Proxy war
against the Soviets in Afghanistan fitted exactly with the Reagan
doctrine as a cheap and effective way to 'give the Reds a bloody
nose' in revenge for Vietnam. Annual US aid to the *mujaheddin*
leapt from tens of millions to hundred of millions by the mid
1980s, making it the largest covert operation outside Vietnam.[9]

The US were not the only supporters – China and Iran were also sending aid. A separate secret fund had been set up in 1981 by William Casey, the CIA Director, for sympathetic governments to contribute to. The biggest donors were the Saudis, who matched US aid dollar for dollar.

In fact, until 1985 when they started sending in Swiss Oerlikon cannon, British blowpipes and US heat-seeking Stinger missiles, changing the whole nature of the war, the whole US operation was supposed to be secret, while despite the vast amount of evidence including training camps on Pakistani soil, Zia regularly denied that Pakistan was helping the resistance. In an elaborate attempt to disguise the CIA's involvement, which was known worldwide, the US obtained Soviet arms from Poland and Egypt and even set up factories copying Soviet weapons, enabling the *mujaheddin* to claim that all their arms were 'captured' from the Soviet invaders.[10]

The US desire to pretend that the war was a purely internal Afghan affair played straight into Zia's hands, as it meant Pakistan, through the ISI, had to be used as middleman. Because the operation was covert there was no paperwork involved, and thus extraordinarily little accountability, enabling many Pakistani generals to get rich and buy ranches in Australia. In between arriving in Karachi, where customs clearance was waived, and reaching the arms camps of the Frontier and Baluchistan, entire truckloads would be diverted, much ending up in Sindh with disastrous consequences for the level of local violence. A Foreign Office official told me that 60 per cent of the arms were going astray, a figure also cited by the Federation for American Afghan Action in 1987, which claimed that not only were Pakistani generals siphoning off millions but also some had been illegally diverted to the Contras in Nicaragua.[11] Not only was the Pakistani army swapping its old-fashioned equipment for the sophisticated hardware supplied to the *mujaheddin*, but it was allegedly selling off some of the best to its allies. After the explosion of the Ojheri camp arms dump, in which almost $100 million worth of rockets and missiles intended for the *mujaheddin* rained down on the twin cities of Rawalpindi and Islamabad, causing thousands of casualties, a government report, never released, said it was the result of deliberate sabotage by ISI because they did not want the US audit team, due to

arrive that week, to discover that some Stinger missiles had been
sold off.

US attempts in recent years to introduce more accountability
and control over distribution failed. In 1989 arms stores were kept
locked for months by ISI refusing to release supplies to the *mujaheddin*
until the CIA stopped trying to interfere. In 1988 Zia, anxious
over what would happen when the arms supplies dried up, had
rallied vociferously against the signing of the Geneva Accord,
which paved the way for the withdrawal of the 115,000 Soviet
troops, calling it 'a figleaf'.[12] General Hamid Gul had members of
Pakistan's Parliament in tears when he gave an impassioned appeal
against signing the agreement, which would, he said, amount to 'a
selling-out of the *mujaheddin*'. For Zia, supporting the *mujaheddin*
was more than just a question of personal survival and forming a
vital block against the formation of a hostile Moscow–Kabul–Delhi
axis. It was a personal mission through which he saw not only the
chance to end the Pushtunistan issue and thus secure Pakistan's
eastern border, but the possibility of an Islamic confederation
comprising Iran, Pakistan, Afghanistan and perhaps even Turkey
and the Soviet Muslim republics, which would form a strong
counterweight to India. Zia was not being romantic when he said,
'I want to pray in the mosques of Kabul.'

The Afghan leader needed to assist in these pan-Islamic ambitions was one who shared Zia's orthodox ideology, who owed all
to Pakistan and was not part of the traditional tribal structures of
Afghanistan, such as the royalist Durranis who when in power
would 'always expand to the West'. The obvious candidate was
Hekmatyar, and from the start there was little doubt that he was
Pakistan's puppet, whom the increasingly Islamicized army would
most like to see in power in Kabul. General Fazle Haq claimed
credit for creating Hekmatyar: 'We told the US you need a worm
to catch a fish and we can provide one. We felt Hekmatyar could
field to the maximum belt and, despite his indiscretions, he delivered the goods.' But Haq admitted Hekmatyar could not be
trusted: 'He's the sort of man who would share your bed then slit
your throat.'[13]

It was no coincidence that Hekmatyar floated the idea of an
Islamic confederation in press conferences and, according to very
senior ISI sources, was the only one of the seven leaders to have

signed a paper pledging that if in power he would respect the Durand line. Initially the US administration had apparently blindly accepted ISI assurances that Hezb was the most effective party, despite the fact that in no province was it the strongest force. But in the face of increasingly conflicting evidence, mostly from press reports, questions began to be raised. Moreover, the US was uncomfortable at Zia's talk of confederation and extending the *jihad*, and just before his death he admitted that the State Department had been 'lobbying at every level for a shift in the balance of support towards the moderates'. Many believed Zia's refusal to budge to be a factor in his mysterious death. If so, his assassin was unsuccessful, for his policy objectives were shared by many within ISI such as General Gul, who was just as religious and complained to me: 'The West think they can use the fundamentalists as cannon fodder – they were all right to win the war but not to run the future Afghanistan. Well, we will not allow that.'[14] The policy did not change despite US claims to the contrary. One US diplomat said, 'The conductor may be dead but the orchestra plays on.' And the playing if anything became more vigorous after Zia's death – ISI unsure of what the future might hold, became desperate to install Hekmatyar in power.

The plan was for Hekmatyar to be in the forefront of a capture of a major town, after which they predicted that the rest of the cities would fall like dominoes. Plans to attack Jalalabad in June 1988 had fallen through, so in September Hekmatyar was sent to the south-western city of Kandahar, laden down with arms and money like Father Christmas to persuade the local *mujaheddin* to fight. Kandahar was selected because of the weakness of the regime in the area. But they could not have chosen a worse place – Afghanistan's second city is a Durrani stronghold, naturally suspicious of this 'urban upstart' and where more than anywhere the Peshawar parties had no relevance and the leaders other than Pir Gilani scorned as 'Made in Peshawar'. Because of their independent nature, Kandahari commanders tended to receive far less arms and aid and in many cases maintained better relations with the city authorities than the Peshawar groups. They were fighting to maintain their traditional way of life, and Hekmatyar's orthodox Islam was just as foreign to them as Najib's communism.

The timing was bad too – although Soviet forces had just

vacated the area, *mujaheddin* morale had been badly shaken by an operation on Argandab, a small orchard town north of Kandahar, where taking a small post had cost 200 dead and caused 30,000 civilians to flee. The fruit crop on which Argandab depends for its livelihood had been almost entirely destroyed. Dad Mohammad, a regional commander, told me that the operation had been carried out only after large payments from Sayyaf's party: 'None of us wanted the attack, but one of the political parties sent money to pay people to fight. I do not call that *jihad*.'

This sort of conflict between commanders in the field and the parties in exile was symptomatic of a growing rift. The outside leaders believed impressive victories to be necessary to prove their worth, whereas field commanders, often reliant on local goodwill for supplies and shelter, were reluctant to risk further civilian lives and property. In Kandahar commanders of all parties had grouped together to form a *shura*, which had agreed that rather than a full-scale attack there should be a gradual siege, replacing the civilian population with guerrillas and cutting off supply routes to government forces. But even this strategy aroused civilian resentment because it resulted in scarcities and rising prices.

During my visit to Kandahar in September 1988 the real reason that Hekmatyar was there emerged. The Governor of the province had approached nationalist forces and tribal leaders to negotiate a surrender. ISI was terrified that the local commanders would agree and then call for the return of the king to this royalist stronghold. Peace on these grounds was totally unacceptable to ISI because it would inevitably cut out the fundamentalists, such as Hekmatyar, whom they had been building up as their future security. Ten years support would be lost. King Zahir Shah would not only harbour expansionist tendencies but would be hostile to Pakistan, which had refused visas to members of his family and prevented the holding of a *loi jirga* (traditional tribal assembly) among refugees, fearing it would demand his return.

Although Hekmatyar was unable to convince the Kandahari commanders to attack, he managed to block peace efforts by creating through money and arms a second Kandahar *shura* which, it seemed, was more directed against the original one than against the Afghan army. There is a Pushtu saying that you can never buy an Afghan, only rent him, but by the time the new Kandahar *shura* had lost interest in fighting, so, it seemed, had the Governor in surrendering and to date the situation is a stalemate.

I was disappointed that even the wild Kandaharis, known as 'Afghanistan's Texans' for their loud-mouthed behaviour, could be bought. Living three weeks with them constantly on the run from bombing campaigns and often spending days in trenches living on stale bread and mud crabs, I admired their tenacity. We were in the midst of war, yet one of the most beautiful moments of my life has to be sitting in the ruins of our shelled-out base in Malajat after a bombing campaign in blessed relief that we had survived, listening to the poignant strains of Louis Armstrong singing, 'And I think to myself, what a wonderful world . . .' as red tracer bullets streaked across the deepening sky.

I thought I had seen the key to the end of the conflict when I accompanied *mujaheddin* from five different parties on a raid to destroy a post in the centre of Kandahar. If commanders could cooperate that closely then they were the hope for peace – these were the real fighters with on the ground support, and some, such as Ahmat Shah Massoud in the northern Panjshir valley, had set up administrations. Massoud had even forbidden smoking. Abdul Razzak, the commander of the 'Mullahs Front' I had journeyed to Kandahar with, was known as the 'Airport Killer'. But aside from his daring attacks on Kandahar Airport, Razzak had set up a camp with a school and clinic which local people would travel to from miles around. It was a start, even if the school was only for boys and taught how to use multibarrel rocket launchers in between Arabic lessons. Surely eventually such commanders would tire of the endless squabbling of the Peshawar Seven and come up with their own solution.

That some key commanders were thinking on these lines was confirmed back in Peshawar where I talked with Abdul Haq, an influential young commander who claimed to have 5,000 men in the Kabul area, and whose house was always a hub of activity, diplomats, and guerrillas flowing in and out suggesting his import-ance in the scheme of things. He found it hard to hide his disillusion-ment at the failure of the Alliance to achieve unity: 'We have been loyal and are still loyal but if the leaders cannot come together for whatever reason we cannot just sit by and let the country be destroyed.'[15] Adding that he was meeting with other commanders, he said: 'We commanders did our job fighting and expected the leaders to do theirs. Now it seems we might have to do that too.'

Haq, a cheerful round-faced chubby man with twinkling eyes and a weakness for ice-cream, did not look at all as one would imagine an Afghan warrior. But a veteran campaigner at thirty, he had been fighting the communists since he was sixteen. Haq loved to tell the tale of how one night, living in the fields around Kabul in 1980, slowly gathering people and capturing arms, he heard on the BBC that he was leading a force of 13,000. In fact there were nineteen of them.

In 1987 Haq had his foot blown off by a land-mine but because of bad relations with ISI for his outspokenness, he found little reward for his sacrifices and when we met in October 1988 he was suffering for his independent views with a cut in supplies. Haq belongs to the party of Younis Khalis, a ferocious henna bearded seventy-year-old with a sixteen-year-old wife, and the only leader to stand up to ISI. Consequently he lost commanders, but Haq had his own sources though he claimed he had always refused to accept 'help with strings', thus earning the wrath of ISI who, having ignored him for nine years, decided early in 1989 after doing a survey of support around Kabul that his participation was necessary in any military strategy. Haq got in more trouble with ISI for telling me, 'If revolutionary wars depend on outside help, this automatically involves intelligence communities which have their own policies. If these policies change the revolution collapses. It's better to be dependent on the inside capturing arms from the enemy.'[16]

But despite Haq's brave words, I was overestimating the commanders or perhaps underestimating the Afghan tradition that 'every man is king'. When it came to it the major commanders, just like the political leaders, would not co-operate because each of them wanted all the power or glory. As the date for the departure of the last Soviet soldier neared, leading commanders all had their own plans for the capture of Kabul, some more elaborate then others. Abdul Haq's, illustrated by an impressive light show in his operations room, involved taking out power stations and securing hotels and embassies for diplomats and journalists. But Haq in the south would not collaborate with Massoud in the north, while other commanders preferred not to leave the luxury of Peshawar and their new found wealth. Homayoun Shah Assefy, the king's cousin and brother-in-law, working as a lawyer just off the Champs Elysées in Paris, was shocked when he returned to his country after ten years, in exile: 'Before the war chiefs and paupers all ate from the same plate. Rich people had to share with their tribes and the worst thing in Afghanistan was to show off. I'm afraid the war has introduced a new element into Afghan society – greed for power and money. It has turned from *jihad* to a business.'[17]

12

SQUANDERING VICTORY

FIGHTING TO THE LAST AFGHAN FOR A DEAD MAN'S DREAM

'Why should we who have never lost a war accept orders from those who have never won one?' (*Mujaheddin* commander Rahim Wardak in Jalalabad, on Pakistani interference in the Afghan conflict)

In the American Club in Peshawar they were chilling the champagne and taking bets on how quickly Kabul would fall. Western embassies were hurriedly pulling out of the Afghan capital in preparation for the final putsch. Five days later, on 15 February 1989, General Gromov, the overall Soviet commander, was due to cross the Oxus river, the last Soviet soldier to leave Afghanistan, signalling an end to a humiliating Soviet military débâcle. In the Haj complex in Rawalpindi, where Muslims gather before embarking on the annual pilgrimage to Mecca, '*Gucci muj*' in designer camouflage and Raybans stood guard as ISI officials shepherded 440 bearded and turbanned men from all over Afghanistan into a large hall in which they were going to decide on a government to replace President Najibullah's in Kabul.

The bets were all lost — the military putsch never came and a year later people would be asking if, rather than when, the *mujaheddin* would take control. It was a stalemate on the political front too. The first session of the Rawalpindi *shura* (tribal assembly) collapsed within forty minutes after a boycott by representatives of refugees based in Iran, and proceedings degenerated into a thirteen-day-long farce which was rather like watching a bad car

accident in slow motion. Reported worldwide, ISI's control of
the Afghan resistance, long denied by Islamabad, could no longer
be ignored as it clumsily tried to force a government of its choosing
on to the gathered assembly. Zia's death and Benazir Bhutto's
subsequent victory in the elections had increased the desperation of
ISI hardliners to ensure a fundamentalist government in Kabul,
worried that Pakistan's new civilian administration would favour
a negotiated settlement which would almost certainly involve agreeing to drop Hekmatyar.

For while the *shura* suggestion had emanated from the Foreign
Ministry, the two organizations for once in agreement, it soon
became clear that ISI saw it as a vehicle for reviving Zia's dream
of a client fundamentalist government. The proposed sixty-member
broad-based council mostly from outside the Alliance was replaced
by a much larger assembly where each party nominated sixty, thus
retaining the 4–3 majority of the fundamentalists. At an Alliance
meeting in January under instruction from ISI head General Gul,
Hekmatyar suggested that the first and only function of the *shura*
should be to approve the proposed interim government of Ahmat
Shah which had been announced in June 1988 and subsequently
forgotten about, being widely considered unrepresentative. Two
moderate parties, those of Mojadiddi and Gilani, walked out but
the third, that of Nabbi, remained, encouraging Gul to think that
he had increased the fundamentalist majority from 4–3 to 5–2.
The Foreign Office was horrified – Ahmat Shah, a member of
Sayyaf's party, was a pan-Islamicist from an extremist sect little
known in Afghanistan before the war, and his government was
described by a senior official as 'a travesty representing all the
worst folly of the alliance'.[1]

With Bhutto and the Foreign Minster both away in China
when the *shura* began, the field was clear for ISI's unsavoury
activities. *Shura* delegates were kept virtual prisoner in the Haj
complex. ISI set up offices inside to direct events and made no
secret of its interference, summoning delegates out from sessions
over loudspeakers. Information was tightly controlled, and all
news sent out from the specially set-up Afghan News Agency
(ANA), staffed by lieutenants of Hekmatyar, was first screened by
ISI officials. A press campaign was launched against Mojadiddi,
who had upset ISI with thinly veiled remarks to an aid community

meeting about the partiality of Pakistan's support. Fearing that Mojadiddi would scupper its plans in the *shura*, ISI put out reports that he had resigned as chairman of the Alliance which he denied, taking to his bed and claiming ill-health. The irony was lost on no one when Mojadiddi later called a press conference at which he announced he was stepping down, saying, 'There was no pressure on me from Pakistan' with an ISI officer sitting in the front row. Though most delegates were afraid to speak out openly, ISI's interference was bitterly resented. One, Saeed Ibrahim Gilani, adviser to Pir Gilani, complained: 'I feel very ashamed that after ten years of fighting we end up the laughing stock of the world in the capital of Pakistan, with Pakistanis making the *shura*, keeping us in chains to the extent that they are even in the dining rooms and bathrooms.'[2]

With victory apparently in sight, Afghanistan was being literally torn apart by foreign interests like the hapless goat in the peculiarly vicious national game of *buzkashi*. One of the few things to have survived the war, *buzkashi* can best be described as rugby on horseback, in which the riders fight to grab a goat which is pulled to pieces in the process. All sorts of forces were at play in the scramble for influence in the destroyed country General Gromov had left behind him, which had never really caught up with the twentieth century but now resembled the movie set for a war film, criss-crossed with tank tracks and trenches and littered with mines and ruined villages.

One disillusioned US diplomat commented: 'Victory had 1,000 fathers and fathers keep popping up all over.' *Shura* delegates claimed that Saudi agents were offering them large sums of money to support Ahmat Shah. Iran's Foreign Minister had flown in to lobby for greater representation for the Shias, who claimed to represent 25 per cent of Afghanistan's population and would vote against Ahmat Shah. The Peshawar-based Sunni fundamentalists were against them having any seats, but Pakistan's Foreign Office feared that with Iran moving closer to Moscow, if the Shias were not persuaded to participate they might instead switch support to Najib, who had shrewdly stepped in with an offer of autonomy for the Shia region of Hazara.

Pakistan was anxious not to jeopardize its close relations with Saudi and Iran, both of which were a source of considerable

aid, bu. proved unable to balance their conflicting interests. A
desper e phone call from General Gul could not prevent the
delega.ion from the mainly Shia eight-party Alliance in Iran leaving after being given fewer seats than promised. As if to rub in
just how little control the Afghans had over the future of their
devastated country, the US ambassador, Robert Oakley, insisted
on presenting the monetary prizes at the *buzkashi* game arranged
to coincide with the final withdrawal and billed the 'Victory
Match'.

Feeling they were being made fools of, the *shura* delegates
were growing increasingly angry that while Pakistan and the US
talked incessantly of 'self-determination for the Afghans', in
reality they were being expected to rubber-stamp a government
many saw as every bit as undesirable as that of the communists.
It seemed that Gul might have overreached himself in his desperation to carry out Zia's mission. Refugees were denouncing the
shura as unrepresentative because of the few commanders and
independents present. The Turkmen and Uzbek communities
produced a petition rejecting it because they were not represented. Rallies in Quetta and Peshawar calling for the return of
the exiled former king were brutally broken up in the presence
of Western journalists.

Although overwhelmingly Sunni Pushtun and dominated by
Peshawar-based party representatives, the remaining *shura* was less
pliable than Gul had expected, and 220 commanders and *mullahs*
signed a petition against accepting the Ahmat Shah option. In
desperation ISI decided to ignore them altogether, and on the
eighth day Sayyaf simply announced that Ahmat Shah was to be
Prime Minister and would propose his cabinet the next day. At a
subsequent press conference, Saeed of ANA, the Afghan News
Agency, said that the Ahmat Shah government had been approved
by the *shura*. In fact the session had collapsed in uproar. When he
was asked the following day by angry journalists why he had lied,
Saeed shrugged his shoulders, held up a postcard of Ahmat Shah
and said, 'What is not true today will be true tomorrow.'

But he was wrong. When Ahmat Shah announced his cabinet
the delegates could take no more. *Mulläh* Nasim of Helmand
spoke out: 'Under Islam in times of war it is acceptable to eat
rotten meat but we have not yet reached the stage where we have

to accept the Ahmat Shah government made in Pakistan.'³ ISI could no longer bulldoze through its wishes and a laborious process of various *shura* committees and subcommittees was begun to come up with an alternative. One member compared it to 'trying to weigh live frogs on scales'. On the thirteenth day they returned with their proposal – *shura* members would each cast two votes for the seven Alliance leaders who then would form the government. After the two-week charade they had ended up with the government they had started with, except that now it was called AIG (Afghan Interim Government).

Sayyaf, having won the second largest number of votes allegedly because he was offering large amounts of Saudi money to delegates, became Prime Minister, while Mojadiddi, who topped the poll, was given the more figurehead position of President. Observers were disgusted. One diplomat commented: 'The whole point of the *shura* was to create a reasonable government people would be happy to defect to. Who's going to defect to something headed by Sayyaf?'

The bad taste left by the *shura* had to be sweetened quickly, and ISI began pushing for an attack on a major city. Not only would this distract attention from the *shura* but, if successful, would strengthen *mujaheddin* claims to controlling 90 per cent of the country and persuade foreign nations to recognize the AIG, and perhaps have a snowball effect on other garrison cities leading to the quick fall of Kabul. It sounded fine in theory. But it is much harder to dislodge an entrenched disciplined army that has the massive advantage of air cover than it had been to retain mountain strongholds against Soviet troops unused to dealing with guerrilla warfare in alien territory.

The March 1989 attack on Afghanistan's second most heavily fortified city of Jalalabad was an unmitigated disaster. Commanders in the area had warned against it, fearing that the pounding of the city with long-range artillery rockets would cause huge casualties among the 200,000-strong population and turn civilians against the *mujaheddin*. Plans the previous year had been ditched for this reason. On a trip to the outskirts of the city a few weeks earlier, I had been told by locals that large sums of money were being proffered to launch an offensive. Some commanders could always be bought, and once the attack was launched by a group from

NIFA truckloads of *mujaheddin* began flooding in yelling, 'Allah-o-Akbar' and 'sensing blood' as the Refugee Commissioner put it.

Initially it was successful. The garrison of Samarkhel, the headquarters of the 11th Division, was overrun with barely a fight, Afghan soldiers leaving behind half-eaten meals in their rush to flee. ISI confidently predicted that Jalalabad would fall within two days.

But when I got there on day three things were already going terribly wrong. My suspicions, raised by the convoy of ambulances screeching towards Peshawar, suggesting heavy casualties, were heightened when I was stopped by Pakistani security at the Torkham border – why should they be trying to stop journalists seeing what was being billed as the key to the end of the war? Finally an Afghan friend arranged for me to be smuggled across under the floor of an ambulance that had been hastily plastered with mud and branches for camouflage. Covered for three hours with blankets reeking of disinfectant, breathing a combination of Dettol fumes and the hashish smoke of the driver, I arrived in Ghaziabad, some twenty miles outside Jalalabad, quite high and partially anaesthetized against the horrors before me.

The road, pockmarked with shell-holes, was packed on our side with *mujaheddin* in pick-ups waving guns and rockets. Coming the other way was a stream of straggling refugees, mainly women and children, many wailing, some with donkeys bearing a precious few belongings for the fifty-eight-mile trek into Pakistan. Ahead we could see columns of smoke rising, and the rumble of bombing was a dull boom. As we neared Samarkhel we heard jets overhead. Sher Ali, a fellow-traveller in the ambulance, picked up a clutch of bullets from the floor. 'See,' he grinned. 'That was last time. An ambush.' He pointed to a string of holes across the rear door.

No one was grinning a second later. The drone of planes was drowning out everything, filling all senses. The ambulance screeched to a halt and we threw ourselves down the slope at the roadside, running to escape that terrible noise until we were in a cave used as a *mujaheddin* camp. There was an eerie moment of complete silence. I thought the world had stopped, then a dog began whining and 'boom . . . boom . . . boom' – cluster bombs were dropping, sending up mushrooms of smoke and seeming to bounce towards us.

The pick-up ahead of us on the road had kept on going, and as if in slow motion we watched it explode in a single orange burst. The government forces were desperate to cut off the main supply route of the *mujaheddin* and were repeatedly bombing the road – and any refugees who happened to be on it.

The regime's airpower was a huge advantage, and one which left the *mujaheddin* as defenceless as in the early days of the war when they were tribesmen with sticks and stones fighting off Soviet tanks. There were other problems too. Begun from the south-east, the *mujaheddin* attack was not taken up from other directions. By the end of the first week it had resulted in the highest one-week death-toll and evacuation of the ten-year conflict – according to Shah Zaman from the Pakistan refugee commission, 18,000 refugees had arrived.

These were the lucky ones – as field commanders had feared, civilians were forming the front line in this bloody battle. Many more were trapped between the bombing of the regime and the rockets of the *mujaheddin*, sent off in a wild kneejerk response to the sound of planes. It was thought that 5,000 rockets were launched in that first week of the resistance bid to take control of this vital city on the main highway to Kabul.

Because of its proximity to Pakistan, the Peshawar parties had more influence in Jalalabad, and the lack of unity and organization among the seven spelt disaster on the battlefield. From initially falling over each other to take the glory, once the tide began to turn the parties began blaming each other. I saw no evidence of inter-party co-operation, and in several cases saw *mujaheddin* killed by their own side because different commanders were unaware of where each others' forward positions were. *Mujaheddin* from NIFA and Khalis, the two largest parties in the area, would not join up and thus lost control of the regime supply route from Kabul. In the deserted state farms of Ghaziabad, where the parties had their basecamps, they had all set up checkpoints preventing infiltration by their Alliance colleagues.

Morale plummeted as it seemed the *mujaheddin* would have to destroy the garden city and all those within it if they were to win, and doubts crept in. Watching a small boy who had lost his entire family in a bombing attack screaming to the heavens before shutting himself off from the world, Sher Ali confided, 'This is not what *jihad* is about.' Commander Noor Haq agreed: 'We don't want to control a pile of rubble and walk on the crushed bones of women and children.'

Within a few weeks the *mujaheddin* had been pushed back first from the woods around the airport, then from Samarkhel. Attacks on the north and west, which should have come at the start, a month later could not restore the *mujaheddin* position, and while ANA was claiming masses of defections from the Afghan army and capture of more posts than actually existed around the city, and Pakistan TV was putting out nightly footage on ISI instructions claiming, 'The *mujaheddin* are stepping up pressure on Jalalabad,' the reality was that the attack had failed, leaving thousands dead or wounded. Next time I journeyed along the road towards Samarkhel, *mujaheddin* were busily salvaging scrap, dismantling abandoned tanks with welding irons and stripping down electricity poles to be sold for a few rupees in Peshawar bazaars. 'We may as well get some benefit,' shrugged one of the human magpies.

The ill-fated attack had exposed a problem in attacking cities that many commanders such as Abdul Haq had already seen, and widened the rift between field commanders and the Peshawar parties. Haq explained the quandary: 'We need to keep up military pressure, but how can we attack in such a way that we only hurt the regime? The people in Kabul are my friends, many work for me and have been jailed or suffered. They shelter or provide food for my men. How can I then launch an attack in which chances are they will die? Are we prepared to take 10,000 lives in Jalalabad, 10,000 in Herat, 10,000 in Kandahar?'[4] For a successful campaign there would first have to be evacuation, though some hardliners maintained that anyone still living in Afghanistan must be a traitor and thus deserved to die.

But ISI claimed that they had never envisaged a major battle in Jalalabad. Because of the high proportion of conscripts in the Afghan army, they apparently believed that once fighting had begun there would be droves of defections, and reports on the low morale of the Afghan air force suggested that they would refuse to fly raids. The whole policy had been predicated on this premise. It was totally false. The air force flew with greater skill and bravado than it had ever been thought capable of, while defections were in their hundreds rather than thousands. No one will jump out of a moving car unless certain it is going over a cliff, and despite Western, and even private Soviet predictions, the Afghan army obviously had greater faith in Najib's chances of survival, while the spectacle of the *shura* could have given no one confidence in the *mujaheddin* ability to govern and created no credible body to defect to.

Barely reported at the time, there had been a critical incident in December 1988 to deter those considering defecting, and partly because of which, negotiations with government forces inside the city, aimed at securing such defections, had broken down. During the *mujaheddin* capture of the Torkham border post, seventy Afghan soldiers who had defected were brutally murdered and their bodies chopped up and sent back in bags. On my first visit to Jalalabad two months later, with two exiles making their first trip home in ten years, villagers could talk of little else. We were taken up a mountain trail to a trench containing charred human bones and scraps of bloody cloth to see the evidence of butchery. The exiles were horrified and one, Homayoun Assefy, predicted: 'No one's going to surrender if this happens. By such actions the *mujaheddin* are forcing regime soldiers to choose between kill or die.' But one of our *mujaheddin* escorts did not agree. 'This is what happens to traitors,' he said. Unfortunately his view was shared by many guerrillas who felt that tribal law dictated an eye for an eye and wanted vengeance for all those friends and relatives killed in the war. During the Jalalabad attack I saw a group of soldiers crossing over, hands up, to one of the parties and immediately gunned down.

Jalalabad was a turning point both in the Afghan war and in civil and military relations in Pakistan. When such an attack had been mooted the previous year, Abdul Haq had warned: 'If we fight and lose, we will lose the war.'[5] By showing that he could survive such a major onslaught, Najib had forced people to reassess their predictions. At the start of the attack a US diplomat had described it as 'time for the *mujaheddin* to demonstrate their manhood'. They had failed, not through lack of bravado, but because of overwhelming odds. In the process ISI had been discredited, to the delight of Bhutto's government, which was eager to clip the organization's wings but had previously been unable to because of the autonomy and American patronage it enjoyed. Awkward questions started to be asked to explain how the intelligence of an agency, described by its US counterparts as the most sophisticated in the Third World, could have been so wrong. An official at the British Foreign Office offered the most widely accepted explanation for the complete misreading of the situation: 'This is what happens when those providing intelligence are also deciding policy. Rather than basing strategy on intelligence coming in, they are providing intelligence to fit their own goals.'

But if that was the case it seemed the US too, with their large CIA presence well aware of the impending attack, had allowed policy motives to blind them to reality. Those most involved in formulating policy at the start of the Bush Administration continued to see the war as a chance to get even for Vietnam. At his first briefing for journalists in Islamabad in September 1988, US ambassador Oakley, who had been involved in drawing up a blueprint for Vietnam and who, with the departure of Armacost, was to become Bush's most powerful adviser on Afghanistan, surprised us by drawing parallels between the two situations. To avenge the 58,000 American servicemen killed in south-east Asia, they had said they were prepared to 'fight to the last Afghan', and as the Soviet ambassador in Kabul, Yuli Vorontsóv, told me the following June, 'The Americans will not negotiate because they want the same humiliation for us as they had in Vietnam. They want to see Soviet Embassy staff clinging to helicopters taking us away – but I keep telling them my roof is no good for helicopters.'[6]

The irony was that to achieve this the US were letting ISI channel all funds and energies into placing in Kabul a man almost as anti-American as he was anti-communist. 'Death to Americans' was a common slogan inside camps run by Hekmatyar or his backers in the Pakistani Jamaat Islami. On one memorable occasion in summer 1989 the American journalists I was travelling with to a Hekmatyar rally pretended to be Australian when we were stopped by his lieutenants, scared of reprisals for admitting their true nationality.

So it was a little unfair to see the CIA sit back and allow ISI to be made a total scapegoat for the Jalalabad fiasco. Had it not been for ISI the *mujaheddin* would perhaps never have got the Russians out. And after all, if the *mujaheddin* had been victorious in Jalalabad everyone would have been claiming responsibility. But while success has many fathers, failure is an orphan, and as the *mujaheddin* attack got increasingly bogged down (despite continued optimistic reports on Pakistan TV) the painful process of apportioning blame began, showing once more the rifts between Pakistan's civil and military establishments.

The Foreign Office got in first, blaming ISI, seeing this as their chance to take hold of Pakistan's policy in the long-running battle between the two organizations. 'The Foreign Ministry never underestimated the regime's strength,' commented a top Foreign Ministry official smugly. 'Other agencies did. We told ISI policies must be predicated on reality, not wishful thinking.'

As the two days predicted for the attack expanded into seven weeks, resistance leaders and even ISI's Washington backers joined the chorus. ISI retaliated angrily with a propaganda campaign to shift the blame on to one of its least favourite resistance parties, NIFA. Hamid Gilani, a NIFA leader, told me that ISI had bought up some of their forces under Commander Pahlawan who, like many commanders belonging to moderate parties, was short of arms because ISI had always favoured the fundamentalists: 'The first we knew that the operation was going ahead was a phone call in the early hours of the morning saying that the attack had begun. We knew it was an ISI trap. If we were successful the radicals would advance, killing our men if necessary, to claim they captured the city. If we failed NIFA would be the scapegoat.'[7]

No one believed that NIFA had attacked against ISI's wishes, so ISI's propaganda changed tack, insisting that the organization itself had been under pressure from the Bhutto government to strengthen the *mujaheddin* position with the capture of a big city which the AIG could move into. General Gul gave an off-the-record interview to the *New York Times*, resulting in an article claiming that the attack was ordered by Bhutto against the advice of ISI.

The story reported a meeting on 5 March, one day before the attack began, at which it said Bhutto had given the order. Some of her advisers were amused by the piece saying, 'At last people think we are controlling the Afghan policy.' But of course they were not. The *mujaheddin*, unable to organize a lunch, could hardly have launched a major attack with one day's notice. Arms had been pouring into Jalalabad for weeks, and Gul had in fact briefed commanders at a meeting on 2 March. At most Bhutto had approved the operation, which would have gone ahead regardless. Gul's attitude to the civilian administration was summed up when after a row at the Foreign Ministry he stormed out saying, 'You know nothing of *jihad*.'[8]

The *NYT* story was the last straw for Bhutto and gave her precisely the excuse needed to remove Gul, as she had wanted to since taking power, resenting his role in the creation of the IDA. One of her first acts had been to launch an investigation into the intelligence services, hoping to disband ISI or at least its domestic wing, which had been used as a tool against the PPP by Zia and had constantly harassed her and her mother during martial law. She had promoted Gul with the intention of moving him 'up and out'. But she had always been thwarted by the CIA, which had trained Gul in the US and relied so heavily on ISI. After the Jalalabad fiasco they were on her side.

On 15 May an Interior Ministry document was presented to the Pakistan cabinet harshly criticizing ISI, though still not by name.[9] Referring to the *shura* it said: 'It was not a realistic posture when some quarters at home and abroad felt that without the participation of the 2 million Afghans in Iran not to talk of field commanders and good Muslims a viable set-up could be created.' The report went on: 'After the Soviet withdrawal there had been disappointment for those zealots who in their naïvety predicted the immediate break up of the PDPA power structure and a victory for the resistance. They failed to realize that for Najib the battle for Jalalabad was the battle for Kabul; that the Soviets had spent money and labour to train the PDPA's armed forces for many years; that while leaving the Soviets left their friends in Kabul with stockpiles of modern arms and equipment and the promise of more; that the *mujaheddin* would take time to acquaint themselves with the methods of conventional warfare under a unified command.' Finally it concluded: 'Doubts are being expressed over the government's control over the Afghan policy of Pakistan.' A week later, in Bhutto's first real move to take Afghan policy into her own hands, she replaced Gul with a retired general, Shams-ur Rahman Kallue, whose brief was to find out exactly what ISI had been up to for the last eleven years.

But what initially appeared to be a direct challenge to the military, later transpired to have also been an involved plan engineered by the CIA to make Gul a scapegoat for the failure of its own Afghan policy. According to both Pakistani and American intelligence sources I spoke to at the time, Gul's interview with the *NYT* reporter Henry Kamm had been set up by the US ambassador, Robert Oakley, who had briefed Gul fully first. US officials in Islamabad who had been fully informed of the Jalalabad attack, and themselves should have seen the idiocy of the plan, were trying to clear their own names and that of ISI as an organization by laying the blame totally on Gul. They knew what the result of the *NYT* piece would be and had deliberately set up Gul and abandoned him, to preserve the reputation of the institution which was so useful to the US for gathering Gulf intelligence, using the many Pakistani soldiers in Oman and Saudi and advisers in Iran. Moreover, realizing late in the day they had been backing the wrong horse, only by removing Gul could they switch support away from Hekmatyar. 'Gul would not jump without their nod, let alone attack Jalalabad or plant such a story. Now they have orphaned him,' said one of his colleagues.

However, Gul was to get the final laugh. While Bhutto was anxious to remove him from the scene altogether, she could not ignore the fact that within the army he had many admirers and was generally regarded as 'a brilliant soldier'. General Beg insisted that Gul be given command of the most important corps – that of Multan, from which Zia had risen to the Presidency. Equally galling, to prevent the transfer looking political Bhutto was forced to give a farewell dinner for her least favourite general – a most uncomfortable event. From Multan Gul was no less threat, continuing to advise Bhutto's political opponents and command the loyalty of ISI despite Kallue's presence as its new head. Moreover, his promotion made him better placed for future ambitions while his treatment crystallized his antipathy towards Bhutto, making him a more deadly threat.

During the army's Zarb-e-Momin exercises the following year, Gul made no secret of his dislike of the PPP government. He told journalists, 'Yes, the Afghan *mujaheddin* were not able to capture Jaialabad. But why were they unable to do so? Because just when the Pakistan government should have been stepping up its material support for the *mujaheddin* it was busy dithering.'

While faces were turning red in Washington over the bungling
of the *shura* and Jalalabad offensive and the exposure of the extent
of Pakistan military control of policy as well as the differences in
civil and military ambitions, in Kabul Najib could have been
excused a chuckle or two. After years of reports of KHAD
(Afghan secret police) and Soviet army atrocities, suddenly Najib,
who had headed KHAD from 1981 until he became President in
1985, could claim the moral high ground. During the *shura* Hamid
Karzay, spokesman for Mojadiddi, admitted to me privately, 'How
can we call Najib a puppet when we have the whole world
pulling our strings? The Soviet forces are gone, yet we are the ones
sitting in luxury offices in Pakistan while he is in Kabul facing the
rockets.' The Jalalabad attack, with its huge civilian death toll, had
given Najib the excuse to appeal to the middle classes, the shopkeepers and urban workers who had remained in Afghanistan, as
their protector against the *mujaheddin*. Most of the *mujaheddin*
rockets fired on Kabul, directed at their main target, the airport,
which is Kabul's lifeline from the Soviet Union, landed on residential areas, while their blockade of roads was causing severe
food and fuel shortages, forcing families to send their children to
scrape bark from the trees for firewood. Reports of executions of
those defecting were causing Kabul residents to fear the consequences of a *mujaheddin* government, and when I visited Kabul in
June 1989 I was told several times, 'At least Najib is a known evil
– who knows what would happen if Hekmatyar came here.'

Kabul was not at all the grey ghost town I had expected. The
plane from Delhi had an almost festival air, with well-dressed
Afghans in designer clothes loading on bags of food and meat that
were stinking in India's pre-monsoon heat. As we dropped from a
great height between snow-topped mountains into Kabul airport,
the plane released potassium flares to deter *mujaheddin* missiles. The
locals called it 'laying eggs', but their contents were deadly. In the
hospitals I was to see many children badly scarred from these
capsules, which burn at 1200°C, and Father Angelo, an Italian
priest who was the only remaining West European diplomat in
the city, gave me several found in his garden after a service which,
with rocket-fire in the background, included a hauntingly fitting
passage from Revelations, 'And there will be no more tears in
Paradise.' At the airport Soviet MIGs were screaming off the

runway bearing their evil load towards Jalalabad. I wondered if
they were the same ones in whose bombing raid I had been caught
in March. There were a few marks in the tarmac where rockets
had landed, but the airport seemed surprisingly intact and a new
terminal building was even under construction.

On that first sunny June day Kabul did not have the appearance
of a city under siege. Bright yellow taxis plied up and down the
paved streets, only their prices reflecting the lack of fuel. My hotel
in the town's main square was on first sight what I had envisaged
– austere, with a sentry on the door and dark crumpled-suited
minders in the lobby. The US ambassador had been killed in a
room along my corridor back in February 1979; the telephone
operator had only one hand and that was enclosed in a sinister
black leather glove. But in the banquet room colourful and noisy
weddings took place every afternoon, often with dancing to Western music. Somehow I had imagined life would have stopped still
– I had not expected to see people enjoying themselves or flowers
perfuming the air.

What struck me most were the women. Extravagantly made
up, often in miniskirts and high heels, with dyed blonde hair or T-
shirts proclaiming 'I'm not with this idiot', they seemed an entirely
different species to those scurrying pitiful creatures hidden in burqas
in Peshawar's refugee camps. I wondered how these women, barter-
ing loudly in the bazaar along the sides of the river or sipping
fizzy drinks and licking ice-creams in the university café, would
feel about Hekmatyar telling them they should be kept locked
away in purdah. Ironically, for a trip to a city under siege, where
secret police lurking behind trees and lamp-posts did not allow
people to loiter, I had an immense sense of freedom after the
oppression of conservative Pakistan.

But there were giveaways that the normality was only a semblance. The fear of conscription meant that there were few young
men on the street. Every morning at dawn large bread queues
would form as people waited for their daily ration of five pieces of
nan per family. Dotted around the city were large orphanages,
where children whose parents had been victims of war were being
indoctrinated and often trained as agents to infiltrate mujaheddin
lines. The large presence of uniforms, the dull boom of the 1,700-lb
Scud missiles passing through the sound barrier five times daily,

the sandbags round the UN club, the constant dropping of flares and buzz from planes overhead – the forty flights that were arriving daily with supplies from Moscow and the jets screeching to war – were reminders that this was the city from which most Western embassy staff had fled four months earlier.

For the aid workers and diplomats who stayed on, trying desperately not to go stir crazy in the town they called 'Kabulistan', the main clue to the fighting outside was that Kabul was shrinking. Although the population had exploded from 400,000 before the war to more than 2 million as people fled the countryside, the area in which residents were allowed to travel was just 12 square kilometres. For expats, entertainment revolved around the UN club, counting rockets and listening to the ravings of a mad Egyptian whose 'wife was in Cairo but heart was in Helsinki'. Adding an Orwellian touch to this prison-like existence was the music and commentary blaring from loudspeakers hung from trees across the city, from 5 a.m. to the 10 p.m. curfew. In fact it was less insidious than it seemed. Rather than the ideological commentary I had imagined it to be, much of the airtime seemed devoted to the Kabul equivalent of Jane Fonda's workout, with frequent performances of the themes from *The Archers* and *Love Story*. The practice was apparently started during the reign of Zahir Shah in the 1960s, when few people had radios. Nowadays many have televisions on which they could watch the bulky figure of Najib, fittingly nicknamed 'The Ox', trying to present a human face over the Japanese-installed TV network.

Glasnost, it seemed, had arrived in Kabul, and every official I met was anxious to admit mistakes of the past and demonstrate their new openness with offers of visits to the notorious Pul-i-Charki prison, where in the early 1980s fifty executions took place per day, though these visits somehow never materialized. The propaganda war had begun with a vengeance. Politburo members with shelves full of Lenin and who until recently had espoused Marxist revolutionary doctrine now had Korans on their desks, and were to be seen regularly praying in mosques to demonstrate their Islamic credentials. The English-language *Kabul Times* printed a speech by Najib on privatization containing almost Thatcherite rhetoric, and another admitting that land reform had been heavy-handed and ignoring the tribes a mistake.

Not everyone was convinced. When Najib announced a state of emergency and martial law immediately following the final Soviet withdrawal in February 1989, the cabinet was purged of moderates. Ruthless house searches by the secret police were continuing, young boys still being forcibly rounded up and Pul-i-Charki, which holds 15,000, still full. While Najib was eager to emphasize that his regime was different, the hundreds of thousands of people whose relatives were tortured or executed in jail would not easily forget his black history as head of KHAD. 'It is not as if he was minister of health or education,' said Abdul Haq, the Kabul commander in Peshawar. 'He was minister of killing.'[10]

I had my first experience of Kabul *glasnost* in action on arriving at the hotel. The road was blocked, not because of tank manoeuvres, but for a procession of Shias mourning Ayatollah Khomeini, whose death had just been announced – the first Muslim demonstration since 1980, when a group of protesting women where shot at. Allowing, even encouraging this was all part of Najib's campaign to woo minority groups who had long felt oppressed under years of Pushtun rule. Najib claimed that now all groups were treated the same regardless of size, while pointing out that the *mujaheddin* AIG was almost entirely Pushtun. Among some of Afghanistan's forty-two ethnic groups a chord was being struck.

Women's rights was another area where Najib was hoping to win the PR war, playing up fears that a *mujaheddin* government would force women behind the veil. To try to win them over he had given women places in his administration and created a special women's militia. To some extent Najib had succeeded. In a government flat, Wajia, a well-known singer, strummed her guitar and, between puffs of her cigarette, said she would leave the country if Gulbuddin came. But while Mrs Esmatee Wardak, President of the Afghanistan's Women's Committee and one of the first Afghan women to graduate, argued that the war had made women 'more assertive and 100 times freer',[11] it was not the PDPA she credited. It was Zahir Shah who gave women the vote and introduced the miniskirt to Kabul, and there were women MPs before the war. The war had made some women vitally important to the economy, with the loss of 1.2 million men and many others maimed, and Mrs Wardak maintained, 'It is suffering and the need to be economically independent that has strengthened us.' Abhorrence

to Hekmatyar did not necessarily translate into support for Najib.
Wajia said she looked forward to the day when she could write
songs about anything with no fear of censorship. At the university
a literature student asked me: 'What is it to have equal rights
under a regime which does not believe in rights?'

Kabul in June 1989 was a very different place to what it had
been four months earlier. Then *mujaheddin* had been pumping in
hundreds of rockets, and the now treacly confident PDPA Politburo members had been worried men with black shadows under
haunted eyes fearing an invasion any day. According to diplomats,
'There was panic, anger and despair within the party.' Just before
the withdrawal ended, a senior member of the hardline Khalki
faction of the PDPA visiting the Soviet embassy to sign the
condolence book for the Armenian earthquake railed, 'You sold us
to the *mujaheddin*,' and envoys were sent to Delhi to ask permission
for party militants to seek refuge if necessary. But Najib had put
party members in uniform, issued them guns, strengthened positions around Kabul and created an élite Presidential Guard to
defend it – men with irremovable blood on their hands who
would be prepared to defend the city street by street, and while
the resistance alliance was falling apart, had convinced the two
feuding factions of the PDPA – his own Parchamites and the
Khalkis – that the only way to survive was to unite. By the time
of my visit, the regime, if still not widely considered viable by the
outside world, certainly had more confidence, and morale among
the few army troops I could meet seemed high. Some even argued
that the Soviet presence had hampered them in the past. 'We
know best how to deal with these *dushman* (bandits). When the
West talks about brave Afghans they should remember we're
Afghans too.'[12]

To search for how far this confidence extended I travelled 400
miles west to Herat, near the Iranian border. A former outpost of the
Persian empire and the country's artistic capital, Herat's exquisite
mosque had become a centre of pilgrimage. But its gardens and
vineyards and turquoise and lapis minarets and tiled poets' tombs,
which brought an oasis of colour to the desert, had suffered the worst
bombing of the war. Known as Afghanistan's Hiroshima, if Herat
had accepted the new face of Najib then he was surely home and dry.
The Soviet forces were only the latest of a series of invaders to

storm the ancient city in its 2,500-year-old history. Their predecessors included Alexander the Great, Genghis Khan and Tam-
erlane the Mongol conqueror. But the Soviets had been the most
brutal, their relentless bombing early on in the war killing or
wounding more that 10,000 of the 180,000 population. They were
believed to be taking revenge for the massacre in March 1979 of
thirty Soviet families, whose bodies were paraded around town on
pikes in the first major rebellion against the communist regime
which had taken power a year earlier. The participation of local
troops in the butchery of PDPA and Soviet citizens was a major
factor in causing Moscow to reassess its position and eventually
send in troops. The Soviet reprisal with massive bombing from
nearby Shindand airbase produced an intensity of feeling which
continues in Herat today, as I discovered from the muttered insults
I received, locals mistaking me for a Russian because of my fair
hair. A UN team visiting the area the previous February had
reported eight-year-old boys regularly ambushing Soviet soldiers
in the bazaar with hand grenades.

  The government must be pretty confident, I figured, to send a
Western journalist to Herat of all places. Accompanied by two
seedy minders from whom I would have been reluctant to buy a
second-hand Kalashnikov, I was taken by tank from Herat airport
to a guesthouse in town. Sitting in its pomegranate-blossom-
scented garden on that perfect summer day, the silence punctured
only by birds singing, the hammering of workmen and tinkling of
donkey carts, it was easy to believe the war was over. I was taken
on a whistlestop tour of committed party officials, who assured
me that everyone loved Najib and the PDPA, and to meet refugees
who claimed to have returned from Iran 'because of Najib's
national reconciliation programme'. The officials were eager to
show me the damage to a minaret of the great mosque, Medresse
Sultan Husain-i-Baiqara, done by a recent *mujaheddin* rocket. 'If
this is the *jihad* they claim, how can good Muslims damage the
house of Allah?' I was told repeatedly. This was such good PR I
suspected it had been a deliberate regime rocket.

  I asked about the UN survey which had reported that 40 per
cent of the houses had been destroyed and almost half the villages
in the province badly damaged. They laughed and said there was
no destruction and the *mujaheddin* had no foothold in the city – we

could, after all, drive around it. The tanks in the bazaar and the army post inside the historic mosque were said to be 'just security measures'. They added that there were no shortages and plenty of electricity and running water – unfortunately we were staying at the only place with neither.

The nights were harder to explain. As the sun went down and the last cuckoo cried we would be treated to a painfully beautiful display of red and green tracer bullets streaming across the sky, picking out suspected *mujaheddin* activity, occasionally followed by the burst of gunfire or white rockets. But the bombers tearing across the sky were, the officials said, simply 'training'.

I was mystified. Ross Mountain, the UN head in Kabul, had described the devastation to me as 'as bad if not worse than Beirut'.[13] I was almost fooled. But when I slipped away to the carpet bazaar while my minders were stocking up on sugar and meat to take back to Kabul, where it was harder to obtain, I was told in whispers amid loud bargaining that everyone was terrified of the government and that the *mujaheddin* controlled half the city, living among the ruins. This was a half which I had not even realized existed, through my guide's clever manoeuvres to fool me into thinking that I had been all the way around. As I wandered in the direction the carpet-seller had pointed, six servicemen surrounded me. According to the carpet-seller, there was a green line dividing the regime side from that controlled by the resistance. If I could cross that the soldiers would not dare come after me. But I was not going to be allowed that far. The only solution was to climb the ramparts of the tenth-century citadel, the headquarters of the regime forces, from which there would be a good view. My minders had told me before that the ramparts were mined, and as I climbed up they called after me angrily that my visa would be stopped. But it was too late to go back and, safely at the top, it was immediately obvious how much I had not been shown. The scene on the other side below reflected merciless bombing: hardly a wall was left standing. Easily a quarter of the town was in ruins and the destruction spread miles around to the west.

The lull in fighting between the government forces and the estimated 13,000 *mujaheddin* under Ismael Khan was because harvest was being gathered, and the resistance feared that the government would take revenge for any attacks by burning the crops of the locals upon whom they were dependent to survive. Herat, which was rebuilt after its conquest by Alexander the Great in the fourth century BC, relies primarily on agriculture to feed its population, though many have fled to Iran. The 2,500-year-old underground irrigation system was destroyed in the war, and the lack of clean water had pushed up infant mortality to one in five live births, according to Dr Farid Hasan, director of Herat's only hospital, as he revealed the starkly empty shelves in his pharmacy.

Snatched conversations in the depths of shops, while examining sacks in the grain market, and even a young army officer who looked at me with sad eyes and asked, 'How long?' revealed the conflict between the depth of feeling against Najib and the frustration with continued war. Playing on this, Najib had begun a strategy of trying to split the resistance between the leaders in Pakistan whom he labelled 'puppets of foreign powers' and the field commanders inside Afghanistan whom he spoke of as 'brave hill-fighters'. He believed that the commitment of the latter was wavering now that the Soviet troops, the main target of their wrath, had gone.

Najib saw the way to peace and his own survival through deals with these commanders, a strategy with limited success so far despite ambassador Vorontsov's claims that three-quarters of field commanders were engaged in the 'very Afghan process'[14] of deals and negotiations on ceasefires. Farid Zarif, a close aide of Najib, told me: 'We have struck deals in Bamyan, Herat, Kunduz, Baghlan and Kandahar. Things are very different to six months ago, when there was a mental block on the other side barring any communication with us.' While in Herat we took tea with some of these leaders who had defected to the government because, they said, they, 'liked Najib's policies'. Outside in the large garden of their rambling house some of their men were fooling around on tanks they had been given. In fact Khair Mohammed, the Deputy Commander of a group which had switched sides in 1987 along with 2,000 men from the Alizay tribe, and now controls the southern part of the defence belt around Herat, encompassing seventy villages, admitted, 'The government gave us everything we wanted. We got well, more than twenty tanks, 100 trucks, lots of guns ...'

It was an open question whether the government could actually control these tribal militia they had bought up to maintain peace,

and who were known back in Kabul as 'Loony Tunes'. Khair
Mohammed's men were certainly enjoying themselves far too
much with their new toys to consider giving them back were the
war to end, and if it continued their loyalty was to no one but
themselves. But in winning them over Najib was exploiting the
fact that most families had relations on both sides, and those in a
mujaheddin-controlled village would have cousins or sons in the
next government-controlled village and thus be eager that there
should be no fighting. Many PDPA officials told me they had
brothers in the *mujaheddin*, but the most extreme example I came
across was Suleyman Leikh, the Minister for Tribal Affairs, whose
brother-in-law is Mojadiddi, an Afghan resistance leader in Pakistan. Tribal connections in traditional Afghan society are as potent
a weapon as money and equipment in persuading a group to
switch sides or stop fighting. Fazal Haq Khaliqyar, Governor of
Herat, a non-party man who had held the same post under King
Zahir Shah, was one of Najib's appointees for precisely this reason.
As he said: 'I am an old respected man of Herat and know all these
people. I attend prayers with the opposition and people trust me.'
Having counted eighteen bodyguards outside his office, I was not
sure the trust was mutual.

Just as in the countryside tribes were being lured by money,
guns, drugs and promises of non-interference in poppy-smuggling
operations, the regime was also using bribery in towns, issuing
food coupons for example, entitling 100,000 families in Kabul to
free or subsidized food. A trip to Mazar-i-Sharif in the north
where, in sharp contrast to Kabul, bakeries were still full of bread
at five in the evening, showed that if people are well fed they are
less bothered about who is in power. Many people there seemed
unaware that the war was even continuing.

I left Kabul believing a military victory for the *mujaheddin*
remote without a total change of strategy. Both politically and
militarily they were in a far worse position than when the Soviet
withdrawal ended, and some were resorting to the psychiatrist's
couch in Peshawar, unable to understand why, when they had
apparently defeated the world's largest army, they could not secure
victory against the Afghan army. The Bush administration was
giving them the summer for another shot at reversing their recent
battlefield fortunes, but time seemed to be favouring Najib's

regime, which found itself in the same situation that the *mujaheddin* had been in before the Soviets left: if you don't lose you win.

But back in Pakistan, Peter Tomsen, the newly arrived US envoy to the *mujaheddin*, was painting a very different picture. To the incredulity of Western journalists gathered in Islamabad for a press briefing in July 1989, he spoke only of the military option and of riding into Kabul on the back of a *mujaheddin* tank, seemingly unaware of how little fighting was actually going on. He told us: 'I'm confident of a military victory. The pressure is growing on Kabul, the regime's control is receding, the lines of communication are under increasing pressure and they cannot recruit troops. Time is on the resistance's side.'

Reality was out of the window. It made no difference us pointing out that the *mujaheddin* in the last three months had lost control of Samarkhel, failed to close supply routes such as the Kabul-Jalalabad road and the northern Salang Highway to the Soviet Union, and been unable to take even a single security post around Kandahar airport. The US had become victims of their own propaganda, and anyone who tried to point out the truth suffered. Ed McWilliams, the first US envoy to the *mujaheddin*, was a fluent Farsi speaker and well placed to know what was going on, having won the confidence of many of the guerrillas. But he was ostracized by the US ambassador, then recalled to Washington, after he sent dissenting cables back to the State Department criticizing US policy, in particular its continued reliance on ISI, which, despite the removal of Gul, had not changed its pro-Hekmatyar stance.

For Tomsen to maintain his belief that the resistance were united but the regime in disarray required an impressive screening-out process. In Peshawar he was carefully steered to party stalwarts but in Quetta, the base for operations in the south-west and where people had always been less afraid to speak out, he faced a barrage of home truths. I breakfasted with him after he had met Mullah Malang, an important Kandahar commander and deputy minister in the AIG, who had publicly told his men not to fight, claiming: 'If we take Kandahar there will be confusion and it will lead us nowhere but clashes.' Malang said he had told Tomsen, 'In Kabul now we have one *mujaheddin* group stopping food going to the people while another is taking bribes to allow it through. If our interim government does not get its act together commanders will lose hope and disappear from the *jihad* or even change sides.'[15]

Tomsen seemed shocked by what he had heard and talked of 'reassessing the situation'. But when we later met back in Islamabad he was back to the official line, discounting Kandahar as 'an exceptional situation'.[16] The hopes of many Afghans, that Tomsen would return to Washington recommending accepting the Soviet offer that both sides halt arms supplies, were dashed. 'Giving us more time just means spilling more Afghan blood,' protested Asim Nasser Zia, a NIFA spokesman.

But plans for a summer countrywide offensive and increased shipments of sophisticated anti-aircraft and mortar to the resistance were shelved by an incident the US could not ignore. In mid-July the news reached Peshawar of a massacre of thirty Jamiat *mujaheddin* by Said Jamal, a commander from Hezb-i-Islami, the party of Hekmatyar, who was still receiving the bulk of US arms. Those killed in the ambush in the north-eastern province of Takhar included seven top commanders, who had been returning to their provinces after a meeting of the supervisory Council of the North set up by Ahmat Shah Massoud the previous year to administer the northern area. There was a long history of rivalry between the two men, who had been engineering students together and before the Soviets invaded had worked together in Pakistan. Hekmatyar saw Massoud, who is known as the Lion of the Panjshir, as a threat and encouraged ISI to restrict his arms supplies as well as spread rumours that he had done a deal with the regime. But analysts continued to argue that Massoud was crucial for any attack on Kabul, and Hekmatyar was worried by what he called 'Massoud's expansionism', which presumably referred to the winning over of many Hezb members. Said Jamal was known to be close to Hekmatyar, and it transpired that during the ambush the two had been in radio contact.

The Takhar incident was a PR gift for Najib, and while ISI apparently persuaded Bhutto that it was 'a tribal feud',[17] the US State Department said it deplored the 'tragic and brutal act'. This time Hekmatyar had gone too far. Massoud captured 300 of his men in retaliation, while in Peshawar five of the seven guerrilla leaders attended a protest rally at which Hezb members were denounced as 'professional terrorists' and Hekmatyar's suspension from the AIG was demanded. In his strongest statement to date, Mojadiddi tore at his old *bête-noire*: 'Those involved in such incidents could not be called Muslim or *mujaheddin* . . . it was not the first time men of this organization killed innocent commanders.'

The pressure was growing on Pakistan and the US to withdraw support from Hekmatyar, who was widely held responsible for a dramatic media shift from describing the guerrillas as romantic heroes, battling bravely on a latter-day Crusade, to narrow-minded anti-West fundamentalists liable to kill each other at the slightest provocation. But the US had allowed ISI to create a Frankenstein. If he was dropped, with his large stocks of arms and money and support from places like Libya, Hekmatyar could cause immense nuisance and sabotage the whole resistance effort, while Saudi's intelligence chief, Prince Turki, had put pressure on Pakistan not to withdraw their patronage of him. Hekmatyar, confident of his friends in high places, began holding mass rallies to demonstrate his support, at which anti-American slogans replaced anti-Soviet ones, and accusing the West of a conspiracy against him. 'Washington,' he declared, 'is deadly opposed to a final *mujaheddin* victory.' In August, at a press conference in Peshawar, he claimed to be in contact with senior Afghan army officers and members of the Khalqi faction to organize a coup, which he implied was the reason for his recent trip to the outskirts of Kabul. As awkward questions began to be raised, he left for well-timed prayers, leaving the distinct impression that this was a warning to his colleagues and backers.

No one took the coup suggestion seriously. The Khalqis were, after all, critical of Najib for proposing deals with the resistance, and thus hardly likely to collaborate with the guerrillas. But ISI hardliners believed that with a military victory increasingly unlikely and fears of flagging interest in the US, a coup from within might be the only way to get their man in power; more money was sent in to buy up members of the Afghan army and airforce, as well as disillusioned Khalqi colleagues of Najib who resented the drift away from communism and talk of coalition government. Nor had the Khalqis approved of the introduction of a multi-party system with elections in April 1988, which reduced the PDPA's representation to 22 per cent, even if the other parties were PDPA creations. Moreover, while Najib had given leading

Khalqis government positions, many had not been allowed to rise correspondingly in the party hierarchy. For although Soviet off-icials were hailing Najib as 'a star performer', there were chinks in his armour. The Khalqis were particularly unhappy about his dismantling of Tsarandoy, the military police, which had been a Khalqi stronghold and played a leading role in previous coups. Just as my Herat trip had shown Kabul's *glasnost* to be superficial, so the supposed new unity of the PDPA was exposed in March 1990 when the Defence Minister and leading Khalqi, Shahnawaz Tanai, initiated a coup, linking forces with Hekmatyar – a most unlikely marriage.

For twenty-four hours Najib seemed in danger. His Presidential palace was bombed, cracking the wall of his office, and he could mobilize no air cover. But he was saved by the crack 15,000-strong Presidential Guard, thought to have been trained in Tash-kent, and sweeping arrests followed with Tanai fleeing to the borders of Pakistan. Having survived this, the strongest challenge to his four-year regime, Najib seemed to be in Kabul to stay. In fact, it was the resistance that had been left more disunited. When the news of the coup broke, ISI had trucks waiting at the border to take in *mujaheddin* for the expected final *putsch*. But for once the other six resistance leaders stood up to them and refused to fight, instead praying in the mosques of Peshawar for its failure. According to a senior ISI official, such was the divergence in opinions between ISI and the PPP government that while it was ISI who were funding Tanai and his colleagues, the government insisted that if they came to Pakistan they would be arrested.

By then, if there was any sense left in the US and Pakistan policy towards Afghanistan it was hard to find. Having managed to turn the *mujaheddin* victory against the might of the Red Army into a fiasco where so confident were they of *mujaheddin* success that they had stopped arms for five months at a crucial time, they seemed determined to compound the error by continuing to push for a military victory, again talking in terms of one last summer. But the military power of the field commanders had decreased, their power undermined by the combined Pakistan–US policy. By mid-1990 the situation on the ground had degenerated into a series of zero-sum games, fighting mostly localized sub-ethnic feuds caused by grass-root rivalries rather than with any political meaning, and where it made little difference whether the winning guy was close to the AIG or the regime.

Congress would not go on indefinitely sanctioning hundreds of millions of dollars, and at the time of writing Washington was no longer insisting on Najib stepping down as a precondition for talks. They had little choice. Moscow, which was fully prepared to drop Najib at the time of the withdrawal and settle for elections or even just representation for 'good Muslims from Kabul' in the *shura*, no longer saw the necessity with the *mujaheddin* in such a weak negotiating postition. But simply firing rockets into Kabul was not the kind of military pressure needed to improve the balance. Some State Department officials believed Moscow would be forced to withdraw their support of Najib because of domestic economic pressures and eagerness to cement the new-found friendship between the two superpowers. But the $800 million a year they estimated is spent by Moscow is far less than the $5 billion it cost to maintain Soviet forces there, and, with increasing unrest in the Soviet Union's Muslim republics, Gorbachev would be anxious to maintain a sympathetic government in Kabul and prevent a fundamentalist regime that might be eager to extend their *jihad*.

Ironically, Bhutto had always favoured a negotiated settlement, but when she visited the US in June 1989 her Foreign Minister was told categorically that the military push and backing of the AIG would continue. 'There should be no fall-back positions,' they said, making sure she was portrayed as an ardent supporter of military aid to the resistance. Convinced of the US role in her father's downfall, Bhutto was not about to argue and continued to take a back seat on Afghan policy. But some US officials say she was mistaken in thinking that her reward would be continued US backing. Robert Peck, now retired, the diplomat who helped negotiate the 1987 Geneva Accords which led to the Soviet withdrawal, said in late 1989: 'Mrs Bhutto believes as long as she is a good soldier in Afghanistan, we will keep her in power. Is Benazir Bhutto necessarily in our interests?'[18]

Bhutto's attempt to take charge by installing Kallue at the helm of ISI achieved nothing. Kallue was continually bypassed, unable to obtain files, while the organization's regional heads indoctrinated by Zia's mission continued to run events. Too late in the day had the US come round to looking at the political option. ISI and

Hekmatyar seemed to be out of control, and ordinary Afghans, while fed up with the war and eager for a negotiated end, would not easily swallow sitting down with Najib. Several refugees described it to me as 'like asking the Jews to pardon the Nazis and form a government with Hitler'.

It was not at all clear that ISI wanted an end to the war, which provided them with rich pickings and justified their continued powerful role. Both Foreign Office officials and government ministers voiced this fear but seemed incapable of acting. So while the positions of the US and USSR were moving closer it was Pakistan, under a civilian administration, causing the block. But Bhutto became increasingly unable to rectify this situation. As relations between the army and the PPP government worsened in 1990, the 'betrayal of the Afghan cause' was a constant theme in the litany of accusations against Bhutto by hawkish generals such as Gul. Referring to Zia's mission, a US diplomat complained, 'We're following the policy of a dead man and the dead man's dream is becoming Afghanistan's nightmare.'

But it was also the nightmare for Pakistan's civilian government. Not only did it give continued power to the anti-Bhutto ISI, but the lull in fighting increased the already wide availability of cheap sophisticated arms, intensifying the carnage in Sindh. Many field commanders had become more interested in drug running, increasing the power of Pakistan's drug barons and the damage to its youth. Moreover, Pakistan feared the Frontier would become uncontrollable with 3.8 million bored, hungry and well-armed refugees showing no signs of going home, while resentment in Baluchistan against the 1 million refugees living there was increasing. The UNHCR, strapped for cash, had already slashed aid, and Happy Minwalla, a close adviser of Bhutto, admitted, 'We fear with the decline in Western interest we will be left with the entire burden of supporting the world's largest refugee population (an estimated $1 billion per day).'

Pakistan also risked losing the immense goodwill it had built up with the Afghans through its hospitality, after years of troubled relations between the two neighbours. On a hill in Paktia province I sat with Abdul Wasei looking down on the road where ten years earlier he had watched Soviet tanks advance. He was sketching crimson tulips to represent *shaheeds*, as he told me. 'I sat here all morning, all afternoon, all evening, and still the tanks kept coming,' he reminisced. 'Many of us had never even seen cars and these things were like metal monsters. I could not believe we would ever turn them back. But we did it. So why is it still all we have are pictures of flowers to remind ourselves of peace? Why can't the world leave us alone now?' As we talked the sun was going down, and I was reminded of the nightly fireworks over the minarets of Herat. For Najib every sunset was another victory. For the people of Afghanistan it meant more sons lost. Among the ruins of Herat, Nadya, who at forty-five had already passed the country's average life expectancy, was no doubt still weeping softly for her country. She was on the other side but had voiced the same emotions: 'I don't care who comes to power. We are all the same people with the same hopes and dreams. We just want to be left alone and the killing to stop.'

13

IN THE NAME OF
THE CRESCENT

INDIA – THE DRAGON ON THE DOORSTEP

'History will be the ultimate judge of Pakistan.' (Mohammad
Ali Jinnah, 1947)

Far up in the top-most reaches of the Himalayas another war was
raging on history's highest battleground. It is a war few know
about, between two countries supposedly at peace.

Since 1984 the élite forces of the Pakistan and Indian armies
had battled to control the Siachen glacier, the world's most
spectacular theatre of war, surrounded by peaks towering above
25,000 ft and including K2, the world's second highest mountain.
Its beauty masks cruelty more lethal than gunfire.

The conflict could be described as little other than senseless: the
battle was for an inaccessible stretch of frozen barren terrain where
the final victor could only be the weather, the killer behind eight
out of every ten victims. Flying over the uninhabitable land, Lt.-
Col. Farooq, the dashing officer who commanded the fleet of
mountain helicopters which is Siachen's lifeline to the rest of
Pakistan, told me: 'We are conducting a war where men must rest
after every four steps.'[1]

Within fifteen minutes of taking off from the sizzling heat and
sprawling mass of Rawalpindi with the then Prime Minister,
Benazir Bhutto, in a C130 like that which killed her predecessor, we
were in a virgin world snaking through mountain passes and
following emerald ribbons of rivers, our plane often lower than the
level of the treacherous road. Every turn brought a breathtaking
new vista, and as we left habitation behind, we entered a forest of

peaks and nature of such staggering perfection that it flooded one simultaneously with a soaring joy and a stark realization of the absolute insignificance of man.

Bhutto, in her role as Defence Minister, was on a tour of frontline positions to demonstrate her new-found solidarity with the army, which had so long denied her power. Arriving at the base camp of Gyari, at the foot of the Bilafond glacier which connects with Siachen, we donned huge padded white snowsuits and boots only two hours from the sweltering capital. Around us were dotted huge boulders painted with slogans – 'Kill them All' and 'Never Surrender' – essential for morale in a battle which Colonel Cheema, the junior Defence Minister, who was with us, described as '95 per cent a war against nature'.

Boarding fragile glass helicopters to Ali Brangsa, the pilot muttered his prayers and we were off skimming over glaciers and skirting the sides of jagged mountains, coasting on air currents to conserve precious fuel. For six months of the year this area is totally cut off, raging blizzards and sub-zero temperatures making even helicopter travel impossible.

Even in the height of summer the weather can change dramatically, but we were lucky. As we journeyed higher the clouds seemed to be tweezed out of the sky, unravelling glittering peaks, like ice turrets, an achingly beautiful land of which no man could ever be master. Below and ahead of us stretched treacherous glaciers, constantly moving like some ravenous being, pushing up rocks and boulders into which men often fall, freezing to death almost instantaneously.

The hollow crash reverberating across the mountains as we arrived with the four-months pregnant Bhutto at the 17,000-ft post of Ali Brangsa made us jump. We could see Indian troops less than a mile away on a peak and imagined they must have fired. But the commander of Pakistan's 56th Baluch regiment smiled wryly – what we had heard was not artillery fire but an avalanche, in which more men perished. Though neither side would release figures, officials had admitted that there had been hundreds of deaths and thousands of casualties among the 4,000 élite troops on either side.

At Ali Brangsa we had to wear dark glasses against the blinding whiteness. The soldiers' faces were burnt black from the glare,

..and several were scarred from frostbite, which sets in within minutes of exposing the flesh, the cold is so piercing. The temperature, which can drop to as low as minus 80 °C and frequently freezes the weapons, was not the only hazard. At 17,000 ft, simply talking makes one's head spin and induces nausea. The air is so thin, with less than half the normal oxygen content, that movements become absurdly heavy and even the fittest men must rest every three minutes. Above 14,000 ft walking is so arduous that to travel fifteen miles takes six days, while on the 19,000 ft glacier it takes twenty minutes to cover 100 yards. According to the battalion medic, the lack of oxygen can cause lungs almost literally to explode, filling with blood and fluid so that the victim suffocates.

The men of Ali Brangsa, living in rock bunkers decorated with religious slogans, were luckier than their colleagues manning Pakistan's two highest posts at above 22,000 ft. There the long isolation caused acute depression, driving men to insanity. One major who had survived such an experience described the desolation: 'There is nothing to do but fire, and after days alone you begin to imagine targets. You need to shoot to reassure yourself you are still alive.'

No army has ever fought in such conditions for such a sustained period. With the ultimate prize strategically useless, the Pakistani troops I spoke to saw themselves as fighting for Islam, with the final honour martyrdom, bodies wrapped in the Pakistan flag of white crescent and star on a green background. Despite the extreme weather, war was definitely under way on the 75-kilometre-long glacier. The difficulty of walking, let alone carrying weapons, ruled out infantry campaigns, but artillery fire was frequent. The day before our visit in August 1989, the Indians had lobbed eight artillery shells and five rockets, a tally which General Imran Ullah, the Rawalpindi Corps Commander, dismissed as 'light'.

The most recent fighting began in 1984, when Pakistan became suspicious at seeing Siachen, which they claim as their territory, suddenly marked on Indian maps. Men dispatched to check found that the Indians had occupied some peaks of the Saltoro range and captured 1,000 square miles. Pakistan's attempts to take back the area lost were unsuccessful, and a senior officer admitted that the failure of the biggest operation in 1987 'only proved the impossibility of conducting a war up here'.

The bitterness left by the genocide of Partition, in which Hindu and Muslim neighbours fell upon each other with ghastly savagery, ensured that relations between India and Pakistan could only begin with hostility. The ideologies of the two nations are diametrically opposed – India is based on secularism and nationalism, while Pakistan is founded on the two-nation theory which insists that religion cannot be separated from politics. So, despite their common history and shared cultural heritage, relations between the neighbours have never normalized. The flashpoint for conflict which has dominated Indo-Pak relations since 1947 is custody of the Muslim-dominated state of Kashmir, of which Siachen is the northernmost part.

Every invader who has ever passed through Kashmir has loved the Himalayan valley with a fierce passion. The Hindus made it a centre of pilgrimage; the Mughal emperors indulged their predilection for gardens around its lily-strewn lakes, on which they lounged among silken cushions in extravagantly carved houseboats; the British stocked its mountain streams with trout from Scotland and built golf courses in the shadow of its peaks. It was the Mughal emperor Jehangir who named this land of snows and clear air, far from the heat and dust of the plains, 'Paradise on Earth'. On his deathbed, when asked if there was anything he wanted, the Emperor whispered 'only Kashmir' in his dying breath.

So it was no surprise in 1947 as the British Empire was dismantled that both sides were determined that Kashmir should be theirs. With its mainly Muslim population, Jinnah needed the state to validate the two-nation theory and pointed out that all its natural links were with Pakistan. The British, having accepted the two-nation theory as the logic for Partition, could not understand that a state with two-thirds Muslim majority might prefer to remain in Hindu India, and in July 1947 the British Viceroy, Lord Louis Mountbatten, even flew to Kashmir to try to persuade the Maharajah Hari Singh to accede to Pakistan. But Nehru, himself a Kashmiri, had no intention of giving up the mountain valley that was a great centre of early Hinduism, and could be used to demonstrate that India's principles of nationalism and democracy were more potent forces than religion. He achieved possession of Kashmir through the support of the great Kashmiri leader, Sheikh

Abdullah. As the rest of the country was torn apart in the rage and brutality of Partition, Abdullah, known as the Lion of Kashmir, kept his province calm with slogans of 'Hindu-Muslim *ittehad ki jai!*' ('Victory to Hindu-Muslim friendship!'). He argued that the real struggle was against feudalism: 'I never believed in the Pakistan slogan . . . we want people's *raj* (rule) in Kashmir. It will not be a government of any particular community but of all – Hindus, Muslims and Sikhs.'

While other provinces were swept by fury in 1947, incredibly there was not a single death through communal rioting in Kashmir, and Nehru proudly declared: 'Kashmir is the laboratory of secularism.' Four decades on, the experiment seemed to be failing. After forty-three years of ignoring the Kashmiris' demand to decide their own future, India was discovering Trouble in Paradise and by 1990 was keeping the state within the union by force and round-the-clock curfew. Clashes between Kashmiri separatists and Indian troops in the first four months of 1990 left more than 300 dead, and brought Pakistani and Indian forces to a state of high alert that could end in a war neither side wanted.

It would not be the first time the two countries had gone to war over Kashmir. The first, in October 1947, occurred when Jinnah, determined that the state should be his and furious that he was no longer allowed to holiday there, sent in Pathan tribesmen and plainclothes soldiers to 'liberate' it, assuming their Kashmiri co-religionists would welcome them with open arms. But the unruly tribesmen were quickly distracted by the lure of looting and pillage, and met unexpected resistance from the Kashmiri Muslims. Before the invaders neared the capital, the panicked Maharajah acceded to India, supported by Sheikh Abdullah, and Indian troops were flown in.

There was a proviso in the accession. The ruling Dogra family had bought Kashmir for 7.5 million rupees in 1846 from the British in return for services rendered during the Sikh wars, in which the British had acquired most of Ranjit Singh's empire in north-west India. Sheikh Abdullah, whose 'Quit Kashmir' movement against Maharajah Hari Singh had landed him in jail on several occasions, could not then allow him the privilege of determining the destiny of its people. So Sheikh Abdullah was promised that there would be a plebiscite to allow the people of

Kashmir to decide their own future. In a national broadcast on 2 November 1947, Nehru stated: 'We've decided that the fate of Kashmir is ultimately to be decided by the people. This pledge we have given . . . not only to the people of Kashmir but to the world – we will not and cannot back out of it.'[2] To persuade Kashmir to stay in India, the state was given a large measure of autonomy in a special status formalized in the Indian Constitution of 1950. Fighting stopped in 1948 when the UN drew up a ceasefire line, leaving Pakistan with only a third – the western wedge, which they called 'Azad Kashmir' ('Free Kashmir'), and the northern wastelands which include Siachen, while India retained the famous resort valley.

Pakistan and India have to this day kept troops stationed in their respective parts of Kashmir, and the referendum to decide its future has never been held. Fearing that the state would vote for Pakistan or autonomy, the central leadership in Delhi continually stalled UN Security Council efforts to arrange a plebiscite, and Kashmir was subjected to a series of puppet governments, beginning with the overthrow and arrest of Sheikh Abdullah in August 1953 after he began demanding 'self-determination' too vociferously. By 1958 the Indian government began to say that the question did not arise, and on 1 July 1965 the Home Minister stated the Indian position categorically: 'Kashmir is an integral part of India. It is a settled fact which cannot be the subject of debate or negotiation.'[3] Despite the betrayal by his great friend Pandit Nehru, Sheikh Abdullah still did not turn towards Pakistan. In 1978, in an interview with Indian author M. J. Akbar, he said: 'The ideals we stood for were more important than Pakistan or India. We had joined India because of its ideals – secularism and socialism. India wanted to build a state where humanism would prevail. So long as India sticks to these ideals, our people have a place nowhere else but India.'[4]

Negotiations over Kashmir began between India and Pakistan in December 1962 but Pakistan, emboldened by India's defeat in the war with China earlier that year and its own consequent new friendship with China, was not interested in talking. Believing India weakened by Nehru's death in 1964, Pakistan ended the delicate peace the following year with a further war. It was no more successful than the first. President Ayub Khan and Foreign Minister Zulfikar Ali Bhutto, repeating Jinnah's failed tactic of sending in tribesmen followed by the Pakistani army, were again unable to change the status quo. Their efforts resulted only in a cut-off in the country's US arms supply, and they were losing badly when the Soviet Union, acting as mediator, brought about a ceasefire.

Indo-Pak relations improved under Pakistan's first elected government in the aftermath of the third war, that time over the secession of Bangladesh, which left Pakistan demoralized and humiliated, having lost half its territory. The resulting Simla Accord, between Prime Ministers Mrs Gandhi and Zulfikar Ali Bhutto on 2 July 1972, included agreement that the ceasefire line would become a line of control and a pact that a final settlement of the Kashmir issue would be by bilateral negotiations. Before it was officially announced, the Pakistan delegation passed on the news of the successful negotiations through the code 'It's a boy!', signifying the low position women have in their society. Bhutto had been in a weak position, with India holding 90,000 Pakistani prisoners of war, and it was a tribute to his bargaining skills that he was not forced to yield more territory, though in achieving this he had priced land above men, reckoning correctly, if somewhat inhumanely as far as their relatives were concerned, that international pressure would force India to release the captives later.

Pakistan under General Zia took a tougher stance, once more declaring Kashmir an integral part of Pakistan, and persistently brought up the subject at international forums. Kashmir was an ideal issue for Zia's campaign to return Pakistan to the faith on which it was based, and became a useful slogan from which to create his Pakistani identity, particularly after 1984 when the Indian troops were found to have advanced into Pakistani territory. The President of Azad Kashmir called for a *jihād* to liberate Kashmir, and border tensions rose, with the fighting at Siachen a natural corollary. Pakistan said it did not accept the ceasefire line, and on maps entering the country stamped 'Disputed territory' in red ink across the area.

Delhi resumed accusations that Pakistan was sending in arms to Kashmir militants. The power of Muslim extremists in the disputed state had been on the increase since elections in 1987 which were allegedly rigged against the Muslim United Front, a group advocating secession. Their hopes of escaping the Indian leash were boosted by the success of the *mujaheddin* in driving out the Soviets from Afghanistan. In the early 1980s a referendum in Kashmir would probably still have opted for India. As late as 1982, at the funeral of Sheikh Abdullah, the dominant slogans were still 'Hindu, Muslim, Sikh *ittehad*' ('Friendship between Hindu, Muslim and Sikh'). But by the end of the decade the Kashmiris had finally had enough of bogus elections and arrests of popular leaders. The secessionist movement for the first time flared into a mass uprising in January 1990 when policemen opened fire on a demonstration, killing fifty people. Subsequent cross-border sniping sparked off a row which brought Pakistan and India to the verge of a new war.

Karan Singh, former Indian ambassador in Washington and son of the Maharajah of Kashmir, recalled an anecdote to explain why a conflict in the 1990s would be far more bitter than those of the post-Raj era, when most senior officers were Sandhurst trained. An Indian officer had been captured in Kashmir in 1948 by the invading Pakistanis and was about to be shot when he was recognized and rescued by his Pakistani opposite number. 'My dear chap, how spiffing to see you!' the two officers exclaimed simultaneously. 'You see,' said Singh, 'they had both been to the same school.'[5]

A third war over the state could be fatally destructive, with both sides conducting an undeclared nuclear arms race. Pakistan's nuclear programme was initiated in 1972 by Zulfikar Ali Bhutto, whose desire for an 'Islamic bomb' was so great that he declared, 'We will eat grass if necessary.' After India's nuclear test explosion in 1974 he ordered a French plutonium processing plant, despite stern warnings from US Secretary of State Henry Kissinger. But delivery of vital final components was halted under US pressure, and eventually the Carter administration cut off aid. However, the parameters of the relationship changed when the Soviet invasion of Afghanistan made Pakistan essential in order to transform the resistance into an effective fighting force. Aid was resumed by the Reagan administration on a far larger scale. On the basis of a Pakistani promise not to pursue nuclear weapons, Congress voted to waive for five years the Symington amendment under which, in order to continue aid, the President must certify annually that Pakistan does not possess 'a nuclear explosive device'.

But few believed that Pakistan's nuclear ambitions had really been shelved. Occasional leaks confirmed that Islamabad was still striving to keep up with its neighbour's progress. In 1984 a Pakistani national was caught trying to export nuclear triggers from the US. Two others were convicted in Canada for export of nuclear-related US electronics. A year later the CIA reported that Pakistan had enriched uranium to above the 90 per cent required for weapons.

Pakistan continued its refusal to sign the Nuclear Nonproliferation Treaty until India does, and in an interview with an Indian journalist in 1987 Pakistan's most prominent nuclear scientist, Abdul Qadir, claimed his country had the bomb, lending weight to Indian accusations that Pakistan was secretly making a bomb with Chinese assistance and US acquiescence. Although the Pakistan government had always maintained that the nuclear programme was for peaceful purposes, journalists attempting to enter the site of the nuclear project at Kahuta were apprehended and badly beaten. The secrecy heightened mutual suspicion, and a delegation from the Washington-based Carnegie Taskforce which met President Zia in August 1988, just before his death, later observed, 'Both India and Pakistan now perceive each other to be capable of deploying nuclear weapons. This has set the stage for an open-ended arms race.'

Pakistan's nuclear programme remained a sticking point in relations with its major donor, but until the Soviet forces left Afghanistan in 1989 the country's strategic importance was sufficient for US administrations to continue overlooking the issue. But on 1 October 1990, aid was suspended when President Bush failed to sign the annual certification assuring Congress that Pakistan's nuclear programme was for peaceful purposes. The dismissal of Benazir Bhutto's government two months earlier had lost Islamabad what friends it had on Capitol Hill to counter the anti-nuclear lobby. Moreover, the *Washington Post* reported that Pakistan had been trying to buy US high-temperature furnaces, usually used in nuclear weapons. The US Secretary of State, James Baker, told his Pakistani counterpart, Sahabzada Yaqub Khan, that objections in Congress made further aid impossible unless Pakistan could provide evidence that it did not possess a nuclear bomb. For any Pakistani Premier to accede to American wishes and sign the NPT or allow an inspection of Kahuta would be political suicide, and the US suspension of assistance was interpreted by many as a warning that elections promised for later that month must proceed.

For the Pakistan army, US aid meant more than the annual $583 million blocked in the autumn of 1990. Since 1982 the US had assisted Pakistan in a massive military build-up. Officially it had received more than $5.5 billion of mostly military assistance, as well as forty F16 fighter jets. On top of this was a considerable cut, usually estimated as at least 40 per cent, from those arms destined for the Afghan resistance. By 1990, then, the Pakistan army was extremely well equipped. But the sheer force of numbers meant that their neighbours had an apparently unassailable advantage – the 1.2 million-strong Indian army was more than twice the size of Pakistan's. Pakistan had already lost three wars against India, prompting a senior US State Department official to warn: 'If I were a Pakistani military planner I'd take a lesson from history.'

The hawkish statements emanating from both sides in early 1990 were in sharp contrast to a year earlier, when, after Benazir Bhutto took office, the talk had been of peace and an end to the glacier war neither side could afford. Although the Soviet invasion of Afghanistan, where the two countries had supported opposite sides, had made relations more uncomfortable, particularly with the accompanying US reinforcement of Pakistani military strength, it was hoped that with two civilian governments in power in the neighbouring capitals, negotiations to break the deadlock could make progress. At the end of December 1988, Rajiv Gandhi made the first formal visit by an Indian Premier to Pakistan in almost thirty years. He had sent warm personal congratulations when Bhutto was sworn in, and the media was quick to draw parallels between the two glamorous young Premiers as the offspring of the subcontinent's two great political dynasties. The meeting was hailed as a replay of 1972, when Mr Gandhi's mother Indira signed the Simla Accord with Benazir's father. In her autobiography, Bhutto points out: 'I symbolized a new generation. I had never been an Indian. I had been born in independent Pakistan. I was free of the complexes and prejudices which had torn Indians and Pakistanis apart in the bloody trauma of Partition.'

But the first meeting proved little more than a photo-opportunity, with neither leader in a strong enough domestic position to afford being seen as kow-towing to the other, and despite the hype and talk of new initiatives, little was achieved other than cultural and trade agreements. However, a personal rapport seemed to have been struck and when the two leaders met again in Paris during the Bastille Day celebrations Gandhi said: 'I feel that with Prime Minister Benazir Bhutto we have for the first time in eleven and a half years an opportunity to solve our problems. We found it very difficult to deal with the military dictatorship.' Gandhi paid his second visit to Islamabad on 16 July 1989 amid full ceremonial honours, and talks were held between the Foreign Secretaries. But peace initiatives ended in disarray when the Pakistan delegation later said an agreement had been reached on Siachen under which Indian troops would retreat to their 1972 postitions, a breakthrough Delhi quickly denied. By the time of Bhutto's visit to Siachen in August, she admitted that talks had broken down and, with Gandhi facing an election that winter, were unlikely to resume. 'Agreement seems very difficult now,' she said. 'Everyone's quite dug in for another winter.'6

The winter passed, and Gandhi lost the election to a coalition led by V. P. Singh. The raised temperature in Indian Kashmir forced both sides to issue warlike words, India accusing Pakistan of training and arming secessionists. V. P. Singh, conscious that the loss of Kashmir would spell the end for his minority government, warned Pakistan that it could not take Kashmir without a war: 'They will have to pay a very high price and we have the capacity to inflict heavy losses,' he told Parliament. His administration, relying heavily for its survival on the Hindu-dominated Bharatiya Janata Party, was under intense pressure to match words with actions.

Bhutto, in an equally weak position with an impotent administration under the thumb of a bureaucracy and army who from the start suspected she was 'soft on India', also found herself forced to take a hawkish stance. Once more politics had run out of her control and back on to the agenda set by Zia, which defined a Pakistani patriot as being anti-Indian, forcing Bhutto to enter Azad Kashmir like a latterday Boadicea, demanding 'self-determination' for Kashmiris 'even if it takes a thousand years to achieve'. Both government and opposition had found a new outlet to demonstrate their political muscle. Instead of holding rallies they tried to outdo each other in 'Pakistan-ness' with statements of support for their 'Kashmiri brothers', and when Nawaz Sharif, himself of Kashmiri descent, set up a fund to 'liberate' Kashmir, Bhutto had to follow suit, causing V. P. Singh to remark snidely that in Pakistan no one seemed in control.

Some of Bhutto's aides pushed for war, in the misguided belief that a war in Kashmir could revive Bhutto's flagging popularity just as the Falklands conflict had for Britain's Mrs Thatcher. Not only would this have been unwise militarily, but it was not clear that Kashmiri Muslims wanted to be part of Pakistan – most interviewed said that their demand was independence, though they did not elaborate how such a remote landlocked state could survive on its own two feet. Moreover, independence would mean Azad Kashmir leaving Pakistan, which would have been as politically suicidal for Bhutto as the loss of Indian Kashmir would be for V. P. Singh.

Fortunately, though both armies were kept in a state of red-alert, wiser sense seemed to have prevailed, the war more one of rhetoric. But for Pakistan, Kashmir is no rallying cry able to pull together a disunited nation. It strikes chords only with the Punjabi-dominated oligarchy of the bureaucracy and military, the *mohajirs* of Karachi who see parallels with their own situation, and with the *mullahs*, to whom it is a holy war necessary to justify Pakistan's basis. The government is dragged in because it cannot afford to go against these powerful lobbies who are the main forces in the country. Bhutto was no exception. In private meetings with journalists some time after losing the Indian elections, Rajiv Gandhi spoke in surprisingly disparaging tones about her and said in their meetings that she had never seemed to be in control of policy. He cited examples of Bhutto expressing one wish and her army-backed Foreign Minister, Yaqub Khan, curtly stepping in to say: 'No, this is our policy, Prime Minister.'

While the Pakistani army has a casting vote, it is hard to see how relations between Pakistan and India can ever be peaceful, as it is in their interests to maintain high tension to justify the large proportion of budget spent on defence (twenty times education expenditure), particularly amid declining US interest after the Soviet departure from Afghanistan. One of the world's biggest armies, it provides valuable jobs to Punjabi youth. Indeed, under Bhutto the defence budget was increased by 50 per cent to 63 billion rupees ($3.1 billion), some 39 per cent of current expenditure, despite her previous stated demand that it should be cut to provide money for development.

The huge amount of money squandered on the Indo-Pak arms race is criminal for countries with such poverty. The superpowers have used the conflict to maintain a stake in the region. South Asia in 1990 was the second largest recipient of Soviet military exports (to India) and the third largest of US military hardware (to Pakistan).

But it is not just the army it suited to keep attention focused on external affairs. The governments of India and Pakistan had long used their uneasy relations to divert attention from domestic crises, such as the insurgency in Pakistan's southern province of Sindh or the Sikh struggle since 1983 for an independent homeland in Indian Punjab. Both sides would take advantage of each other's weak spots: India, which until Kashmir flared up had two-thirds of its troops concentrated on the Sindh border, frequently alleged that Pakistan was arming Sikh militants, while Pakistan blamed India for causing unrest in Sindh.

To the uninitiated the anti-Indian rhetoric could seem little short of obsession. More than half Pakistan's population is under fifteen, and thus a second generation after Partition untainted by the memory of genocide. Yet the press and educational material of both countries continued to deliberately distort each other. The Pakistani press appeared unable to mention the word India without using 'hegemony' in the same breath. India depicted Pakistan as a US satellite out to destabilize India, while the majority of Pakistanis seemed seriously to believe that India was just waiting for an opportunity to invade, despite the fact that all three wars have been started by Pakistan and there seems no earthly reason imaginable why India should want another 110 million hungry people, with yet more languages and regional differences, to add to an already troublesome population. A Canadian who attended Quetta staff college in the early 1980s told me he was amazed that while the Soviet forces seemed an imminent threat just over the border in Afghanistan, strategy at the military academy focused entirely on India.

The tortured relations between the two neighbours created a

bizarre situation where the two countries have no direct air link
between their capitals, a train runs only weekly, communications
are poor, and it is extremely difficult for those with relations
across the border to obtain visas. These obstacles have little effect
on the lawmakers, who can afford the *bakshish* or pull strings to
secure a visa. Despite the antagonism, there is tremendous curiosity
among Pakistanis about their fellow Indians. I was frequently
asked to compare the countries and soon learnt that the correct
answer was 'Pakistan is more hospitable and so much cleaner. No
one sleeps on the streets.' For the most part that is true, but I could
have added that India is freer, women are treated more fairly, it
has a stable political system and a solid industrial base and is more
advanced technologically, but it would not have been tactful. My
Pakistani friends were seeking reassurance that splitting up from
India had at least made them better off economically.

In many ways Pakistan needs to maintain hostility with India to
justify its own existence and to define itself. The country invented
in the name of the crescent would be a deep disappointment to its
founders, who envisaged a modern state. But the very *raison d'être*
they used has prevented that advance, the debate between the
fundamentalists and the liberals over what it means to be an
Islamic state never having been resolved. Jinnah talked of a secular
state and a country free of discrimination, but for some outside the
mainstream of Islam, the land of the 'pure' turned into a nightmare.
The Ahmadi sect, for example, were declared non-Muslim in
1974 by Zulfikar Ali Bhutto under pressure from Arab leaders and
in an attempt to win over the clergy, who as early as 1953 had
taken to the streets to demand their expulsion. Ahmadis (also
known as Qadianis after the Punjab town where the movement
began) are an Islamic sect who believe that a man called Hazrat
Mirza Ghulam Ahmad, born in 1835, was the Mahdi or Messiah,
whereas Muslims believe that Mohammad was the final Prophet.
There are nearly 10 million Ahmadis worldwide, of whom around
4 million are in Pakistan, where the movement was founded in
1889. Persecution of Ahmadis on a grand scale began in 1984,
when General Zia promulgated an ordinance denying freedom
of religion and transforming many Ahmadi activities into a criminal offence; this led to a widespread campaign of harassment,
partly documented by the human rights organization Amnesty

International. Under Zia, Qadiani became a dirty word. In his message to a conference of the 'Finality of Prophethood' in London in August 1985, Zia promised to 'persevere in our efforts to ensure that the cancer of Qadianism is exterminated'.

Many Ahmadis were arrested simply for professing their faith, and their mosques were demolished or desecrated. Rashid Ahmad Chaudry, Press Secretary of the Ahmadi association, claimed: 'The teachings of Ahmadiyat were misrepresented so as to create hatred among the members of the community. The *mullahs* were let loose by the government and they roamed about in cities and villages, using the pulpits of mosques to incite the people to kill the Ahmadis and burn their property.'[7]

Benazir Bhutto's People's Party pledged in its manifesto to 'ensure security and protection of life, honour and property of every citizen irrespective of his political affiliations, religion, caste, race and sex'. But after they took power the killings and intimidation of Ahmadis continued, while the Minister of State for Religious Affairs, Khan Bahdur Khan, declared that the restrictions placed on Ahmadis would not be removed even if the 1973 Constitution was restored and Zia's amendments annulled. According to Rashid Ahmad Chaudry, the Minister issued instructions to provincial Chief Ministers on 30 January 1989 to implement all laws against Ahmadis: 'As a result, well-organized attacks on the Ahmadi population were made and hundreds of Ahmadi houses looted and set on fire by armed hooligans led by religious fanatics and aided and abetted by police authorities.' The Ahmadi organization alleged that Bhutto agreed to keep to Zia's ordinance in order to persuade religious parties such as Jamaat ul-Islami to drop their insistence that a woman cannot be head of government under Islamic law.

In April 1989, riots against Ahmadis took place in Punjab and Sindh. The small town of Nakana was ransacked after rumours were spread that an Ahmadi had burnt the Koran, and the story of Amatul Naseer Sultan, who was one of the many women attacked with her children, was typical: 'A large group of people broke into our house shouting slogans, shattering the door and demolishing the wall and started throwing stones and sticks at us. I locked myself and my children in a room but the culprits broke the door and the windows and set the house on fire. My young children became extremely scared and fearful and took protection under the bed. At this they set the beds on fire. Pieces of glass were showered on us from all directions. Two of my children were crying and screaming and these cruel and brutal people were asking the innocent children to be thrown in the fire.'[8]

While members of the Ahmadi sect were suffering such persecution in Pakistan, ironically in London their exiled leader was preaching tolerance. For in Britain, too, home to 2 million Muslims, the moderate side of Islam was being forgotten. The publication of Salman Rushdie's *Satanic Verses* had sparked off numerous demonstrations, endorsing the late Ayatollah Khomeini's call for the author's death and burning the books. Previously tolerant non-Muslims were asking what it says about a religion that one book could provoke such a wave of international terror.

It was in Islamabad, perhaps fittingly, that the anti-Rushdie protests had started, with a riot in February 1989 in which eight people died and the American Centre was attacked by rampaging Muslims incited to march at the morning prayer meeting. Passions were so high in the wide Jinnah Avenue, on which they descended, that the men seemed almost rabid with their smouldering black eyes and panting breath. Pushed and squeezed in almost every part of my body, it was impossible to equate this frenzied mob with the exquisite art and spectacular architecture that Islam had inspired, which, like the Taj Mahal, above all exuded serenity. Nor did it seem possible that these people were motivated by the same religion as the swirling dancers and pipers in the Sufi shrines of Sindh.

Mirza Tahir Ahmad, the Ahmadi leader, said in London that he had scoured the Koran but could find no mention of a death penalty for blasphemy such as Muslims see in Rushdie's book. But the tolerance Jinnah envisaged in his Pakistan is far from present in today's Pakistan. Christian leaders say they have been deliberately stopped from building a church in the capital. The emphasis has been on the penal side of Islam, with harsh laws discriminating against women and minorities rather than the compassionate nature of the Koran. It seems curious that a state created as a homeland for Muslims would feel it necessary to issue edicts telling people how to say their prayers, or police the streets to ensure that fasts were being kept during the month of Ramazan, as happened in Zia's regime.

For most Pakistanis, the creation of their country meant simply swapping domination by an overwhelmingly Hindu population for domination by a Punjabi majority and landowning élite, backed by a clergy determined that others should follow their orthodox path. It should have been predictable. Just as in the 1940s the movement for Pakistan was the province of the élite, so politics in Pakistan today continues as the preserve of a few landlords and *mullahs* with little mass support. In fact the power of the religious lobby is so strong that had it not been dismissed, the Bhutto government, which had pledged to remove discriminatory Islamic laws, would almost certainly have had the Shariat Bill forced on it. Passed by the Senate in May 1990, this would bring everything from media to education to economic policy under the purview of the Shariat committee (an Islamic body set up in 1980 by Zia, chosen by the President) and enable them to question any government action. Kamal Azfar, an eminent Pakistani lawyer and minister under Ali Bhutto and again in Jatoi's caretaker cabinet, wrote in 1987 of the implications of the Shariat Bill: 'If all cases are to be decided in accordance with the Shariat, then not only the existing laws become redundant but there will be no occasion for the Parliament and provincial assemblies to enact any law in future. In other words these legislative bodies will become defunct.'[9]

M. J. Akbar, in his excellent study of why India has stayed together and Pakistan fallen apart, has harsh words to say about Pakistan's leadership: 'It is quite clear how the landlord–clergy alliance shared out Pakistan. While the landlords and capitalists allowed the clergy to make Pakistan a religious state, the clergy allowed the landlords guaranteed property rights and the capitalists unbridled control over the economy. Theocracy and landlordism/capitalism are the two pillars of Pakistan. No matter who comes to power, whether the leader be in uniform or not, these two things will never be tampered with. Anyone making even a mild effort to challenge these two "rights" will be removed from power.'[10]

14

THE EMPIRE STRIKES BACK

'We apologize for this temporary democratic interruption. Normal martial law will be resumed shortly.' (Graffiti on Karachi wall, August 1990)

On the morning of 6 August 1990 the headline staring out of the *Nation* newspaper told Benazir Bhutto that her government was about to be dismissed. The end was swift. By 4.30 that afternoon, troops had surrounded the ministries and television and radio stations. In a press conference at 5 p.m., the President, standing alongside the three unsmiling service chiefs, announced that Parliament had been dissolved and the government dismissed for 'corruption, mismanagement and violation of the Constitution'. After just twenty months in power, the Muslim world's first female Prime Minister had been deposed. Within six weeks she was in the dock facing four charges of corruption and maladministration.

It was an unceremonious end to Pakistan's second experience of democracy, and the curtain on the country's best opportunity since Ali Bhutto's election victory in 1970 to rid itself of the military shackles that plagued its history. Once more, it seemed, the vested interests of the military, *mullahs*, landlords and bureaucrats had conspired to prevent democracy taking root. When the end came no one but Bhutto herself was surprised. Rumours had been circulating for two months that the breakdown of relations between the government and GHQ had reached the point of no return. Immediately after a corps commanders' conference in the last week of July, the military conveyed to President Ishaq its decision to remove Bhutto if the President himself did not do so.

It was a revealing insight into the extent of Bhutto's isolation that right up until troops surrounded her secretariat she refused to believe that she could be ditched. Arif Nizami, the editor of the *Nation*, who had written the scoop story predicting her fall, tells how that morning he received a call from Bhutto's office.[1] Tariq Rahim, the Parliamentary Affairs Minister, was on the line. Rahim asked him where the material had come from for his article, then accused him of running information planted by the military intelligence. In the meantime Bhutto had sent her close aide, Happy Minwalla, to see the US ambassador and the President, who told him he was not about to do anything 'extraordinary'.

Apparently reassured that the dissolution story was untrue, Bhutto continued to prepare for a forthcoming visit by Britain's Princess Diana and her speech for the World Children's Summit that she was due to co-chair. The rest of the morning was taken up with presiding over the monthly meeting of the cabinet Economic Co-ordination Committee.

Tariq Rahim was less convinced. As the day progressed and the President's office continued to delay returning the file allowing him to summon the next session of Parliament as he had planned on 8 August, his fears grew. He explained, 'I had given them the file on 5 August so I could announce the next session on television on the 6th. When they did not return it by 9.30 a.m. as promised I called and they said it would be there at 11 a.m. When at 11 a.m. it was still not ready I spoke to Benazir. She said everything was all right and that Happy had met the President and he had sworn to abide by the Constitution. But at 2 p.m. when I phoned the President's office again they told me the file would not be available. I said whatever you are doing history will not forgive you. By 4 p.m. the first army trucks were appearing on the horizon.'[2]

Had Bhutto suspected what was happening, she could have dissolved the assemblies herself and called fresh elections under her own supervision, giving her the advantage of incumbency and guaranteeing against rigging by her opponents. To avoid that eventuality the army high command had told Jatoi, then leader of the opposition, to table another no-confidence vote against Bhutto for 15 August. The motion was duly announced on 5 August at a hastily called press conference which surprised even Jatoi's close colleagues. After that, for Bhutto to dissolve the Parliament would have appeared an act of cowardice, suggesting that she did not believe she could survive the vote. In the event the ploy was unnecessary, because Bhutto's own naïvety and arrogance could not accept that a second Prime Minister was to be dismissed within little more than two years. Referred to as 'Alice in Blunderland' even by some of her own ministers, as the government's problems grew, Bhutto, who prized loyalty above everything, had increasingly surrounded herself by sycophants. Insisting to the end, 'I'm the only people's leader,'[3] she had distanced herself from the people by constructing around her house in Karachi towering twenty-foot steel reinforced concrete walls mounted with machine-gun turrets, the structure resembling a Foreign Legion fort.

It was inside these high walls that I spoke to Bhutto for the first time after her dismissal. We met within hours of her first court appearance and I was shocked by her loss of poise. Gone was the ice-cool maiden whose courageous fight against a dictator had captured the imagination of the world and who just that morning had sat upright in court, face unmoving, while the prosecution read out charges that she had given a British company a contract to buy cotton at a below market price. Serene despite the oppressive humidity and the crush of supporters from the slums of Lyari, dirty underfed men around a white queen, Bhutto had played the martyr role superbly, her only sign of tension the constant fiddling of her long fingers with the plastic top from a mineral water bottle. It was hard to believe such a screen goddess figure guilty, and in comparison the small mumbling man from the prosecution seemed cheap and sordid.

But later, inside Bilawal House, a very different Bhutto descended the stairs, her pallor accentuated by the deep cerise *shalwar kamiz* in which she was dressed. The scene seemed specially created to show an unruffled family house. On the lawn outside, the donkey belonging to her two-year-old son Bilawal was munching hay. Inside, her two children played noisily with their *ayah* at the other end of the elegant silk-carpeted room. Occasionally Bhutto cooed rather falsely at the son who would one day, no doubt, be expected to carry on the Bhutto dynasty.

In spite of her perfect make-up and the carefully arranged set, it was impossible for Bhutto to hide the tension she was going through. The fairytale was over. Suddenly Bhutto seemed just another young woman who had lost her job. Her face blotchy and her voice just one note off hysteria, she protested, 'This is the most dishonest act I've seen and that's why I've stayed in the political arena to fight. What happened was a sneak attack on democratic institutions.'[4]

While we talked, in sauntered the dashing husband many believed had brought Bhutto down with his interference in the running of Sindh and his alleged use of influence to secure lucrative contracts for himself and his friends. To the horror of many of her colleagues, Bhutto had insisted that Zardari was to represent the party in two constituencies in the forthcoming elections. Other PPP members felt he would be a greater liability with a definite role inside Parliament than when he was simply First Husband, whose major distraction was the polo-field. His presence in Islamabad would increase charges of nepotism and 'family raj', as their opposition termed it, with husband, mother and father-in-law all in politics.

But Bhutto refused to accept the allegations against the husband with whom she was obviously deeply in love. Her voice rising, she protested, 'Our government tried to honestly and efficiently serve the people. A lot of people said there was hanky panky going on. What hanky panky? Tell me about it. Are we living in the civilized world or are we back in medieval times when people were burnt as witches. If there was corruption why did no one bring me facts?'[5] A week later Zardari was behind bars, arrested for embezzlement, involvement in kidnapping and using influence to obtain illegal bank loans.

Bhutto was equally adamant that she deserved no blame for the snuffing out of democracy. 'It's a clear case of the old order striking back at the new,' she insisted. 'Those who supported dictatorship could not accept the idea of a young woman Prime Minister making all these important social and economic strides.' But was that the case? Could Bhutto really be said to have challenged the old order, to have acted against the interests of theocracy and landlordism? Was the whole episode, as she insisted, a plot to discredit the Bhutto name by elements within the army and bureaucracy who, she claimed, had tried to undermine her from the day she was sworn in? Was the President's version more accurate, depicting an incompetent government out to make as much money as possible to compensate for its eleven years of sacrifice? Or was it simply a case of an inexperienced government, incapable of building consensus, and led by a Prime Minister whose popularity abroad blinded her to the reality of chaos at home?

Whatever the cause, what was certain was that Pakistan had been plunged back into political crisis. The last thirteen years had seen eleven of military rule and the dismissal of two governments. The army, it seemed, while content to return to barracks, still wanted the upper hand in any power-sharing arrangement. The question was how, under such conditions, could democracy function? As Bhutto said, 'All this talk of corruption becomes irrelevant when one looks at the wider issue that now two governments have been dismissed after two years. If you can't accept Junejo and you can't accept Benazir Bhutto who can you work with?'[6]

Outwardly the President and army chief continued trying to demonstrate a semblance of democracy. General Beg said, 'Personally I think there should be elections every six months to cleanse the political system.' But the all too familiar promise of elections within ninety days following the government's dismissal sounded hollow, particularly while there was a risk of Bhutto returning to power. As she herself said, voicing the thought obviously tormenting her mind, 'You don't dismiss an elected government to allow it back three months later.'

Perhaps Bhutto's government, as she said, never had a chance. Having reluctantly transferred power to Bhutto, many in the military remained unreconciled to her government. For eleven years they had been indoctrinated to regard Bhutto as public enemy number one, not a view that could be shaken off overnight. After her fall she complained, 'From the day I was sworn in I was aware of many attempts to destabilize my government. Each time an attempt failed there would be a gap of two or three weeks before they tried again.' She added, 'I was walking a tightrope which the President, Nawaz Sharif and others were always trying to pull.'

But Bhutto played into their hands. Despite her weak political position, with a cobbled together majority and governments in only two provinces, Bhutto's attitude was confrontational rather than consensus building. It was not easy for Bhutto to forget that the army had hanged her father. Nor could her cabinet easily forgive their ill-treatment and torture under the long years of martial law. Once in office, remarkably, they did not seek vengeance against their former enemies but equally they were quick to forget former allies. By 1990 the PPP government found themselves in a similar situation to that which had confronted Benazir's father in 1977 — Bhutto against the rest. This, combined with the government's poor record of achievements, meant that when the army finally struck there was little public objection. In fact law and order had deteriorated so much that in some southern cities demands for martial law were rife by June 1990.

Outside Pakistan the news of Bhutto's dismissal was greeted with shock. Only the timing, coming just four days after the Iraqi invasion of Kuwait, lessened the outcry. Much of the West had never removed their rose-tinted spectacles, and despite the turbulence and incompetence of Bhutto's rule as well as reports from their ambassadors of their countrymen in Pakistan being openly asked for commissions for contracts by ministers, had refused to see anything wrong with the courageous young woman who stood for democracy.

But inside Pakistan the exuberance which had greeted Bhutto's assumption of office had rapidly dissipated. On few occasions in history has a ruler squandered so much goodwill so quickly. Like her predecessors, Benazir had quickly become obsessed with Machiavelli's axiom that 'the first rule of politics is to stay in power'. From day one her government concentrated on destabilizing Nawaz Sharif's government in Punjab and increasing their own national majority, through cash rather than consensus. The day to day running of the administration took very much second place and was often forgotten. To criticism at their lack of social and economic policy her ministers protested that they were 'consolidating democracy'. But Sharif, whatever his background as a Zia protégé, was democratically elected too. Rather than enhancing democracy, the PPP was doing its reputation considerable damage by the spectacle of buying and selling of elected MPs to the highest bidder.

Any remaining moral high ground left to the 'party of

democracy' was cut from under them by the increasing tales of corruption. During the 1988 election campaign Bhutto had main-, tained that 'corruption can only be stopped from the top'[7] and repeated her father's advice that 'Caesar's wife must be above suspicion.' Yet within a few months in office the clink of glasses in the colonnaded houses of Karachi and Islamabad to celebrate the conclusion of deals had become a familiar sound. Corruption – always a deeply rooted feature in Pakistani politics – was rife with the return of democracy and more blatant than ever before. Having been on the outside for so long, many of Bhutto's colleagues felt it was their turn to make money, receiving pay-offs for passing on lucrative contracts. 'They're about as subtle as a train wreck,' a Western banker in Karachi told *Newsweek* in May 1990. And, at least in the public perception, Caesar's husband Asif Zardari was the worst offender of all.

To the Pakistani people, then, the PPP government seemed no different to previous regimes, and behind their fine words and past democratic credentials its politicians as dedicated as their predecessors to the icon of self-interest. In spite of all the promises and expectations, Bhutto's twenty months in power saw no legislation other than the annual budgets. Not a move was made to repeal Zia's repressive Hudood ordinance, under which women could be jailed for being raped, even though 3,000 women along with their children were languishing in Pakistani jails for 'crimes' against Hudood. The government had shrunk too from endorsing draft legislation to end the medieval practice of bonded labour. Some of Bhutto's own MPs owned businesses employing bonded labour so the proposal was allowed to die, though after their dismissal PPP officials claimed that a draft law would have been retabled in August 1990. The population was predicted to double in the next twenty years but Bhutto dared not offend the *mullahs* with the introduction of family planning.

Yet the way Bhutto told it, her twenty months saw a social and economic revolution. She claimed, 'The IMF austerity programme had been implemented successfully, the budget deficit brought down, inflation halved. Profitability of banks was up 70 per cent, tax collection by 20 per cent. Investment had increased four-fold. We had arrested seventeen top drug barons, our poppy eradication programme was a success and we had overcome a war threat with India.'[8]

In fact World Bank disbursements to nationalized credit institutions had stopped because of distribution of loans without collateral, the IMF suspended payments in June because of failure to meet fiscal targets, literacy worsened, development was minimal, while the defence budget, which together with debt servicing eats up 80 per cent of current expenditure, was actually increased – something Bhutto oddly cited as 'a great achievement'.[9] Rather than risk the ire of the country's big landlords by suggesting they pay tax for the first time in their lives, the bills were paid by slashing state spending and introducing sales taxes which affected most the lower strata of society. Time and again the interests of the masses who had voted Bhutto in were ignored, even insulted, in order to appease her own Parliamentarians and the *mullahs* and *zamindars*.

Other PPP leaders were more honest, admitting that if the government had not been dismissed it would have collapsed anyway. Farooq Leghari, the former water and power Minister, and perhaps the most respected senior PPP member, said ruefully, 'We made many mistakes. Even when we tried to do things right they turned out wrong.'[10] Salman Taseer, who as a Punjab provincial MP was less in the firing line, could be more scathing: 'We had no clear directives, no overall strategy and poor man management. It was a chaotic situation.'[11] However, he added, 'Twenty months is not an opportunity. Benazir did not know how government worked for six months.'

In her defence, Bhutto was undoubtedly faced with tremendous pressures. A lot of people had suffered and a lot of hopes had been built up during eleven years of military rule. People like the young men who were dancing and letting off fireworks into the sky the night Bhutto was announced as Prime Minister were soon crowding the entrances of ministries waving their red, green and black party cards and demanding to know where their jobs were, their expressions contorting from jubilance to sullen anger. To reward those who had sacrificed in the fight against Zia, Bhutto appointed so many ministers and advisers, regardless of their competence, that it appeared even she could not keep track. On one famous occasion at a reception she asked a guest, Father Julius, what he did, to be told, 'I'm your Minister for Minorities,' while a gentleman by the name of Naveed Malik achieved

notoriety when he was sworn in as Bhutto's Adviser for Tourism
and only some time later discovered to be the wrong Naveed
Malik. The said Mr Malik was immediately picked up by the
IDA and began holding press conferences at which he claimed he
had been removed because he had 'uncovered scandals about Asif
Zardari'.

Bhutto's own background militated against her success. Brought
up as a feudal princess, surrounded by servants and having spent much
of her life outside Pakistan, perhaps she did not even know the
country's problems. Though educated enough to have vision, her
Western education was alien to Pakistan, and even where she could
identify the needs of the population her inexperience meant she did
not know how to tackle them.

To explain the lack of law-making, Iftikhar Gilani, the Law
Minister, argued: 'We were busy sweeping away the cobwebs of
martial law.' Bhutto's human rights record was undoubtedly the
best in Pakistan's history. But the government, particularly the
Interior Ministry, continued to use some of the apparatus of martial
law such as Intelligence Bureau agents to monitor activities of
opponents and journalists, even tapping the phones of some of
their own ministers.[12] It was a far cry from the early Zia years,
however, when journalists who dared to step out of line would be
lashed, leaving them with terrible scars.

Instituting a free press was an uphill task in a country where
intelligence agencies, the government, the opposition, those with
political ambitions and even the President all had journalists in
their pay, creating a reverse kind of chequebook journalism where
those who could pay most or threaten most effectively would get
more statements in the papers regardless of their importance.

Bhutto made a promising start, appointing Javed Jabbar, a flamboyant advertising director and independent senator, as junior
Information Minister, retaining the full portfolio herself. But Mr
Jabbar took the policy too literally, and fell from favour by showing the anti-Rushdie riots on television while Bhutto was on a
state visit to China. He said later, 'I was disillusioned as early as
March 1989. Far too many people were brought in to run information, many of whom thought news bulletins should be used solely
as a party platform.'[13] In August that year he spoke out and was
promptly transferred, leaving the nightly television news to revert

to its old pattern of 'what the Prime Minister did today', showing little of the opposition, though just enough (and where possible showing Sharif in a bad light) to claim that all had access. Promises to disband the National Press Trust, which controlled the national news wire service and several papers, were conveniently forgotten when it was found too useful a vehicle.

While insisting that her hands were tied from the start, Bhutto was reluctant to portray herself as heading an impotent administration. Instead she said it was because she took tough action and thus stepped on toes that the Establishment (by which she meant the President, military and bureaucracy) could not accept her. 'I was not a Prime Minister without portfolio. I did make decisions, we did get things done. The President thinks that political government should just be the frill, the icing on the cake, while the real government is run by the civil servants. I was not prepared to be that kind of Prime Minister.'[14]

In fact, had Bhutto moved straight in and imposed drastic reforms no one could have stopped her. The army, having lost sixteen top generals in the air crash that killed Zia, was demoralized and eager to restore to its uniform the honour that had been lost by too long in the forefront of running the country. Despite suggesting otherwise, the army really never had any choice but to hand over power, and the new high command was not wholesale against Bhutto but evenly divided. At the start many civil servants were enthusiastic about the new regime. Moreover, there were many non-controversial but crucial areas in which reform was desperate and to which no one could have reasonably objected, such as education, reform of which would have built the party a stronger popular base from which they would have been better placed to take on past foes.

But the government seemed interested only in increasing its power, and thus allowed and even encouraged the forces against it to consolidate. The more Bhutto appeared undemocratic in her fight to topple Sharif, the more General Beg could present himself as the good guy, the Supreme Arbiter keeping the politicians in check. The PPP's biggest handicap was its black and white 'you're either with us or you're against us' view of the world. This was evident, as I learnt from personal experience, in their dealings with press. When the media, which had always given the PPP a sympathetic hearing in opposition, became critical of them in government, the leadership apparently unable to understand the concept of objective reporting, turned hostile. As the earliest Western critic of the government's lack of initiative, I began receiving calls asking if I was being paid by their opponents. When my visa expired in September 1989 the Interior Minister, Aitzaz Ahsan, took advantage of an army denial of my story of unrest against Bhutto in GHQ, to deport me, giving me a few days to leave the country and announcing his decision to a press conference. Calling me to his house to explain his decision a hysterical Mr Ahsan, known within the PPP as 'Little Master', accused me of 'coming to Pakistan to jeopardize the fragile democratic institutions',[15] quite forgetting that I had arrived during military rule and indeed that my first visit had been to attend Benazir's wedding at her personal invitation. Not content with this, Mr Ahsan's men in the Intelligence Bureau put two cars and a motorbike on to tailing me and ransacked my flat, planting ludicrous stories in the local press that opposition leaders had bought me mountain bungalows, that in fact I was an agent for Soviet, Indian and British intelligence, while the *Financial Times* was owned by 'a well known Indo-Jewish lobby'.[16] On returning to Pakistan in September 1990 I was given a file by the caretaker administration headed 'Activities of Christina Lamb'. Dated from as early as January 1989, it contained copies of all my post, incoming and outgoing, personal and professional. Hardly the act of a democratic government.

The PPP's 'us and them' mentality was perhaps a natural hangover from their past persecution, but suspicion that the army and bureaucracy and President were against them quickly became a self-fulfilling prophecy. Yet with no secure political base, Bhutto was in no position to take on such power lobbies. Her relationship with the President was the first casualty. Having been forced to elect him, as part of the deal by which she took office,[17] Bhutto always maintained that he was not neutral and grew increasingly irritated at seeing him in frequent meetings with opposition leaders while not calling her own ministers. For his part, he said her ministers had not asked to see him. Senior civil servants would pass on files to the President before the Prime Minister, and as the business of government grew more chaotic the President took to sending notes to Bhutto advising her that certain acts were unconstitutional. Bhutto said, 'All the time with his nasty little notes he was building a case against me. His role was absolutely immoral. He acted as the leader of the opposition and spent all his time wondering how can I get Benazir Bhutto?'[18]

As if one powerful enemy was not enough, Bhutto began doing exactly what her sceptics in the army feared. Ill-advised moves to curb their power all backfired, as Bhutto forgot her own description in her autobiography of the army as the 'single most organized and smoothly functioning institution in fractious Pakistan'[19] and tried to create lobbies within it, a move guaranteed to infuriate such a hierarchical organization.

The first major clash came in the summer of 1989, when Bhutto made both a clumsy and a public attempt to remove Admiral Sirohey from his position as Chairman of Joint Chiefs of Staff. The Defence Secretary, the senior bureaucrat in the Defence Ministry, informed the President of her intentions before she could summon Sirohey. The President was livid and insisted that according to the Constitution, dismissing as well as appointing generals was his prerogative. The army feared that if Bhutto got away with this act a precedent would be set by which she would move out all those officers whom she was suspicious of – the 'bearded generals', as her father had called those religious officers such as had been promoted by Zia. Zia had instituted Islamic training of the army, and there was a strong fundamentalist faction in the armed forces close to the Muslim Brotherhood organization and reluctant to see a woman, particularly another Bhutto, in power. Bhutto had only eventually succeeded in removing her greatest foe, General Gul, from the head of military intelligence because it suited the country's US backers. Afterwards some of Gul's colleagues had instigated propaganda that the move had been on Indian instructions, pointing out that the announcement followed a visit by the Interior Minister to India. Moreover, to oust Gul she had to promote him to Multan, where as corps commander he was in one of the army's most powerful positions and from where he continued to keep contact with and advise her opposition.

Bhutto, it seemed, did not learn from these unsuccessful attempts to take on her old adversaries in khaki. The following year she tried to secure an extension of office for Lt.-General Alam Jan Mahsud, the Lahore corps commander, to push him up to be a full

general and Vice Chief of the army. Clearly the PPP were hoping
that their own appointee would replace Beg when he retired in
August 1991, rather than Beg's choice, who could be one of their
great enemies such as Generals Hamid Gul or Asif Nawaz. The
army complained to the President that Bhutto was trying to create
'extra-institutional loyalties' to politicians, and pointed out that
Beg had already made it clear that no one would be given an
extension. Extensions during the Zia era were a major cause of
malcontent, blocking promotions and frustrating junior officers.
General Beg, always the cool guy, simply ignored Bhutto's machi-
nations and posted a new corps commander at Lahore, leaving
Mahsud with no option but to retire on 18 July and worsened
relations between the army and PPP.

It would have been a very different story had the People's Party
won a large majority in the 1988 elections. Like Charles II after
the Restoration, many of Bhutto's colleagues would have called
for the blood or at least for the trial of army officers involved in
the long suppression of the PPP. As it was, with their fragile hold
on power they were forced to give these officers continued privileges such as plots of land and scholarships for their children.
Despite the continuing patronage, such anti-PPP officers were
well aware of the party's true feelings, and while Bhutto was
touring Siachen proclaiming 'the generals and people are one
now', they were hatching plots. The first, as early as summer
1989, was discovered and stopped.[20] In fact, if there was any
truth in her words it was the more chilling thought that the army
was controlling the government. Bhutto's words brought to mind
the title of the autobiography of Ayub Khan, Pakistan's first military dictator, who promoted himself to Field-Marshal and ruled
the country from 1958 to 1968. The book was called *Friends Not
Masters* and fooled no one.

What ultimately decided the fate of Bhutto's government was
that fateful combination of the armed forces and Sindh. Unable
really to rule Pakistan, through fear of upsetting lobbies to which
she was hostage if not a part, Bhutto increasingly found that her
only role was to maintain law and order. It became equally clear
that for this she needed military help, causing a resurgence of the
old comment that if the army was having to act as policemen for
the government they might as well take over the whole show. I

frequently came across army officers who would repeat that Bhutto had been given power in the belief that she was the last hope for keeping Sindh in the federation. The implication was clear. She had not only failed to end the violence in the southern province — it had worsened, and once more it was the army keeping peace. Bhutto must have known that there was a limit to how long they would quell riots with tanks on the streets of Karachi, arrange swaps of political prisoners and sit at roundabouts with machine-guns guarding the population, without asking why they were doing a civilian government's dirty work.

Bhutto herself admitted that relations with the army chief broke over the Pucca Qila incident in Hyderabad at the end of May, in which more than thirty *mohajirs*, including women and children, were brutally shot down on breaking curfew. While Bhutto described it as an act of defiance by MQM 'terrorists' in which 'only fourteen people died', Beg saw it as a massacre under the auspices of the PPP Sindh government. From then until their last bilateral meeting on 24 July, differences between the two over how to deal with Sindh became irreconcilable. Saying that the Sindh government had botched up its clean-up operation, the army asked for a free hand to sort out the situation, demanding constitutional powers under Article 245 which would allow them to suspend high court jurisdiction in the area and set up army courts. This would have been seen as a virtual state of martial law, and as Tariq Rahim explained, to allow it would have been the death of the party: 'We knew the aim was to go just for the PPP. We would have lost all credibility in Sindh and that was our powerbase.'

With so little trust between the two main forces in the country, the end was just a matter of time. The 5–5 split in attitude towards Bhutto among the army high command shifted to 7–3 in favour of ditching her. General Beg told colleagues, 'It was most unfortunate that the government could not trust the armed forces.' But given Pakistan's history, the lack of trust was understandable. The government was hardly unaware of comments such as one which raised my gooseflesh less than a year into their rule. At a reception at the Indian embassy a senior army officer remarked of the government, 'We're just letting the children play for a while.' Nor could Bhutto forget that it was allowing the army full powers which had led to her father's downfall. At the Sindh briefing in that

fateful July corps commanders' meeting, as a row broke out between the Interior Minister and the Karachi corps commander,
Bhutto could no longer restrain herself and, according to one of
those attending, burst out, 'It was the army that killed my father.'

In the midst of this constitutional controversy over the army's
role in Sindh, despite not having consolidated her political base
either in Parliament or among the public, Bhutto began interfering
in army promotions, refusing to agree recommendations made by
the army promotions board, usually a routine matter. An alleged
remark by Bhutto to the effect, 'We should have some of our own
people in the army' caused an outcry in the senior ranks, while
public complaints by her ministers about the role of the military
intelligence in undermining government activity were seen as an
attempt by the PPP deliberately to malign the armed forces, as it
was felt they had tried with ISI. In fact, there is considerable
evidence that both agencies did work against the government, but
Bhutto had badly misunderstood the armed forces if she thought
she could criticize one branch without upsetting the whole balance
of relations in such a hierarchical institution.

To the military, then, Bhutto's intervention in promotions was
the last straw, breaking the commitment she had given on taking
power that she would not interfere in army matters. For the
army's part, they were no longer bound to their side of the
bargain, and the generals decided the show could no longer go on.
The President needed little persuasion to act, having hardly spoken
to the Prime Minister for over a year. His reputation as a man
who kept to the book lent credibility to the charges cited as
reasons for the government's dismissal, and there was little outcry.
By that time the popular perception was of a corrupt government,
and there was mounting resentment that the new dawn promised
by Bhutto's administration had never come.

The question was what next? By September 1990 the mood of
the country had rarely been so depressed. Pakistan seemed to be
running out of options. As one Karachi businessman put it, 'At
least during the last martial law there was always Benazir Bhutto
as the light at the end of the tunnel. Now there is only darkness
ahead.' Sitting one evening with friends in Lahore watching the
news, such was the uncertainty that when the screen went suddenly
blank there was an almost collective sigh of relief. 'Martial law,'

they said. 'Now we know where we stand,' was the unspoken thought. When the broadcast resumed a minute later, having apparently been affected by only temporary interference, I could have sworn my companions were disappointed. Amid such instability only one thing was clear. The army would not let Bhutto back. One hawkish corps commander almost grimaced with disgust as, refusing to voice Benazir's name, he told me, 'We can't stand her. We don't even want her in the country or the Parliament, let alone in government.'

But just as the PPP government had seriously miscalculated in its dealings with the military, so had the generals underestimated the bravery of Bhutto and the loyalty of some of her politicians. The lack of principles demonstrated by politicians over the previous two years, changing parties to the highest bidder, had led the army to expect that if the PPP was seen to be clearly out of favour its members would desert like rats from a sinking ship to an army-backed IDA which could then move in. But suddenly, once more given a cause to fight, the PPP showed it could still be the only party with soul.

With corruption charges mounting against her and her husband in jail, Bhutto could return to the Joan of Arc role she played best. The charges raised sympathy rather than anger, and with the so-called accountability process directed solely at the PPP it seemed nothing more than a political vendetta aimed at preventing them campaigning or possibly even disqualification. The charges laid against Bhutto and her ministers increased and became more ridiculous. In the week before the election two more charges were placed against Bhutto, accusing her of using secret funds and state planes to buy and then transport MPs during the attempted no-confidence vote. Had Nawaz Sharif never used Punjab government planes for campaigning? Bhutto's predecessors were hardly angels, even if they were more subtle about rake-offs. Farooq Leghari quite rightly claimed, 'The manner of our dismissal has washed away the bad name we were getting.' Moreover, in a country where even *mullahs* steal electricity, corruption is a way of life and hardly enough to discredit a government. This was no repeat of the Bofors arms scandal, which had brought down Rajiv Gandhi in neighbouring India the previous year. Speaking at an election rally in late September in the desert town of Nawabshah, from which Zardari was contesting, Mr Jatoi's outraged comments on the corruption of the Bhutto government evoked little response. His audience were far more interested in whether he was going to give them the schools, roads and electricity every politician promised and none delivered. In the meantime they were happy to have a free lunch.

Moreover, with power apparently inevitable, the divisions in the anti-Bhutto alliance became harder to paper over despite the weight of military, bureaucracy, religious and business backing. Was their candidate for premiership Nawaz Sharif or Jatoi? Even the army was split over that. Jatoi had the advantage of being Sindhi but had lost his own seat in the last election,[21] whereas Sharif had a considerable powerbase of his own. Whoever was at its helm, few expected an IDA government to hold together for long and most believed the army would then step in, saying we've tried out all the politicians. With the men in khaki always on the sidelines, was there any future for democracy? Salman Taseer expressed the unpalatable truth: 'One thing is clear – if you want government in this country you must do a deal with the army.' Realizing this, as elections neared, Bhutto began withdrawing her vitriol towards the army and directing it towards the President, who she demanded 'must step down'.

However, the party had already done one such deal and found themselves left unable to rule. This time, with even less trust on both sides, the terms were likely to be even stricter. For the army to let Bhutto back would involve them in considerable humiliation and bring with it the fear that having fallen victim at their hands again, Bhutto was likely to be vindictive this time. For the PPP's part, as Taseer asked, 'Can you let the bear into the tent and expect to survive?'

Forty-three years of constraints militating against democracy had been built into the Pakistani system and Bhutto, it seemed, was not the person to undo them. Much tragic truth could be read in what Mountbatten wrote privately after securing agreement on Partition: 'The responsibility for this mad decision must lie squarely on Indian shoulders, for one day they will bitterly regret the decision they are about to make.'

The regret is evident in real Pakistan, from the riot-torn streets of Karachi to the gnarled old man seeing the land on which he scrapes a living turn to salt. Nowhere is Rousseau's comment, 'Man is born free but is everywhere in chains', more strikingly true. From the dawn of Pakistan's creation to the second birth of democracy, the old Sindhi has seen a life of cheated expectations. Promised freedom from oppression by Jinnah, he got new oppressors – that they were of the same religion was of no consolation. Promised land by Bhutto, he was rewarded only with rhetoric. Promised law and order by Zia, he got ruthless subjugation, army units sweeping through the villages killing cattle and shaming women. Promised respect by Benazir, there was no end to the bondage he and his sons slaved under, struggling to pay off a debt to the *zamindar* which only increased.

Further away than the old man can imagine, further even than the crushing glaciers which feed the river that refuses to water his land, the brave men of Siachen are fighting for his country and religion. But their regimented night prayers among the icy peaks seem unconnected to the old man's tears and trance in the nearby Sufi shrine. They are fighting for a mythical national interest, which politicians ignore in everything from the tax system to water distribution to drug addiction to demographic trends. To the country's power-brokers they are fighting to maintain hatred of India on the boil. Pakistanis fear that the day they stop thinking of their neighbours as evil Hindus, there will be no uniting factor left and awkward questions will arise about the socio-economic distribution of the country and the benefits of Partition.

As the sun goes down over the Khyber Pass, for the Afghans victory slips further from their grasp. Like the Pakistani masses they are suffering from their leaders' yearnings for power – leaders who dwell in grand houses cushioned by overseas bank accounts while refugees bear the indignity, hunger and blistering sun of life in camps.

Pakistan's political system may be irreparably stunted, but from rickety teahouses to glitzy business dinners all over the country the 'gobshop' is incredibly politicized. From the disco-loving son of a scion to the leathery man sitting crosslegged in the street dust, rolling *bidis*, everyone has a strong view. Zulfikar Ali Bhutto is usually credited as having given the people of Pakistan a voice or political consciousness. But he did not. Instead the master magician created an illusion because of which many see political activity as a substitute for economic activity. Politicians had long since received plots of land as a privilege of power, but Bhutto took such perks to new extremes and for the first time political workers also benefited. Thus the attitude long held by feudals — that political power is necessary to maintain economic power — permeated down through society, the masses believing that the only way they could survive economically was to lend political support to the local bigwig. The system continued under Zia, Junejo and Benazir, and today's society is obsessed by politics because it is seen as the easiest way to make money, whether it is the rickshaw-wallah who flies the flag of the local MP's party so that the police will not give him a ticket, the shopkeeper who joins the party to retain his licence, or the big businessman who pumps in party funds to ensure future contracts.

Commitment to democracy, then, is solely another means to secure one's share of plunder. Hence those who were ministers under martial law joined the PPP just before the 1988 elections to ensure their slice continued. And every time there was an attempt to destabilize Bhutto or Nawaz Sharif, there would be a crazy reshuffling between parties, a kind of political musical chairs as people tried to ensure they remained on the winning side.

The feudals have always survived the game because, largely due to their own deliberate suppression of education, no leading politician has ever emerged from the lower or even middle classes. An analysis of the Pakistan Parliament from 1970 till 1990 reveals that 80 per cent of members had landholdings of more than 100 acres, whereas in India's Lok Sabha the same proportion has no land at all or less than fifty acres. While politics remains the preserve of the rich, living insulated lives from the country's myriad problems and educated in an alien context, it is hard to see how the needs of ordinary people can be truly represented. Ironically, in his social background, General Zia was perhaps the most representative if least legitimate of all Pakistan's rulers. The only election to have been fought (and won) on economic slogans was that of 1970, and the man calling 'roti, kapra aur makan' was a wealthy zamindar.

The odds against democracy taking root under such conditions are long. The cause lies in the country's origins. Pakistan did not come about from a political movement and a long struggle and ideological commitment, but was more of a byproduct of the

Indian struggle. Pakistan was a demand of the élite, not the masses, and was more of a bargaining position to ensure this section's share of power and the accompanying loot. Today the cry for democracy serves the same purpose. While these people continue to run the country and prevent the emergence of a strong middle class, the needs of the masses will remain ignored because the gulf between the two groups is too wide. The Koran preaches tolerance but the society which has emerged from its pages is one of intolerance, with no commitment to democratic principles. Everything is seen in black and white, and it would take a revolutionary to challenge the entrenched power structures. The only other way for these to be dismantled now would be for the country to break up, a possibility increasingly discussed. Ironically, it is perhaps because they were never secure about their country's future that those in power have always been obsessed by self-interest rather than national interest.

In his last letters to Jinnah, the poet Allama Iqbal wrote that Pakistan was formed to solve the problem of bread for the Muslim masses. Yet less than half a century later it was not uncommon to see stories in the newspapers of peasants burning themselves to death because they could find no food or employment. As the *muezzin* calls evening prayers, signalling another day's survival of the invented nation, millions of men touch their foreheads to the dust and millions of women locked away inside four walls like caged birds squabble hysterically. Outside on the village street all is quiet except for a shuffling noise coming nearer. Gradually it is distinguishable as the sound of beating on a cracked drum as the monkey dance man limps along the dirt street. As he jerks the moth-eaten monkey to attention and holds out a quaking claw of a hand for a few *paisa*, vultures circle over the dome of the small sand-walled mosque. But no one in the village has any more to spare. The white salt has eaten up their crop, and as night tolls for many it is time to surrender to death under the crescent moon. Pakistan is still waiting for Allah.

GLOSSARY

ajrak	printed Sindhi shawl
ayah	nanny
bara bazaar	market for smuggled goods
bazaari	small shopkeepers and traders
bhai	brother
bidi	cheap paper cigarette
burqa	tentlike garment which covers women from head to foot
chador	woman's veil
chai	tea
chaikana	teahouse
charpoy	string bed
dacoit	bandit
dupatta	woman's headscarf
fatewa	religious pronouncement
ghairat	honour (Baluchi)
hari	landless sharecropper
hookah	pipe for smoking tobacco through water
jeay, jiye	long live
jihad	holy war
jirga	tribal assembly
lathi	wooden staff
malik	tribal head (in Frontier)
mohajir	migrant from India
muezzin	mosque official who chants prayers
mujaheddin	man fighting for Islamic cause
mullah	priest
non	flat unleavened bread
paan	betel-nut paste

pagri	turban
paisa	one hundredth of a rupee
petou	woollen shawl
pir	holy man, descendant of the Prophet
pukhtunwali	tribal code practised by Pathans
purdah	keeping women behind a veil or within four walls
roti	bread
sardar	tribal chief
shaheed	martyr
shalwar kamiz	pyjama-like garment worn throughout Pakistan
shamiana	canopy
shura	consultative assembly
tamasha	spectacle
ulema	body of religious functionaries
wadera	feudal landlord (Sindh)
zamindar	feudal landlord

NOTES

CHAPTER 1: INVENTING A COUNTRY

1. In the 1937 elections the Muslim League won only two out of eighty-six Muslim seats in Punjab, none out of thirty-five in Sindh, and was crushingly defeated in Bengal and the Frontier – all the areas that became Pakistan.
2. For a full account of the 1946 Cabinet Mission, led by Sir Stafford Cripps, see P. Moon, *Divide and Quit*, Chatto & Windus, London, 1961, pp. 42–64.
3. M. J. Akbar, *India: The Siege Within*, Penguin, Harmondsworth, 1985, p. 36.
4. Tariq Ali, *The Nehrus and the Gandhis*, Pan Books, 1985, p. 83.
5. The Law of Evidence, passed in 1984, means that in many legal situations the evidence of one man is equivalent to that of two women. In murder cases the amount of compensation payable for a murdered woman is half that for a murdered man.

CHAPTER 2: 'GANGSTERS IN BANGLES' COME TO ISLAMABAD

1. Conversation with author, Aiwan-e-Sadr, Islamabad, 2 December 1988.
2. ibid.
3. Conversation with author, 2 December 1988.
4. Benazir Bhutto, *Daughter of the East*, Hamish Hamilton, London, 1988, p. 86.
5. Interview with author, Karachi, 10 June 1988.
6. Interview with author, Rawalpindi, 23 July 1988.

7. Conversation with author, Shandur Pass, July 1989.
8. Interview with Oriana Fallaci, *L'Europeo*, April 1972.

CHAPTER 3: TICKETS TO THE MASKED BALL

1. Bhutto admitted that a committee had been set up for negotiations with Jamaat Islami during an interview with author, 10 June 1988.
2. Interview with author, Karachi, 11 June 1988.
3. Interview with author, Karachi, 11 June 1988
4. Conversation with author, Shandur Pass, July 1989.
5. ibid.
6. Interview with author, Karachi, 12 June 1988.
7. ibid.
8. Quoted in interview with Oriana Fallaci, *L'Europeo*, April 1972.
9. Interview with author, Karachi, 12 June 1988.
10. Interview with author, Islamabad, August 1988.
11. Conversation with author, April 1989.
12. Press conference, Rawalpindi, June 1988.
13. Interview with author, Rawalpindi, 23 July 1988.

CHAPTER 4: THE SUPERPATRONAGE ROADSHOW

1. Interview with author on train from Lahore, October 1988.
2. Interview with author, Lahore, 15 November 1988.
3. Charges against Bhutto included awarding a contract to a British company to buy cotton at below market prices, using secret government funds for political bribes, selling cheaply an area of reserved land in Islamabad for the construction of Lakeview Hotel by associates of Asif Zardari, and awarding a contract to produce cooking gas on favourable terms to friends. Many more charges were laid against her and her ministers, but to date nothing has been proved.
4. Interview with author, Islamabad, 26 September 1990.
5. Interview with author, Bilawal House, Karachi, 30 September 1990.
6. Conversation with author, Multan, April 1989.
7. Interview with author, Lahore, 17 November 1988.

CHAPTER 5: A SUBCONTINENTAL DYNASTY

1. Akbar S. Ahmed, *Discovering Islam*, Routledge, London, 1988, pp. 82–4.
2. Interview with Oriana Fallaci, *L'Europeo*, April 1972.

3. Benazir Bhutto, *Daughter of the East*, Hamish Hamilton, London, 1988, p. 86.
4. US Arms Control and Disarmament Agency; World Military Expenditures and Arms Transfers 1966–75.
5. White Paper on performance of Bhutto Regime, Vol. 3, P.A. 68, Annex 24, Government of Pakistan, Islamabad.
6. Asghar Khan, among others, had appealed for military intervention.
7. B. Bhutto, op. cit., p. 78.
8. Interview with author, 23 July 1988.
9. ibid.
10. Conversation with author, Islamabad, July 1988.
11. Press statement, Karachi, 18 August 1988.
12. Interview with author, London, April 1990.
13. ibid.
14. ibid.
15. Interview with author, Rawalpindi, August 1989.
16. ibid.
17. *Financial Times*, 16 January 1990.
18. Interview with author, Karachi, 23 September 1990.

CHAPTER 6: 'BUT MINISTER . . .'

1. Press conference, Information Ministry, Islamabad, March 1989.
2. Press conference, Islamabad, November 1988.
3. Source requested confidentiality, April 1990.
4. Interview with author, Islamabad, 5 December 1988.
5. Conversation with author, Islamabad, December 1988.
6. *Los Angeles Times*, 5 June 1989.
7. 'The Politics of Ethnicity', *Asian Affairs*, February 1990.
8. Told firsthand confidentially by an Indian official, London, April 1990.

CHAPTER 7: SINDH – LAND OF ROBIN HOODS AND WARRIOR SAINTS

1. Interview with author, forest near Dadu, September 1989.
2. Interview with author, Mehar jail, September 1989.
3. Interview with author, jail in upper Sindh, April 1989.
4. Interview with author, Karachi, July 1988.
5. Interview with author, April 1989.
6. Interview with author, September 1989.
7. A. Ahmed, *Discovering Islam*, Routledge, London, 1988, pp. 82–4.

8. Interview with author, Karachi, September 1989.
9. ibid.
10. Interview with author, Karachi, July 1988.
11. Interview with author, Sann, September 1989.
12. ibid.
13. Interview with author, Karachi, July 1988.
14. Interview with author, Dadu, September 1989.
15. Interview with author, Larkana, April 1989.
16. Interview with author, Islamabad, July 1989.
17. At a press briefing, Rawalpindi, 13 September 1989, General Beg said, 'Even these days I get letters mostly from Sindh urging me to impose martial law.'

CHAPTER 8: DIAL-A-KALASHNIKOV

1. Reconstructed from interviews with eyewitnesses of Black Friday, Hyderabad, October 1988.
2. Reconstructed from conversations in Orangi.
3. Interview with author, Karachi, April 1989.
4. *Journal of Asian and African Affairs*, Washington, December 1989, p. 106.
5. The MQM improved on these results in 1990, winning some seats in interior Sindh.
6. Quoted in *Time* magazine, 12 March 1990.
7. Conversation with author, Karachi, September 1989.
8. Interview with author, Karachi, September 1989.
9. Interview with author, Karachi, September 1990.
10. Interview with author, Prime Minister House, Islamabad, 23 September 1990.
11. Interview with author, Orangi, September 1989.

CHAPTER 9: PROPHETS AND LOSSES

1. Ministry of Finance figures, 1988.
2. State Bank figures.
3. Interview with caretaker Prime Minister G. M. Jatoi, Islamabad, 25 September 1990.
4. Figures from interview with V. A. Jaffarey, Islamabad, 24 June 1989.
5. Interview with author, National Assembly, Islamabad, 4 June 1989.
6. Figures from V. A. Jaffarey, op. cit.
7. Dr Mahbub ul Haq, Planning Commission, 1968.
8. International Bank for Reconstruction and Development, report on Industrial Development of Pakistan, 1966.
9. Interview with author, Islamabad, December 1988.

10. Interview with author, Islamabad, 24 June 1989.
11. Interviews with shipbreakers, Karachi and Gadani, April 1989.
12. See *Economic Survey of Pakistan*, 1982–3 and 1988–9.
13. Interview with author, Lahore, August 1989.
14. Interview with author, Murree, June 1989.
15. Press conference, 3 August 1989, Islamabad.
16. Newsline, August 1990.
17. Interview with author, Nawabshah, 28 September 1990.
18. Interview with author, Karachi, 29 September 1990.
19. Interview with author, Bilawal House, Karachi, 30 September 1990.
20. Interview with author, Lahore, 24 September 1990.
21. Interview with author, Karachi, June 1988.
22. Interview with author, Islamabad, 28 August 1989.
23. Interview with author, Karachi, September 1989.
24. Interview with author, Karachi, September 1989.
25. *Time* magazine, 12 March 1990.
26. See debate on 'Women and Islam', Christian Study Centre, Rawalpindi, 1984, p. 18.
27. 1981 Census.

CHAPTER 10: THE GREAT GAME REVISITED

1. Interview with author, Khyber Pass, March 1989.
2. Interview with author, Peshawar, March 1989.
3. Pakistan Narcotics Control Board figures; also see Melvyn Levitsky, US Assistant Secretary of State for International Narcotics, on Drug Trafficking to House Committee, Washington, 8 January 1989.
4. Confidential interview with author, Khyber Pass, August 1989.
5. Interview with author, Quetta, 9 July 1989.
6. Interview with author, Islamabad, 11 July 1989.
7. Interview with author, Quetta, 9 July 1989.
8. Interview with author, Quetta, 8 July 1989.
9. Interview with author, Quetta, 10 July 1989.
10. Pakistan Economic Survey 1981–2. See also S. R. Poonegar, History of Economic Development in Baluchistan, Department of Information, Government of Baluchistan, 1988.

CHAPTER 11: 'RESISTANCE TOURS LTD'

1. Interview with author, Rawalpindi, 15 February 1989.
2. Pushtu poem by Abdul Bari Jahani.
3. At the time of writing, *mujaheddin* hold only six out of thirty-one provincial capitals.

4. See *Financial Times*, 18 February 1989.
5. Told to author by NIFA commander and confirmed by Hezb commander and Pakistan Foreign Office.
6. Interview with author, Rawalpindi, 15 February 1989.
7. Figures from Chief Commissioner Afghan Refugees, Islamabad, compiled 15 May 1989.
8. Conversation with deputy to one of the leaders, February 1989.
9. See Bob Woodward, *Veil*, Simon & Schuster, New York, 1987.
10. *Wall Street Journal*, 16 February 1988.
11. 'The Missing Millions', *Far Eastern Economic Review*, 5 March 1987.
12. Interview with author, Rawalpindi, 23 July 1988.
13. Conversation with author, Islamabad, September 1988.
14. Interview with General Gul, Islamabad, October 1988.
15. Interview with author, Peshawar, 22 October 1988.
16. ibid.
17. Conversation with author *en route* to Jalalabad, February 1989.

CHAPTER 12: SQUANDERING VICTORY

1. Interview in Foreign Ministry, February 1989.
2. Interview with author, 12 February 1989.
3. Mullah Nasim in Rawalpindi *shura*, 18 February 1989.
4. Interview with author, Peshawar, 4 June 1989.
5. Quoted in *Time* magazine, 31 May 1988.
6. See *Financial Times*, 19 June 1989.
7. Interview with author, Islamabad, May 1989.
8. Much of this comes from discussions with confidential sources in Pakistan and US intelligence and AIG members.
9. Made available to author by Cabinet member.
10. Interview with author, Peshawar, 4 June 1989.
11. Interview with author, Kabul, June 1989.
12. Conversation with army officers, Kabul–Jalalabad road checkpoint, June 1989.
13. Interview with author, Kabul, June 1989.
14. BBC World Service, 9 July 1989.
15. Interview with author, Quetta, 10 July 1989.
16. Interview with author, Islamabad, 11 July 1989.
17. Conversation with author, Shandur Pass, July 1989.
18. See *Financial Times*, 22 December 1989.

CHAPTER 13: IN THE NAME OF THE CRESCENT

1. Conversation with author, Siachen, 21 August 1989.
2. Government of India White Paper on J&K, New Delhi, 1948, pp. 52–3.

3. Lok Sabha debates, 3rd series, 1 July 1965.
4. M. J. Akbar, *India: A Siege Within*, Penguin, Harmondsworth, 1985, p. 250.
5. 'Militants fan war fever over Kashmir', *Sunday Times*, 15 April 1990.
6. Interview with author, Siachen, 21 August 1989.
7. 'Persecution of Ahmadis and Their Response', Press and Publication Desk, Ahmadiyya Muslim Association, London.
8. ibid.
9. Kamal Azfar, *Pakistan: Political and Constitutional Dilemmas*, Pakistan Law House, 1987, p. 143.
10. M. J. Akbar, op. cit., p. 31.

CHAPTER 14: THE EMPIRE STRIKES BACK

1. Interview with author, Lahore, 24 September 1990.
2. ibid.
3. Interview with author, Karachi, 30 September 1990.
4. ibid.
5. ibid.
6. ibid.
7. Interview with author, Lahore, November 1988.
8. Interview with author, Karachi, 30 September 1990.
9. ibid.
10. Interview with author, Lahore, 24 September 1990.
11. ibid.
12. Tariq Rahim and Javed Jabbar, both ministers in the federal cabinet who had joined the PPP belatedly, allegedly had their phones tapped.
13. Interview with author, Karachi, 22 September 1990.
14. Interview with author, Karachi, 30 September 1990.
15. Interview with author, Islamabad, 19 September 1990.
16. See press reports in *Daily Jang, Pakistan Times, Dawn, Friday Times*, 20 September to early October 1989.
17. Bhutto had agreed that her party would support Ishaq in the elections for President by the Assembly.
18. Interview with author, Karachi, 30 September 1990.
19. Benazir Bhutto, *Daughter of the East*, Hamish Hamilton, London, 1988, p. 79.
20. That there was a move against Bhutto within the army in September 1989 was told to me by two ministers, Tariq Rahim and Aitzaz Ahsan, and confirmed by intelligence officials. Indian Premier Rajiv Gandhi, in a private conversation with journalists, later said he had been given a warning of this.

21. Jatoi lost his own home constituency in Sindh in 1988, but in 1989 won a seat in a by-election in Punjab in a stronghold of his friend Mustafa Khar.

SELECT BIBLIOGRAPHY

AL-QURAN, translation by Ahmed Ali, Akrash, Karachi, 1984.

AHMED, A. S., *Discovering Islam*, Routledge, London, 1988.

AKBAR, M. J., *India: The Siege Within*, Penguin, Harmonds-worth, 1985.

ARNEY, George, *Afghanistan*, Mandarin, London, 1989.

AZFAR, Kamal, *Pakistan: Political and Constitutional Dilemmas*, Pakistan Law House, 1987.

BHUTTO, Benazir, *Daughter of the East*, Hamish Hamilton, London, 1988.

DUNCAN E., *Breaking the Curfew*, Michael Joseph, London, 1988.

FISCHER, Louis, *The Life of Mahatma Gandhi*, Harper & Row, New York, 1976.

HART, David, *Guardians of the Khaibar Pass*, Lahore, 1985.

KIPLING, Rudyard, *Kim*, Penguin, Harmondsworth, 1987.

KIPLING, Rudyard, *Poems*, selected by James Cochrane, Penguin, Harmondsworth, 1977.

MASON, P., *The Men Who Ruled India*, Pan, London, 1985.

MATHESON, S., *The Tigers of Baluchistan*, Oxford Books, Karachi, 1975.

MINTJES, H., *A New Debate on 'Women and Islam'*, Islamabad, 1984.

MOON, Penderel, *Divide and Quit*, Chatto & Windus, London, 1961.

NOMAN, Omar, *The Political Economy of Pakistan 1947–85*, KPI, 1988.

NAIPAUL, V. S. *Among the Believers*, Penguin, Harmonds-worth, 1987.

INDEX

Printed in India by Rekha Printers Pvt. Ltd., New Delhi.